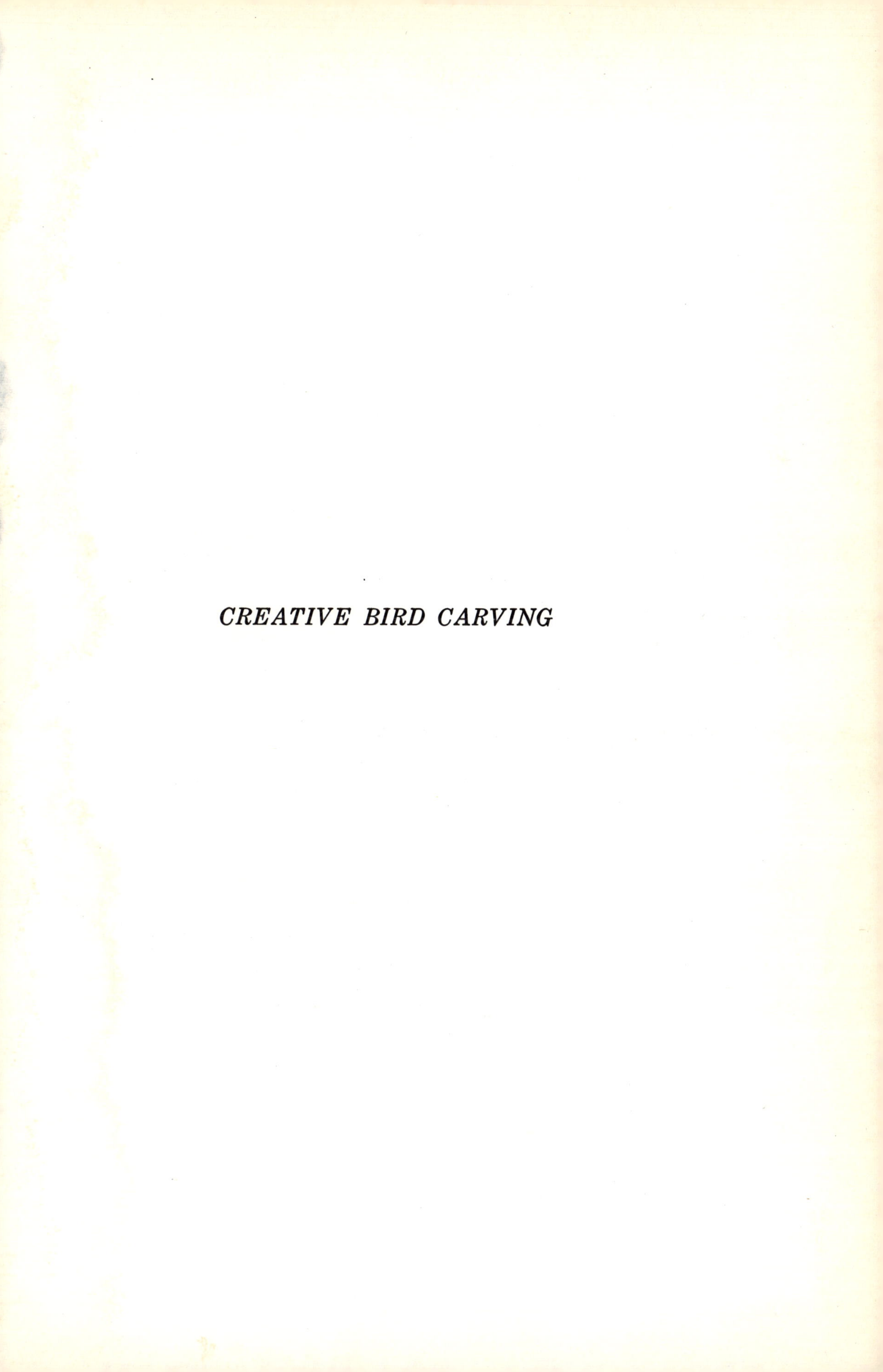

CREATIVE BIRD CARVING

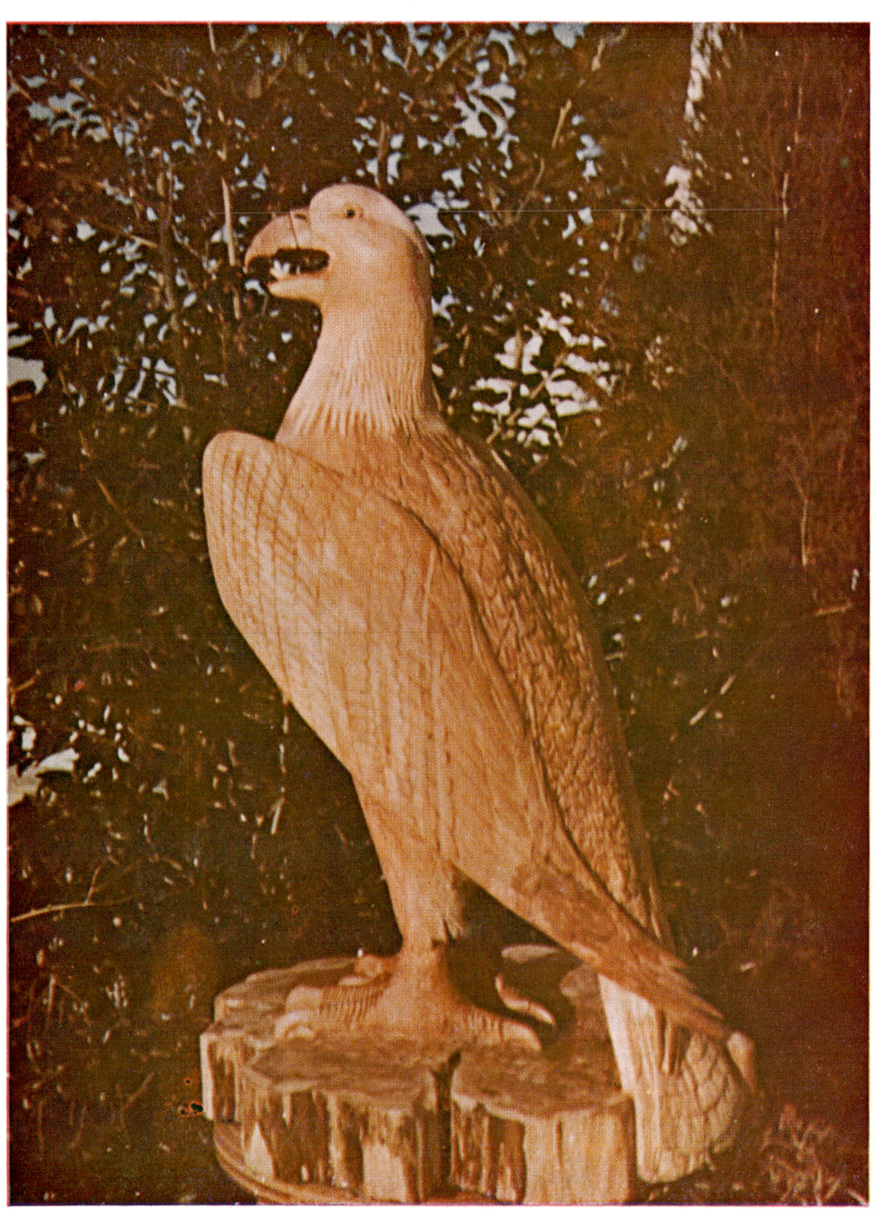

Creative Bird Carving

By

WILLIAM I. TAWES

Illustrated

TIDEWATER PUBLISHERS

Cambridge 1969 *Maryland*

Standard Book Number 87033-141-8

Library of Congress Catalog Card Number: 79-107781

Printed in the United States of America

For My Sons:

William Stanley, killed in action in Korea, and Walter Richard, who died of a World War II disability in a V.A. hospital.

They would have appreciated this book.

Also by William I. Tawes

GOD, MAN, SALT WATER AND THE EASTERN SHORE

CONTENTS

ACKNOWLEDGMENTS

Many individuals have offered suggestions and encouragement in my efforts to create this book. I wish to especially thank the many bird-carvers whose works are represented in Chapter 17. Their kind cooperation contributed much to the contents of this volume. Among them, Mrs. Gladys Black deserves special mention. She read the chapter on polychroming birds and offered many helpful suggestions and much constructive criticism.

Mr. Bruce Burk is probably the best-known professional bird-carver on the Pacific Coast. His carvings have won many prizes in national contests and Kerr's, of Beverly Hills sells his work. Bruce kindly consented to review the manuscript and write the Foreword. His invaluable criticisms and suggestions are reflected in the contents of the book. His help is deeply appreciated.

Several manufacturing concerns generously permitted the use of their literature and illustrations from their brochures or catalogs. Proper credit is given these establishments in appropriate places. Mr. R. A. Link, Technical Information Specialist of the U.S. Department of Agriculture, Forest Service, kindly permitted the author to use the findings of his laboratory, located at the University of Wisconsin, concerning Polyurethane Resin finish to wood stabilized with Polyethylene Glycol (Leaflet No. 24) and the literature and pictures concerned with the stabilizing process of green woods.

Mr. John Rood, author of *Sculpture in Wood,* who recently retired from the University of Minnesota, graciously contributed the photograph of his near-abstract bird without charge, and permitted its use in the Picture Gallery chapter.

Obtaining photographs from various museums required considerable correspondence but eventually the authorities of the respective institutions permitted their pictures to be used.

Mrs. Mary Jane Cornell of Tidewater Publishers deserves a special vote of thanks for her labors, beyond the call of duty, in creating order out of the chaos of my manuscript. Such patience is seldom witnessed in these days of "root hog or lose your tater."

Finally, I wish to express my appreciation for the help given by all individuals who have not been specifically referred to in these paragraphs.

W. I. T.

FOREWORD

The need for a hobby or an avocation which will provide relaxation and pride of accomplishment for both the young and the old has never been greater than it is today. Almost daily we read or hear of people of all ages suffering heart attacks, ulcers, nervous disorders or breakdowns, alcoholism and drug addiction. These are symptoms of tension, or, in many cases, just plain boredom. Leisure time is being increased. Retirement ages are being lowered, but little is being done to prepare people who have led active, busy lives to occupy themselves during the so-called "inactive" years. The man, woman, or child who acquires a rewarding, relaxing, lifelong hobby is to be envied.

One of the greatest sources of personal satisfaction to an individual is seeing his own idea grow from rough material into a finished object of beauty or usefulness—strictly as a result of his own efforts. However the opportunity to do this is limited in these days of mass production, automation, and specialization. More and more the average man is being made to follow a pattern established by someone else. There is a growing tendency for a man to regard himself as just a cog in the big wheel of industry. In his own workshop or studio, however, he is king, for there he can formulate the idea, create the design, and with his own two hands make the finished product. He can look at his accomplishment with pride and say, "I made it myself."

Of all the hobbies or avocations involving creative work, I think wood carving, bird carving particularly, is one of the most fascinating and rewarding activities.

I once read that if ever you even attempted to paint a picture, you would from then on be unable to walk past a painting without stopping to look at it. I have personally found this to be especially true in regard to bird carving. Not only will you be unable to ignore another's carving, you will find it impossible not to observe in great detail each and every bird you see daily. You will want to know more and more about these truly remarkable creatures, about their great beauty, their tremendous power and endurance, their wonderful adaptability on the ground, in the air, and—in the case of waterfowl—on and under the water. When you try to capture in three dimensions their graceful forms and attempt to duplicate the beautiful complexity of their plumage, you will find it impossible to ignore the existence of the Master Carver.

Bill Tawes, like myself, discovered the enjoyment and satisfaction of bird carving fairly late in life. I am sure we both wish that we could have been introduced to this creative outlet at an early age. Bill Tawes, also like myself, found that hard work, study, and stick-to-it-iveness can take the place of inherent talent—if there is such a nebulous quality in man.

Motivated by the desire to help others, Bill Tawes has now applied his recognized carving talent and his many years of teaching experience to the task of showing how a novice can take a rough block of wood and transform it into a thing of beauty. You will find that he has masterfully achieved his purpose. Clearly and concisely he starts out with simple projects and progresses to more complicated, professional types of carving. He gives the tyro a brief history of wood carving, one of the oldest art forms; he guides him in the selection and care of his tools; he informs him of the various woods available and of their advantages and disadvantages; he shows him how to plan his work, how to introduce originality into his carvings, how to finish his carvings, and more.

Even if your interest in bird carving is only casual, I am sure you will enjoy this book. However, don't be at all surprised to find yourself on the way to the hardware store and lumber yard for tools and materials.

BRUCE BURK

PREFACE

At a recent bird-carving exhibition, probably the most complete and representative of such a show ever assembled, I was invited to give daily demonstrations in the art of wood carving. One of the most frequent questions asked by my observers concerned information as to where a good text on the subject might be purchased. The publisher of my recent book visited the show and because of this experience he also felt the need for an elementary guide for individuals interested in carving birds He suggested that I write such a book for he believed there was not only a large sales potential, but an opportunity to make a worthy contribution to the art by stimulating interest in preserving, for posterity, the realistic likenesses of the birds and wildfowl of America.

The promise of success of the projected book was based mainly on current demands for interesting pursuits for retired persons, not otherwise gainfully employed, to fill in their long hours of leisure time. Also, there was felt a need for further instruction for individuals already engaged in whittling activities, and finally, helpful information and guidance for young people in search of a suitable medium in which to express their creative abilities.

Woodworking is a medium with which almost all persons are somewhat familiar. The possession of a jackknife is as much expected of a boy as is a ball; so for most male adolescents and men a small beginning, or initial step, has already been taken in fashioning wood toward some preconceived end. Of course, the jackknife was laid aside in most instances when the boys became older because of more urgent demands upon their time. But the urge to whittle is never entirely lost with age, for when the pressures of office, factory, or the job have been released there is a frequent return to the basement to putter with tools in the creation of wooden objects. These individuals are potential wood-carvers. Then, there are others who never lost the urge to use a knife, and who have continuously filled in the chinks of their leisure time with whittling in one form or another. This book has been written for all of these groups.

My first aim is to teach (or inspire) an activity which will profitably occupy the leisure of both our young people and our senior citizens; and the second objective is related to the first: to encourage the ardent whittler to further develop his carving skills so that he (or she) may express his creative yearnings in a suitable medium and make life more satisfying and worth the candle.

Bird carving has already become a national creative pastime for a host of men and women. For some, this activity has become a unique and profitable vocation. The work of ornithological societies of the various states, the conservationist, and literature published by such groups, have created a broad base of interest in American upland game, waterfowl, and shore birds. Through the efforts of these nature lovers, all of us have become more conscious and appreciative of the beauty and mystery of the wildlife in our fields and along our streams and waterways. Such interest has inspired many talented craftsmen to exercise their skill in reproducing in sculptural form the birds of our nation, and have instilled such enthusiasm for their work that the public is willing, in many instances, to pay fabulous prices for their creations.

With the foregoing thoughts in mind the idea of this book was conceived. After more than twenty-five years of teaching woodworking, plus a hitch at public school administration, I was encouraged to apply my tools to the art of bird carving by such craftsmen as Bruce Burk, Wendell Gilley, Homer Lawrence, the Ward brothers, and others whose works are illustrated in this text. No less talented is Mrs. Gladys Black whose sensitive expressions of her art in carving are overwhelming to persons who feel deeply concerning such creative efforts. Her carvings are an encouragement to the many, many women who have aspirations in this direction. I am personally acquainted with many of the craftsmen mentioned in this book and with their work, so I should be excused for making use of their experience as references. There are no better teachers than the masters.

Finally, I hope to create with this small volume additional interest in the art of wood carving. I have tried to supply the information that has been requested by the beginners who feel the compelling urge to express themselves in wood. I present my material with the feeling that it is simply done, and in straightforward manner, so that the neophyte will have little difficulty in following my directions. I trust that my descriptions and expositions will inspire and direct the most inexperienced persons to pick up their chisels and mallets with confidence and determination, and grow in their carving skills until they too are numbered with the best.

The beginner must realize, however, from the very start, that talent, as someone has said, is nine-tenths perspiration and one-tenth inspiration. The skilled craftsman already knows this fact. Only consistent industry, seasoned with intense interest, will develop the budding carver's powers to professional dimensions.

WILLIAM I. TAWES

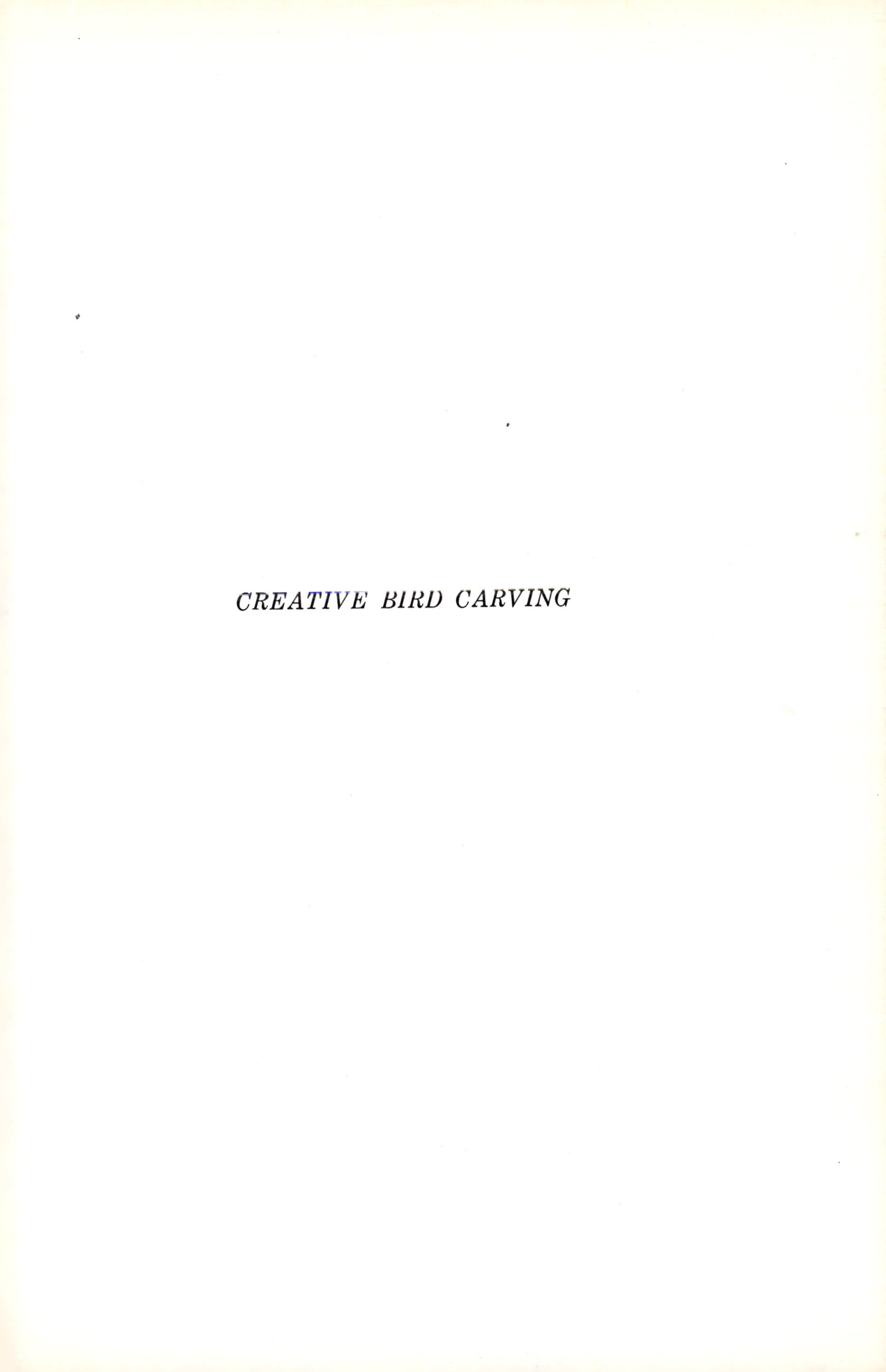

CREATIVE BIRD CARVING

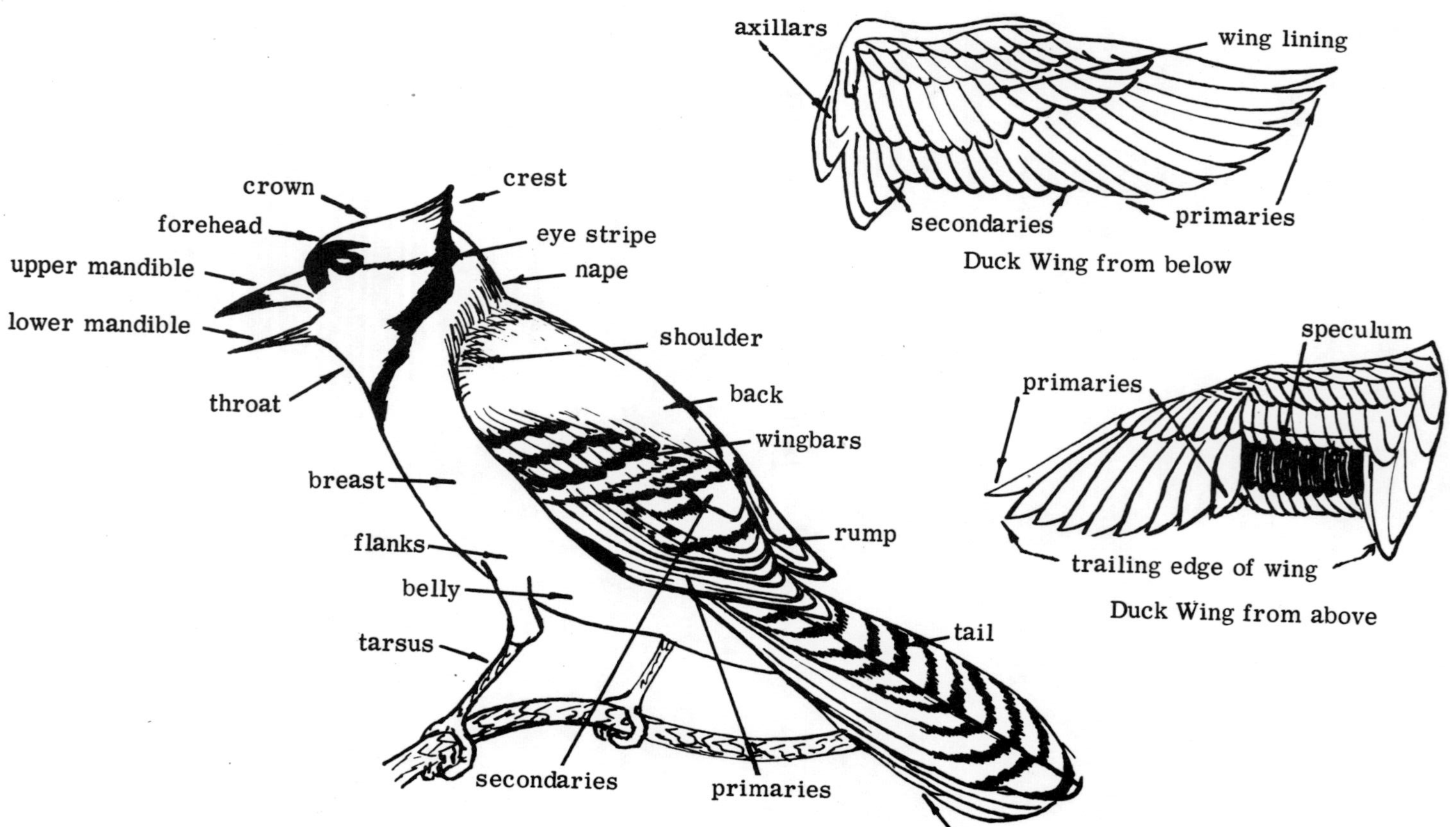

Figure 1. Topography of Birds and Ducks.

Chapter 1

A. *WORK AS A SOCIALIZING INFLUENCE*

During the era when the author was a public school teacher there was an old principle of instruction which still is considered of utmost importance in the learning process. The principle was known as *motivation*. This technique of arousing the attention of a child in the subject matter to be taught usually consisted of interesting material incident to the lesson, and so exciting that even the dullest pupil would be "hooked"—at least for the moment. The dessert, so to speak, was served before the meat and potatoes.

While this method may conflict with the cookbook recipes, it was a cardinal procedure of the effective teacher. It still is! The author heartily believes that the presentation of related subject matter, designed to stimulate the interest of the learner, is essential to good instruction. So firmly does he believe in this procedure that the habit has become ingrained in his pedagogical thinking. Therefore, the initial chapters of this somewhat technical book have been planned to include a warming-up period of discussion in preparation for the basic instruction that follows.

Indeed, the excellent material available pertinent to the subject of this book is voluminous, covering many fields of human endeavor. Of course, only the surface of a small portion of the literature will be scratched here, but the budding carver should know something of the historical significance of his art, its place in religion and in the more utilitarian pursuits of primitive man, to help him flower in his appreciation of the carver's impact upon civilization—his rise to Parnassus. Perhaps even more important than wood carving's historical impact is its importance as a leisure-time activity to occupy the hours not taken up by the job of earning a living. For the retired person there are few more worthy and suitable hobbies than wood carving. For many people it is a challenge bringing out latent talents. For both, the pursuit can be a satisfying experience and in some instances a means of supplementing the lean income.

The therapy of working with the hands is of first consideration in rehabilitating patients afflicted with varying degrees and types of emotional disorders. Work of any sort is good preventive medicine, and did not Froebel say many, many long years ago that work with the hands builds character?

To all civilizations that have had their day in history, the time came when the people weakened in their will to survive. They sold their birthrights for a mess of sensual pleasures. The children professed to know more than their elders, forgetting that the labors and insights of their forefathers were responsible for their nation's greatness in the first place. The people lost their perspective of good government. The *liberals* wasted their nation's wealth in grandiose schemes of social welfare, wrecking the financial structure upon which their country's commerce with other peoples rested. The vision of the leaders dimmed, descending from lofty heights of strength and prosperity to the low level of deadening charity, worldly indifference and indolence. They dedicated themselves to the Mammon of the arena. In Rome, feeding Christians to the lions became a national pastime, irrespective of the fact that the people had forsaken their own gods long ago. The student of history will recall that while Nero fiddled in his palace, wine and bread were free for the lazy rabble in the streets, for none of them would work. Outside of the city walls the barbarians patiently stood like jackals, waiting for the final dissolution. The people never had it so good—but they perished!

Strangely enough, the eggheads and do-gooders were largely to blame for the decline and fall of all past civilizations we know anything about. Historians believe that the Priesthood of Babylon opened the gates of the city to the enemy.

From all of these past civilizations the works of the creative artists and craftsmen alone remain and are remembered. The scribe who sank his stylus in the soft clay brick or chiseled his message in stone is remembered, too, but to be a good penman in those far-off days required the ability of a sculptor. The poetry of Shelley is appropriate here:

> I met a traveler from an antique land
> Who said: Two vast and trunkless legs of stone
> Stand in the desert. Near them, on the sand,
> Half sunk, a shattered visage lies, whose frown,
> And wrinkled lip, and sneer of cold command,
> Tell that its sculptor well those passions read
> Which yet survive, stamped on those lifeless things,
> The hand that mocked them, and the heart that fed;
> And on the pedestal these words appear:
> "My name is Ozymandias, king of kings:
> Look on my works, ye Mighty, and despair!"
> Nothing beside remains. Round the decay
> Of that colossal wreck, boundless and bare
> The lone and level sands stretch far away.

This poem seems to show the futility of power and greatness; how the sands of time break up and obliterate the vain glory of mighty kings. The theme is true—not only for this ruler, but for all of the kings and their times throughout the ages. Ozymandias, or Rameses II, whose fallen image at Thebes inspired the poem, is but an example of all the mighty kings whose reigns were but watches in the night that is past. But the fallen, broken stones of the sculptor, indicative of past greatness, were not entirely covered by the desert sands, and provide for us a significant lesson. We learn that the king was a mighty monarch, "king of kings," who ruled with a heavy scepter; that he was seemingly a cruel man with paranoic tendencies, for such characteristics were carved upon his visage.

The fragments of pottery, *steles,* broken images, and crumbling architecture are all that is left of ancient peoples to tell of their flash of greatness in the dark night of antiquity. But from these artifacts research scholars, students of past civilizations, and archaeologists have learned many things and have pieced together a brief history of the particular nation's days of glory. This history was written by the craftsmen and artists during their days of grandeur.

Wooden sculptures and carvings that have come down to us are, in many instances, better preserved than the stone kings, gods, and goddesses. There are few works which do not have a broken nose, a missing ear, or lack a whole member (including the head). The fragments of Rameses II are striking examples of both the ruin of the images and the light they shed on the people who made them. It is from these fragments that we know so much about the life and times of ancient cultures. For example, from such fragments we learn that a ruler named Hammurabi drafted a moral code for his people more than two hundred years before the Lord commanded Moses to leave Jethro's flocks and go down into Egypt and free his people from bondage. Even before Hammurabi, the last great king of Sumer had carved such laws on tablets of stone. Hammurabi borrowed from the Sumerians and the Israelites borrowed from both to write their Ten Commandments. Appropriately enough, the *stele* of Hammurabi has at its top a relief carving of the sun god Shamash, patron of justice, delivering to the king the official symbols of authority. It is no accident of history that this period was during the golden age of Babylonia. It is interesting to note, too, that the ancient rulers received their powers from the gods and were commanded by them in performing every significant act of their reign. In many instances they were considered gods themselves, as was the case of the Pharaohs of Egypt. What is still more important to us at this juncture is the fact that many of these rulers were carved in wood or stone by their royal sculptors and are now reposing in museums all over the civilized world, or scattered on the sands of the desert too large to move away. These colossal works may be found from the Easter Islands to the banks of the Nile, and in Asia to the forsaken fields of Korea.

About one thousand years after Hammurabi, a skilled Egyptian carver of wood and bronze formed the sacred *Ibis* (Figure 2), the symbol of Thoth, god of wisdom, and Maat, goddess of truth and justice, wearing the feather of authority upon her head. This relic, still in excellent preservation, resides in the Kestner Museum at Hanover, Germany. It was carved during the period of the Middle Kingdom, about the 7th or 6th century B.C. The sculptors and painters received special privileges under the Pharaohs, so their arts waxed and flourished. The tomb of Tutenkhamon yielded sculptures of remarkable form and technique. Some were skillfully carved in the round with probable likenesses of the models (1366–1357 B.C.). But even these sculptors had the benefits of thousands of years of development in the art. Scenes of birds, antedating King Tutenkhamon, have been discovered painted on the walls of burial vaults. Significantly enough for our theme, one famous mural depicts a fowling scene of birds and fish with heron *decoys*. While our richest discoveries have been made in desert countries like Egypt, all peoples, everywhere, have practiced the art of carving. Such a medium of artistic expression has been universal, going back into the dim past before history. For more than 15,000 years stylized birds have been carved (cave art at Lascaux, France), and how long before this period no one knows.

According to tradition, Moses commissioned Bezaleel, a cunning artisan, to carve of shittim wood the ark, pillars, and other phylacteries of the tabernacle. Bezaleel and his pupil, Aholiab, carved all of the sanctuary furniture (1491 B.C.). Bezaleel was the Hebrew version of Leonardo Da Vinci—"filled with wisdom of heart, to work all manner of work, of the engraver, and of the cunning workman, and the embroiderer, in blue, and in purple, in scarlet, and in fine linen, and the weaver ..." Not only could he carve wood, but he cast bronze, silver and gold, and cut precious stones (Exodus 35).

Our own aborigines in America had developed wood carving to an advanced stage before Columbus visited our shores. Again, most of the carvings took on religious significance, but the more utilitarian bowls, mortars and other domestic articles were also in evidence. The Indians' pipes were carved and otherwise decorated with wampum, seashells, feathers and hides of animals. Totem poles of the Northwestern tribes were

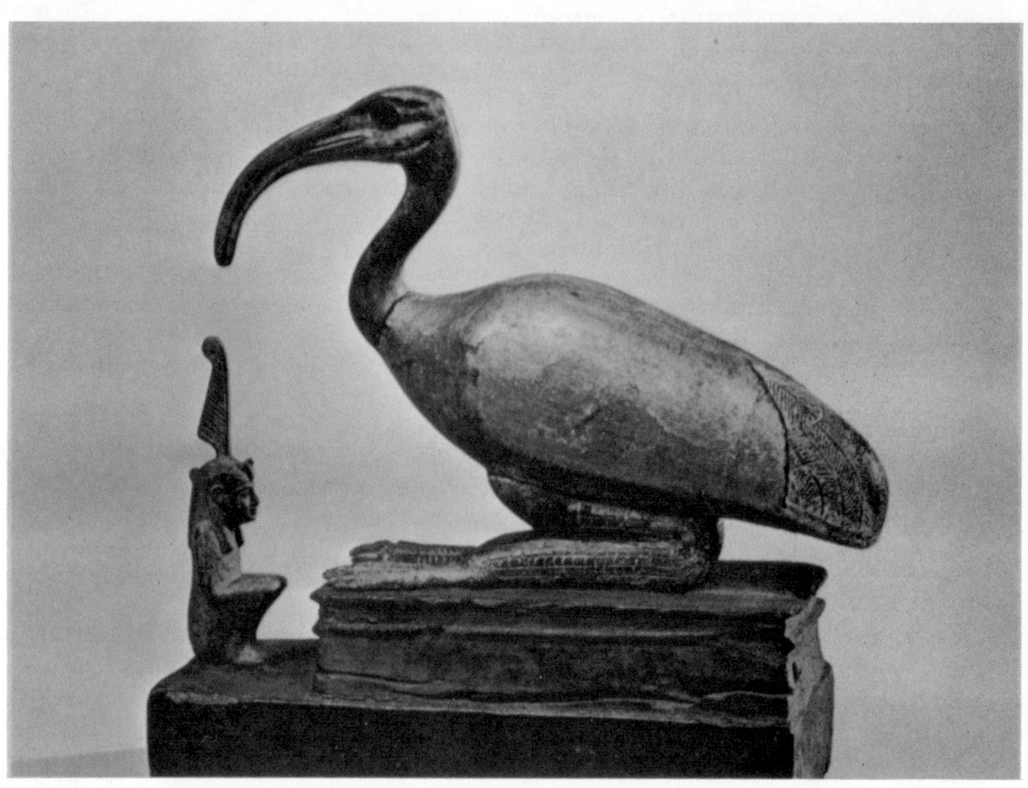

Figure 2. Ibis, the sacred bird of Thoth, God of Wisdom, and Maat, Goddess of Truth and Justice. Gilded wood and bronze. 7th-6th centuries B.C. Kestner Museum, Hanover.

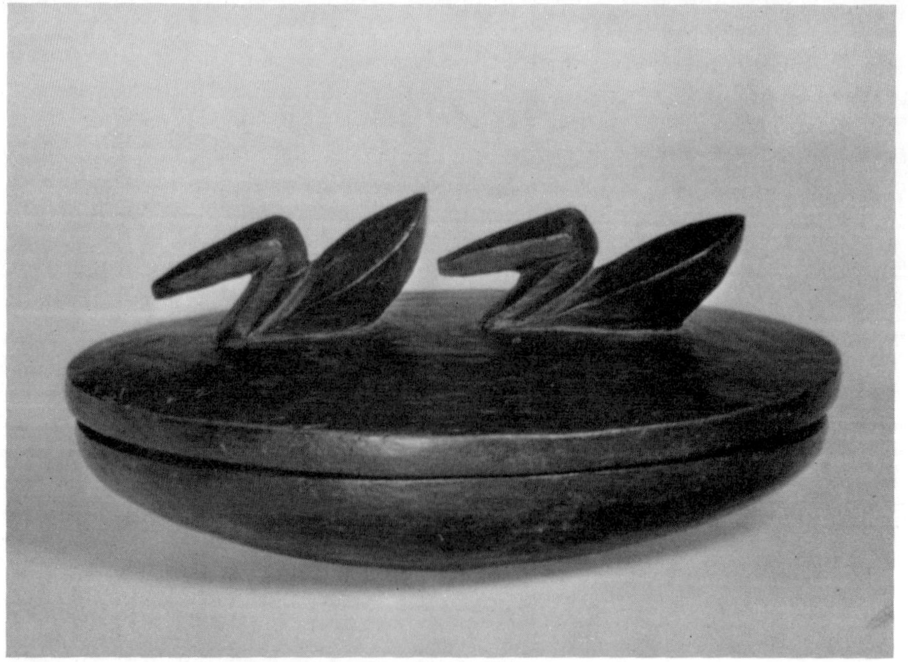

Figure 3. A wooden-lidded meat and vegetable bowl carved by a native of the Kwanga tribe (Barotseland). Northern Rhodesia. Rietberg Museum, Zurich, Von der Heydt Collection.

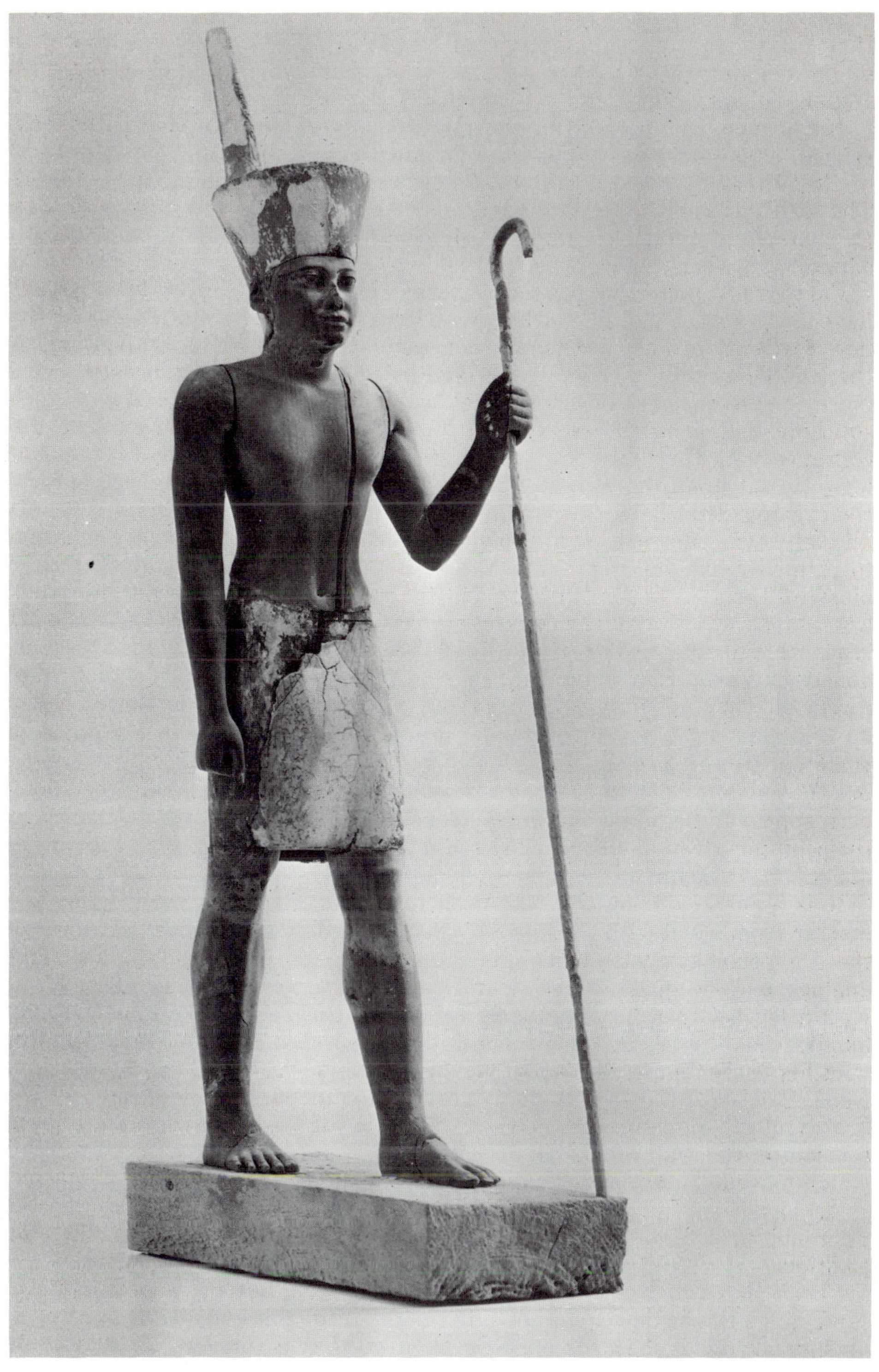

Figure 4. Statuette: King Se'n-Wosret I, wearing the Crown of Lower Egypt; cedarwood, painted; from the tomb of Imhotep, Lisht. *Courtesy*, The Metropolitan Museum of Art, Museum excavations, 1913-14; Rogers Fund, supplemented by contribution of Edward S. Harkness.

sometimes more than fifty feet high, carved with symbols and figures along their entire length, reading from top to bottom. These messages have little or no meaning to us now, but before the white man came they were the Indians' history books and genealogical records.

In our own time-period the Kwanga wood-carvers of Northern Rhodesia, Africa, have told more about their primitive lives and their times than all of the other tribesmen combined. They were, and are, the history makers. The skillfully carved and designed meat and vegetable bowl in Figure 3 is an example of their skill and imagination. Could ever ducks be so simply carved with such characteristic poise!

Carvings of primitive peoples, whether in our own time or in ages past, have always intrigued the author, both because of their simplicity and manner of execution. They are usually compact; the figure well contained within the log. Their subjects were conceived because of a utilitarian need or the more compelling urge of religious expression. They were carved with tools so crude that even the most ambitious of modern carvers would be discouraged with their use. The carver's only vise was formed by his toes and legs. He sat upon the ground with his log between his knees. Yet, most of the carvings that have survived are truly fascinating and possess a beauty all their own. They are often copied by modern craftsmen who are sensitive to primitive art and appreciate the skill of their creators. Unfortunately, most of them were not stabilized after carving. Having been carved of unseasoned wood in most cases, many have cracked seriously, and some are ready to fall apart. The crude finish that some received helped tremendously, but even they show the wear of the ages. Figure 4 is a picture of a very old carving, King Se'n-Wosret I, wearing the crown of Lower Egypt on his head. It is a skillfully carved statuette discovered in the tomb of Imhotep. It is marvelously preserved after a period of nearly 4,000 years, but the entire length of the body is seriously split. Cracks along the shoulders appear to be joints that have opened where the arms were attached by the sculptor after having carved them separately. What a pity the carver did not know about polyethylene glycol!

It is a far cry from the forgotten primitive man who carved the first mortar from wood with a crude tool of stone and the sophisticated carver of the Egyptian statuette with his more efficient bronze tools. The same analogy may be made of the primitive wood-carver on the Zambezi River with a log between his legs, hacking away with his adz-like tool (without handle) held firmly in his strong skilled fingers, and the modern sculptor with his finely tempered tools of steel and a rugged vise to hold his block of wood. Yet, all of these individuals are of the same mold, so to speak, for art knows no age, no language, no race. The urge of the predawn man to paint a bison on the wall of his cave (Figure 5) was of the same cerebral stuff which moved Michaelangelo to sculpt King David from a block of marble.

As has been suggested before, the spirit of creativity is akin to the religious urge and early man did not differentiate between the two emotions—if indeed, they are two in number. Only in modern times has art been shorn of some of its religious trappings, but no modern concept can change the basic yearning—only its direction. So, when the tyro picks up his carving tools he is obeying an urge that is ageless. He is joining those immortals who have helped to pull man up to his civilized state by his own boot straps. For generic man is still a barbarian, a complex creature possessing potentialities for both good and evil. These positive and negative powers are so integrated in his personality that even the Saints probably have their full share of these earthly attributes. But in every generation there are a few saviors who have attempted to pull man up from the mire in which he was stuck fast or was sinking. The rest of the masses were fighting among themselves, selfishly pursuing their daily activities, callously ignorant of the finer things of life. They did not care a damn for a sonnet, a *Moonlight Sonata,* a *Mona Lisa,* or a *Pieta*. But to those who developed a liking for good literature, an inner ear to hear the strains of an angelic choir, a vision to create, their reward was the kingdom of heaven.

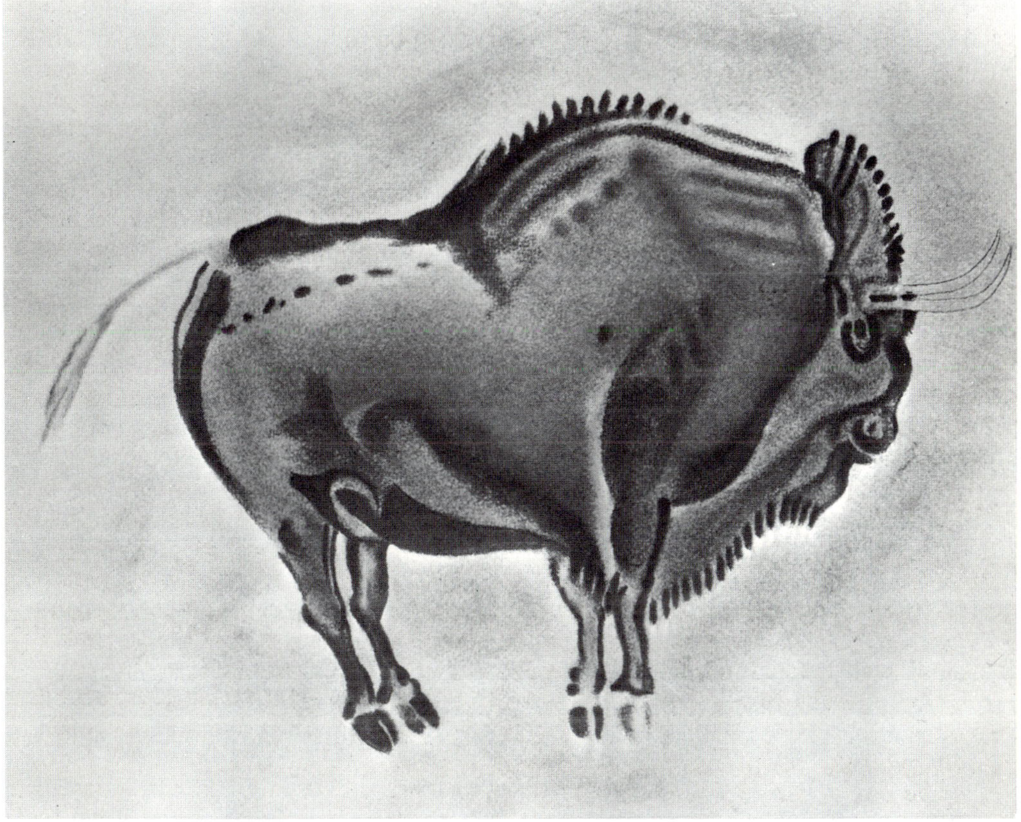

Figure 5. Bison in cave. ***Courtesy*** **of The American Museum of Natural History.**

B. *THE HISTORICAL SIGNIFICANCE OF BIRDS*

Although this book has been written with the thought of interesting individuals in bird carving, the central theme, thus far, has been to emphasize the socializing influence of such an activity; to avoid the dangerous vacuum of idleness on the one hand, and to satisfy the emotional urge on the other. Now the thought will be directed to a closer aspect of the subject: the birds themselves.

Birds should have a special historical and psychological meaning to everyone, especially to those persons interested in carving them. They are much older than man and were a well developed species long before he appeared on the scene. Their impact upon the race cannot be fathomed. They have been represented as being God's messengers to and from heaven throughout the ages, and were thought to have powers equal to the angels, who were themselves conceived as virtuous young men with snow-white wings. Egypt's god of the resurrection, Osiris, was the father of Horus, a god of light and heaven. Horus was always represented as a *falcon,* or a man with a falcon's head. He was conceived by his mother, Isis, while flying over a swamp in the guise of a *hawk.* Our own Christian diety is often thought of as a *dove.* In three of the Gospels the Holy Ghost takes this form: ". . . in a bodily shape like a dove. . ." The sacred *Ibis,* representing Thoth, god of wisdom, has been mentioned before. Among our Northwest Coast Indians the *raven* was thought to be the creator of the universe. At Tacoma, Washington, ravens peer from an 83-foot totem pole, topped by an *eagle,* the clan symbol. Down through the ages, from the stylized birds carved on cave walls to the *sea gulls* of the Mormon temple, birds have had a reverent place, equaled to that of gods themselves. Even now artists use birds to symbolize the soul leaving the body and the confines of the earth. The *peacock* was once the symbol of immortality throughout all Asia, and in our own time the *goldfinch* is thought by many people to protect one from the plague. All in all, birds are holy subjects, all 9,000 species of them. They represent the carver's most interesting and inspiring models. They offer the least resistance to his unskilled hands, and his greatest challenge after he has mastered his craft. In the development of his carving skills to produce their likeness his greatest aspirations should be achieved. They are in this book the source of his salvation in learning the carving skills, and his hope for a future life in the creative art.

So closely does the sensitive artist feel toward his subjects that he is likely to consider them animated figures being born of his chisel and mallet. As the bird emerges from the shapeless block it speaks to him in unheard words of promise, and is as much solace and meaning to him, perhaps, as the divine birds of antiquity were to their votaries. I have often felt this way. So closely did I associate myself with my most recent work that I found myself talking reverently to the eagle I had carved.

"Acquilla," I said, stroking his head, "you are a majestic bird. How proud you stand, and yet how sad! You must rest immobile upon your perch forever, and never, never fly away."

The eagle stared ahead bravely and boldly, unmoved. His open wings were poised in sacred rest and not in restless flight. He seemed resigned to his fate, content and unafraid. Perhaps he knew that he, like the two young lovers on Keats' Grecian urn, could never fade away, and that he would be forever young.

> Thou, silent form, dost tease us out of thought
> As doth eternity: Cold Pastoral!
> When old age shall this generation waste,
> Thou shalt remain, in midst of other woe
> Than ours, a friend to man, to whom thou say'st,
> "Beauty is truth, truth beauty—that is all
> Ye know on earth, and all ye need to know."

No wonder Moses said to his people: "Thou shalt not make unto thee any graven image, or any likeness of anything that is in heaven above, or that is in the earth beneath, or that is in the water under the earth." The impulse to worship idols is still very much with us. It is easy for an artist to become psychologically involved and identified with his creations but, oh, what a wonderful way to become an idol worshipper!

Chapter 2

TOOLS REQUIRED AND HOW TO CARE FOR THEM

There are some wood-carvers who claim that only a few tools are necessary to carve birds. They are correct if they refer to whittlers who carve small models. They can do expert work with limited implements. The author recently observed such a carver whittling a decoy duck from white cedar with only a hatchet, a coarse rasp, and a pocket knife. After the bird was carved and painted with the markings of a drake mallard it was really beautiful—for a decoy duck. In this particular case the craftsman was a very clever individual who had carved decoys all of his life and had learned to use his few tools with the skill and precision of a professional.

The objective of this book is to produce more than a mere whittler. It is designed to advance the beginner through several stages of increasing difficulty far beyond the skills necessary for making a decoy duck. Becoming acquainted with the tools of the trade is a vital part of this instruction. If the carver learns their uses from the beginning he is more likely to become more familiar and proficient with them as he progresses. Therefore, the list of tools suggested here for the novice might be more than sufficient, but is, nonetheless, fundamental and deemed necessary for a favorable start. There is little pride evoked from using a chisel, rasp, and jackknife because these tools are common to most homes for general purpose work. The psychological advantage of possessing a good kit of tools cannot be overstressed, and this concomitant help is seldom realized. Yet, these unconscious aids are real and the neophyte is in greatest need of them. The more experienced carvers know the thrill of working with good tools and they are eternally tempted to buy more of them, even beyond their particular needs. The beginning carver should avoid the danger of having too few tools with which to work on the one hand, and a reckless collection of them, on the other. Some tools suggested in this chapter may be used infrequently, but when they are needed no other tool is quite so desirable. Certain tools will become favorites and be used more than all of the other tools combined. Therefore, until the beginner knows his way around, the suggestions in this chapter should be seriously considered.

The American craftsman demands a full kit of tools. They are not only desirable, but required for satisfactory results. Most carvers of wildfowl have very elaborate shops equipped with power tools and machines. The professionals must have these laborsaving facilities to be successful. Most of them have a table saw, band saw, drill press, and other motorized machines. My workshop is equipped with hand power tools and machines which I find convenient for the most picayune jobs. But I am one of those craftsmen who must have a whole kit of tools to make and install a button for the stable door. In any event, this chapter will stress good tools, a number of them, for the beginner. Chipping a chip is not the only operation involved in carving. Getting the log or block ready for the carving operation is quite a task in itself, sometimes requiring several specialized tools. (I find the chain saw a very useful machine.)

As this book has been designed primarily for the use of beginners in the carving arts, two groups of tools will be listed. The first consists of those tools a neophyte should possess; the second group is for the more experienced carver and is, therefore, more sophisticated and extensive. Neither list is conclusive, however. The beginner may pick and choose or add to his group; the skilled craftsman will certainly expand his tool supply, adding to his kit more and more tools as the years go by (Figures 6 and 7). This urge is

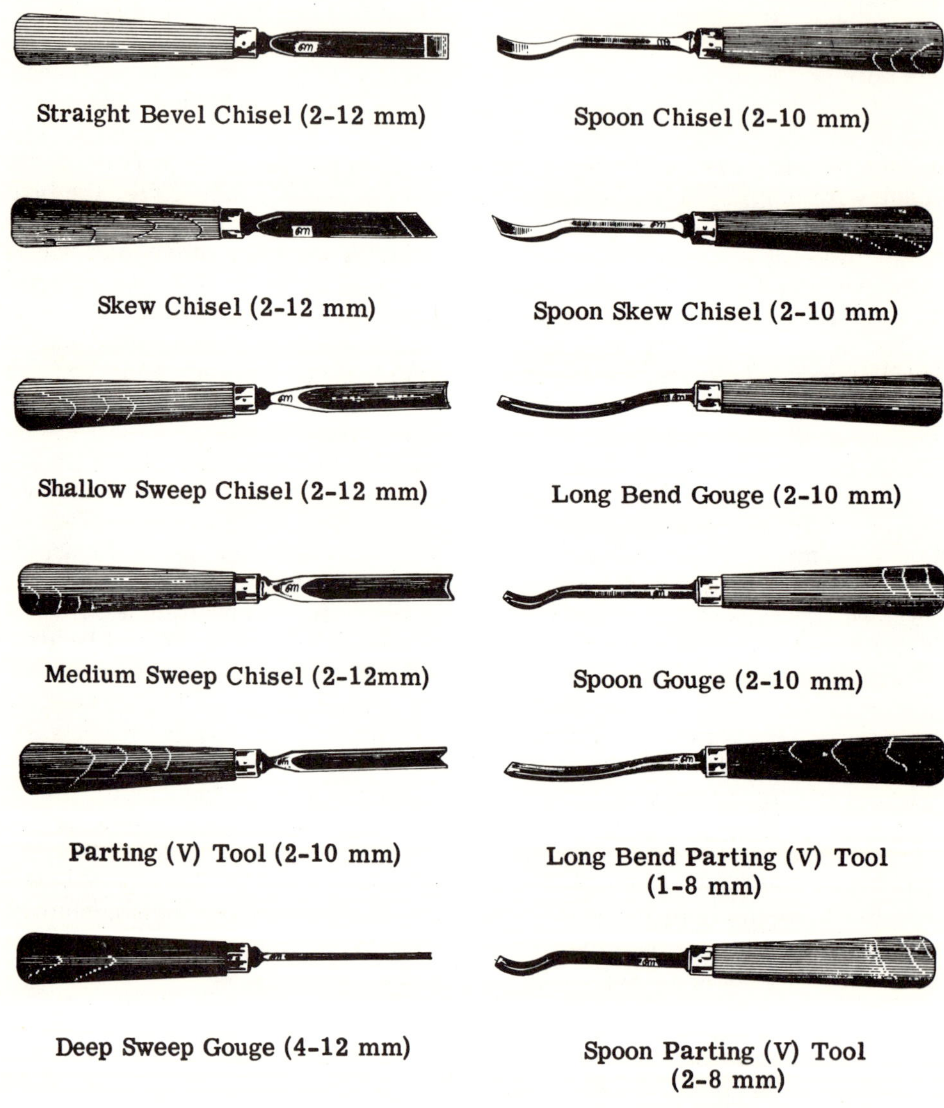

Figure 6. Amateur carving chisels. *Courtesy,* Frank Mittermeier, Inc.

in the right direction for it not only increases the stature of the carver psychologically, but also his potential to excel in his craft.

Even the basic group of tools is elaborate as compared with those possessed by carvers of other countries less affluent than ours. But the American can afford better tools and carving conditions and he will seldom settle for less. In the first place, the beginner is not likely to be as nimble of fingers as those carvers with a long ancestry behind them who used primitive tools, and know no other way. The path they follow has been worn smooth by generations of skilled craftsmen. In the second place, there is little point in starting the difficult way when a simpler, more direct, and easier method is readily accessible.

The first requirement of a carver is a suitable room in which to work—away from the family. An individual who has decided to dedicate himself to the task of creative efforts cannot have his emotional drive brought to an

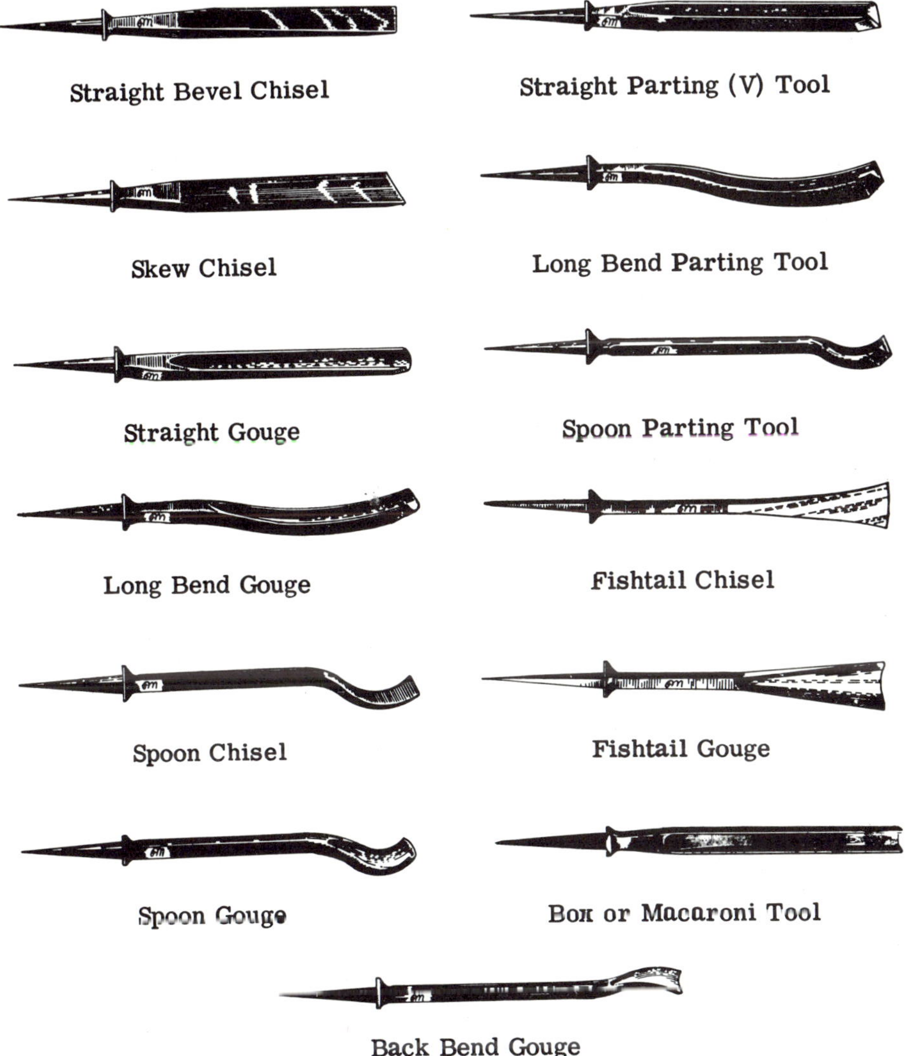

Figure 7. Professional carving chisels. *Courtesy,* Frank Mittermeier, Inc.

abrupt stop by a command from the kitchen to peel the potatoes. The room may be the *dry* cellar of a home, but more preferably another building cut off from the mainstream of domestic activities. This environment may not always be possible, but it is the kind a dedicated carver, or painter, should have. The room should be large enough to accommodate the machines (to be added later), a large workbench, sawhorses and working space. There should be plenty of natural light available and provision for artificial lighting. The spirit of the artist moves him to work during all sorts of unscheduled hours, at night as well as in the daytime. In fact, the breadwinner may have no other choice than to practice his hobby at night. A room 20 × 30 feet with a 10-foot ceiling is not too large and will, like the tool list, meet the carver's needs for many years to come. A suitable heating device or system in cold climates is also necessary during the winter months. Heating a room does not present the problems it did in former years; there are excellent electric units that are not only convenient but efficient. There are portable oil burners reputed to be reliable and suitable for shops. Oil burners present a fire hazard, however, and must be kept away from oily rags and shavings; carvers should be ever fire-conscious when using them. Not so hazardous is a fireplace with a curtained grill. Some of my friends have such excellent waste-disposal facilities in their shops or studios. If made of masonry materials (advisable), it is rather expensive but worth the cost over a long period of use. It is a comfort on a damp, chilly day and an inspiration to those sensitive to the meaning of fire. One is, indeed, rewarding and as cheerful as a cricket.

The following tool list is suggested:

General Tools

Saws—1 crosscut, 8 points, carpenter's
1 rip, 5 or 6 points, carpenter's
Squares—1 steel framing square (or aluminum)
1 try square
Boring tools—1 set of augers, ¼″ to 1″
1 brace (ratchet)
1 hand drill with drills 1/16″ to ¼″
1 Carpenter's hatchet
1 Draw knife

Carving Tools*

2 Carpenter's gouges, ½″ and ¾″
2 Carpenter's chisels, ½″ and ¾″
1 Spoke shave
1 Coping saw (with blades)
1 Pair of roundnose pliers with cutter jaws
1 Set of carving tools (minimum)
  2 Chipping knives
  1 Skew chisel, 8 mm
  3 Chisels, 12 mm, 6 mm and 3 mm
  6 Gouges, 12 mm, 10 mm, 8 mm, 6 mm, 5 mm and 3 mm
2 V-chisels (parting tools) 10 mm and 3 mm
1 Fishtail gouge 1½″, shallow curve
1 Lignum vitae mallet 18 ozs
2 Slip stones (Arkansas), one for gouges and one for V-tools (knife edge)
1 India fine- and coarse-surfaced oilstone
1 Strapping block, laminated leather to wood; same size as oilstone
1 Cabinet scraper with handle

* In some cases, the beginner may feel that the suggested carving set costs too much money before he knows for certain whether he will want to carve or not. These individuals should purchase the small Japanese set of 12 tools now available. They cost about $1.50 and are made of tool steel. The bits are sheet-metal thin and short, but hold a good edge. Also, to supplement these tools, an x-acto set of knife blades with a handle should be purchased. Even the professionals use these knives. They may be purchased for less than $2.00.

Carving tools are usually imported, so the sizes are always in millimeters. They come in amateur sizes with handles, and in professional sizes without handles. A supply of hardwood handles may be purchased for about $.25 each. Professional carving tools may be purchased in all sorts of sizes and sweeps (form of cutting edge), from very shallow to very deep (Figure 8). The shanks and/or blades come straight, long bend, spoon, and back bend. The shanks terminate in a tang suitably shaped for inserting into the wooden handles.

OTHER TOOLS A CARVER SHOULD HAVE

1 Power grinder equipped with light, safety shield, and water-cooling well
1 Pr. tin snips (compound-leverage)
1 Oilcan
An assortment of rasps,* rattail files and other similar tools, rifler files, etc.
1 Hacksaw with blades
1 Tap and die set, U.S. Std. coarse, ¼″ to ½″
1 Tap and die set, 1/16″ to ¼″

If the beginner advances normally to the more difficult carvings, still other tools will be desirable, but they are not necessary. They will help to streamline the carver's efforts and otherwise facilitate his work. Other tool suggestions and machines for the advanced carver are as follows:

A number of fishtail gauges, various sizes and sweeps
One or more offset gouges
One or more additional V-tools
A motorized carving kit
A power drill press, table saw and band saw
A hand power drill, ¼″ capacity
A hand power drill, ½″ capacity
A saber saw
A shaper, if formal bases are contemplated for the carvings

HOW TO SHARPEN AND CARE FOR TOOLS

After the carver has become accustomed to his art, his tools will be almost sacred to him. One mark of distinction between the neophyte and the skilled craftsman is the care he takes of his tools. Last summer (1967) I observed a sculptor carving a woman's head from the largest bole of osage orange I had ever seen. The occasion was an outdoor art show in which I participated. The sculptor had his tools wrapped in a sheepskin with the wool still intact and carried in a basket. A child became interested in the basket of tools and began to finger the sheepskin. The sculptor immediately stopped his work and bent over the child and by kindly persuasive words turned her attention in another direction. The tools were razor-sharp, but the sculptor was as much interested in the care of his tools as he was in the child's safety. "They belonged to my father," said the sculptor.

Many years ago I applied for a job at Grey's Ferry, Philadelphia. A con-

* Recently a rasp has been designed of expanded metal with razor-sharp edges. It may be purchased with removable blades, flat or convex. The carver should have this tool; it cuts fast and clean. "Surform" is the trade name of one popular tool manufacturer.

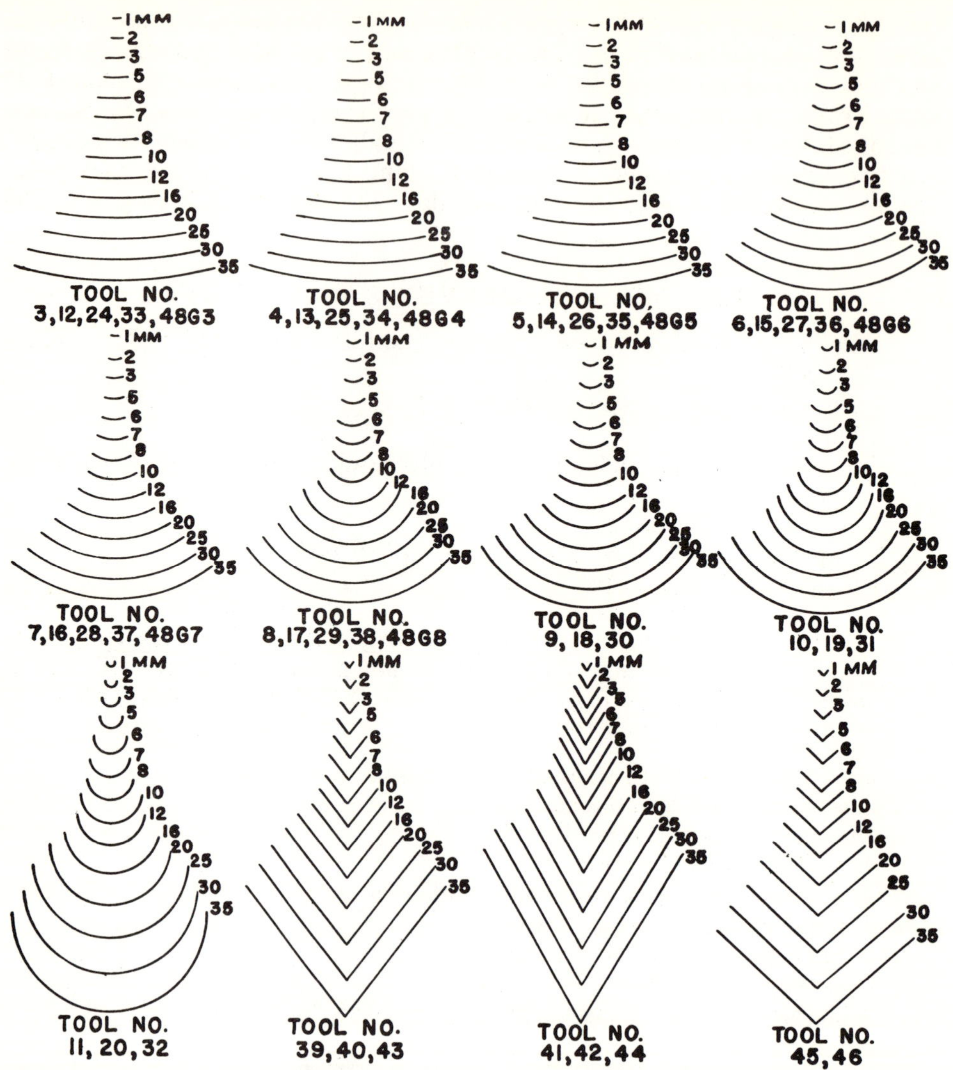

This chart shows the sizes and sweeps (form of cutting edge) of the professional carving tools. The number at the right of the drawings indicates the tool's width in mm—millimeter. The numbers below the drawings are the tool numbers of the different types—**Straight** No. 3 to 11, 39, 41, 45 and 48G 3 to 8. **Long Bend** No. 12 to 20, 40, 42 and 46, **Spoon** No. 24 to 32, 43 and 44, **Back Bend** No. 33 to 38—in which the above sweeps are obtainable.

Figure 8. Carving tool chart of different sweeps. *Courtesy* Frank Mittermeier, Inc.

struction company was converting an old factory along the Schuylkill river into a paint manufacturing establishment. The carpentry foreman inquired if I had my tools with me. I did not. "Bring them with you tomorrow morning and I'll let you know if we want you," he said. The next morning I presented myself at the gate with my box of tools. Fortunately, the foreman was just checking in himself. He recognized me immediately and asked to see my tools. With one studied look he turned and said: "You're hired." He then gave directions for signing up with his company and where to report for work.

This same experience was repeated several years later when I applied for a job in lower Delaware. The contractor asked to see my tools. He examined them more carefully than the foreman had and observed that the saws "needed touching up a bit." But he was otherwise satisfied. These men were interested in (1) learning if the tools were new or used regularly, (2) how they were sharpened, and (3) the kind of care they had received while in use. If the tools had not met all of these qualifications I would not have been hired in either instance.

The sculptor is considerably more "fussy" with his tools than a regular carpenter. His tools must be not only sharp, but properly ground and honed. Following the slightest contact with metal or abrasive surfaces, the edges must be resharpened. The sculptor's tools must be kept razor-sharp, so great care must be exercised in protecting them. Still another consideration affects the serious craftsman: he "loves" his tools almost as much as a mother her newborn child. Of course, this attachment is not developed overnight but results from a long association with them. The time comes when parting with an old tool is like losing a dear friend.

Chisels, gouges, and knives are usually ground sharp at the factory, but not honed. This is the task for the carver after his tools arrive. To perform this operation at the factory would in many instances be a case of love's labor lost. There is no assurance that the tools will arrive without their edges being damaged. Also, the cost is extra. Some carvers do not attempt to sharpen their own tools. This shortcoming is unfortunate and works an unnecessary hardship in both time and convenience. The neophyte is urged to study this phase of his work as much as the art of carving. It is a reasonable conformity to his task and is just as important in his training as any other operation, if not more so. This skill, like carving, must be learned by practice and it certainly is no more difficult. Following the directions religiously and experience are the tricks of sharpening tools.

The primary tool in the sharpening process is a power grinder. The model recommended is a two-wheel type, ⅓ h.p. motor, with safety glass shields, a light, and a water-cooling device. One wheel is fine and the other coarse-grained. They are usually made of carborundum or aluminum oxide, about 6″ in diameter, depending upon the size of the machine.

The first requirement when grinding an edge on a tool is to keep the bevel in one plane and at the proper angle with the wheel. The angle recommended for soft woods is 12° to 15°. Harder wood might require a steeper angle. To maintain the angle while grinding the tool, I hold the blade with the fingers of my right hand, so that they serve not only to hold the chisel against the wheel but as a stop against the tool rest. When the chisel is removed from the wheel to cool the edge in water, the fingers are not moved but held in their original position. When the blade is again pressed against the wheel, the same angle is achieved. The tool is ground until a burr begins to form on the top edge. A skilled mechanic knows when this point is reached by observing his work closely. When no light is reflected from the edge, he knows that the chisel is ready to be whetted. The next operation is the whetting procedure. The surface of the India oilstone is flushed with light oil (kerosene will do) to float off the steel particles left from the previous job and during the present operation. Hold the bevel flat on the stone. The bevel is slightly hollow-ground so lifting the blade is not necessary. Move the chisel forward and backward in a figure-eight movement covering the entire surface of the stone. The cutting stroke is forward; that is, the edge advances across the surface of the stone with some pressure. After a few strokes, a burr (wire edge) will appear on the top of the blade. Turn the chisel over (not quite flat) on the surface and wet it off. The burr will reappear on the beveled side. Again turn the blade over and repeat operations until the burr is removed. If the burr is persistent, the edge may be drawn through a piece of soft wood which will remove it. The chisel should now be sharp and ready for honing and stropping.* Honing is done with the hard Arkansas slipstone, and is usually done while holding the slipstone in the left hand and the chisel in the other. The angles already established should be followed. The leather laminated block may be used for the stropping operation. When stropping a tool, the edge should always *retreat* over the surface. Otherwise it will bite into the leather and ruin the strop. Strop first one side and then the other until no burr appears. Again, if there is a persistent burr, repeat the operation suggested above. The chisel should now be razor-sharp.

Sharpening the gouge is much more difficult, but the operations are fundamentally the same. The bevel is maintained on the wheel of the grinder in the same manner as in the case of the flat chisel, but rotated so that the curved bevel is cut evenly. Some carvers hold the gouge in one hand and the India stone in the other to whet the bevel, while holding it against the vise or some other steady-rest. I prefer to use the stone as in the first case, but hold the blade of the gouge at right angles with the oilstone and advance it over the surface with a rotary reciprocating motion. The burr is removed during the honing operation with the Arkansas slipstone, the flat surface being used for the outside bevel and the convex edge for the inside of the gouge. Stropping is done in a similar manner but with the edge always retreating from the leather. In both instances the gouge may be held against a steady-rest while the slipstone or leather block is held with the other hand.

The V-tool is the most difficult one to sharpen. It should be conceived as two flat chisels coming together to form a sharp-angled "V." A teat is apt to form at the point where the flat surfaces come together. This projection should be carefully whetted off after the grinding procedure. The bottom of the "V" should be slightly rounded and not allowed to remain at a sharp angle. The heel of the tool should be given a slightly smaller angle. Otherwise, sharpen as in the case of the flat chisel. When sharpened correctly the V-tool is the most useful of all the carving tools.

In summary, the tools should be held against the grinding wheel lightly. Be careful not to burn the edges. Keep the tools cool and do not rush the procedure. Carefully performing the sharpening operation will pay off both in time and ease in carving. The neophyte should practice with band iron until he achieves some skill in the grinding procedure. Tool steel is much too expensive for exercise, especially when formed in carving tools.

Read other authorities' directions on how to sharpen tools to get other perspectives of how the job is done. Some tool suppliers have good suggestions printed in their catalogs. With the kind permission of Frank Mittermeier, Incorporated, the directions printed in the company's brochure are reproduced (Figure 9). Read these directions carefully as they conform with the techniques used by the experts.

Sharp tools should be carefully protected from abrasive substances, especially the edges. The park sculptor, referred to previously, appreciated this aspect of his work. Some carvers keep their tools in racks on their

* There is some confusion concerned with honing and stropping the tool. Some authorities hone their tools with an Arkansas slipstone while others use leather. The author hones his tools with an Arkansas slipstone and strops them with the leather laminated block.

After the proper bevel (angle) and sharp cutting edge has been ground on the grinding wheel. The carving tool has to be hand whetted, honed and stropped for a keen edge.

A carving tool should have two cutting bevels, outside and inside. The so called outside bevel should be ground on the grinder, the inside bevel must be hand whetted or honed.

The amount of whetting to be done, depends on the sharpness of the cutting edge after grinding.

Chisels: Whet the 12° to 15° bevel in a circular or "8" shaped movement on a flat India oilstone, till a fine bur (wire edge) has turned up. The other side of the chisel with the blade almost flat, should be rubbed on the oilstone till a short bevel can be noticed. Follow with honing, hold the tool in one hand and the Arkansas oilstone in the other hand. Rub the oilstone in an up and down movement, with the pressure on the downstroke — against the cutting edge — Hone the large bevel first, then the small bevel. The bevels should be flat and the cutting edge square, do not round the corners.

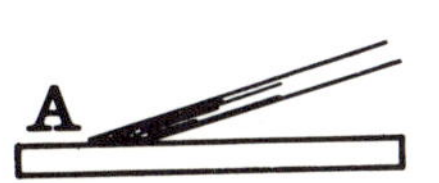

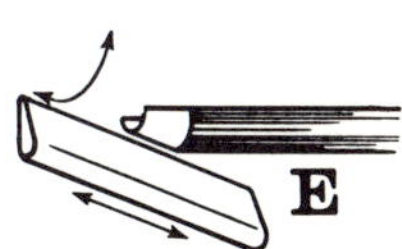

Straight Skew Chisel: Should have a 12° to 15° angle on both sides, as the tool has to cut right and left in sharp corners. Whetting and honing is the same as on the chisel, except that both angles should be equal.

Gouges: The outside bevel can be best whetted by rocking it for and back on the inside of an India gouge slip. For the inside bevel use an India round edge slip. Stroke the oilstone up and down till a bevel has been formed all around the curve (sweep) of the tool. On gouges with the No. 9, 10 or 11 sweep, use a round or pointed oilstone, to prevent rounding the corners of the tool. For honing use a hard Arkansas round edge slip, the flat side for the outside bevel and the rounded edge for the inside. On tools with the No. 9, 10 and 11 sweep use a round or pointed Arkansas oilstone. When honing, apply the pressure on the downstroke.

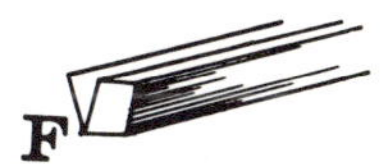

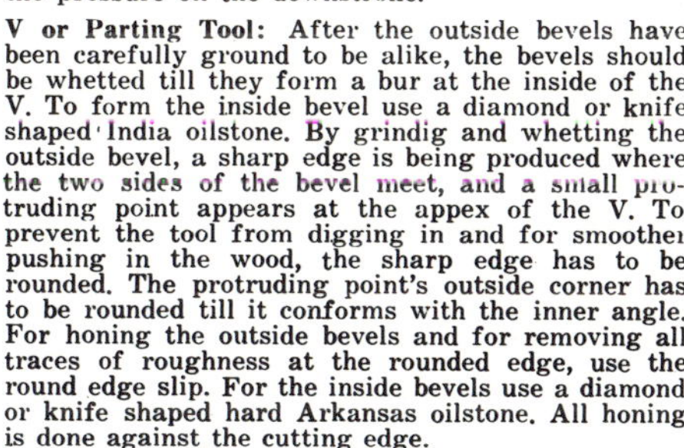

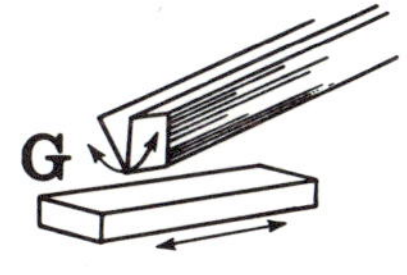

V or Parting Tool: After the outside bevels have been carefully ground to be alike, the bevels should be whetted till they form a bur at the inside of the V. To form the inside bevel use a diamond or knife shaped India oilstone. By grindig and whetting the outside bevel, a sharp edge is being produced where the two sides of the bevel meet, and a small protruding point appears at the apex of the V. To prevent the tool from digging in and for smoother pushing in the wood, the sharp edge has to be rounded. The protruding point's outside corner has to be rounded till it conforms with the inner angle. For honing the outside bevels and for removing all traces of roughness at the rounded edge, use the round edge slip. For the inside bevels use a diamond or knife shaped hard Arkansas oilstone. All honing is done against the cutting edge.

When a bur has formed, which cannot be easily removed by honing, draw the edge of the tool a few times across the corner of a woodblock or cork, that will remove the bur completely.

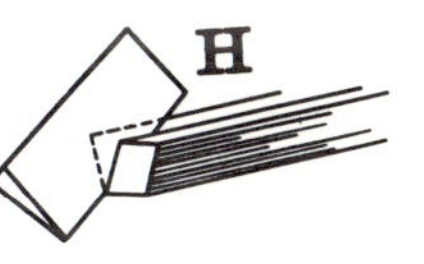

To prevent glazing of India and Arkansas oilstones use Pike Oil or a light oil mixed with kerosene. A few extra drops of oil on the stone is better than letting the stone get dry.

All tools should be stropped before using. The tool is drawn across the strop with the cutting edge trailing, to prevent the tool from cutting into the strop.

Drawings

A) Whetting of chisel's outside bevel.
B) Whetting of chisel's inside bevel.
C) Whetting of gouge's outside bevel on the inside of gouge slip.
D) Whetting and honing of gouge's inside bevel.
E) Honing of gouge's outside bevel.
F) Protruding point on V tool.
G) Rounding of sharp edge and protruding point V tool.
H) Whetting and honing of V tool's inside edge.

Figure 9. Whetting, honing and stropping. *Courtesy*, Frank Mittermeier, Inc.

workbench; others use cloth pack rolls with a pocket for each tool. Whatever method is used, avoid injury to the sharp cutting edges.

Tools that are not to be used for a long period of time should be given a coat of oil, applied with a soft cloth, and stored in a dry place. Hardly anything can be more frustrating to a "fussy" craftsman than rough, rusty tools. Tools are his best friends and they will never fail if given proper care. The carver is advised to be "fussy" in caring for all his equipment.

Chapter 3

BEFORE THE CARVING BEGINS

A question often asked by interested observers of my work is: "How do you begin?" or words to this effect. The answer resolves itself in my own mind by trying to answer a question of my own: "Which came first, the chicken or the egg?" While my first efforts would appear to be thinking out the idea in all of its ramifications of form, pose and perch, I am conscious of the fact that whatever I imagine is conditioned by my research about the birds and ducks I carve. My initial plans, therefore, are influenced by books, pictures and statistical data upon which I rely for references. All of this background work must be considered in the project and, of course, it constitutes a reserve from which to enlarge or to otherwise enrich the subject as it progresses toward completion. Which of these techniques came first, the idea, or the supporting related information, is a moot question. But the query is not really important, for like all other such matters, the end results are what count—the integrated whole, preconceived in any psychological pattern or direction. Background material permeating the germ idea, taken together, is my first step.

In a few instances, the mental image is further supplemented by observation of a living model. This experience might even result in a revised conception of the idea itself. Whenever possible, a live model is studied before the carving begins. Observing a live model is rarely possible, but when the opportunity is available, notes and sketches are made of the living bird or duck. Usually, the background material consists mainly of books and pictures—good books and pictures by the authorities in their respective fields. A carver cannot go far wrong by using this material for color, markings, form and general characteristics of the particular bird he carves. By faithfully following the colors and form of such realistic painters as Peterson, Singer, Weber, and a few other recognized illustrators of birds of our streams, waterways, and fields, the carver is relatively safe in the natural portrayal of his work. The experienced carver should not plagiarize an artist's work, but the neophyte should proceed cautiously until he has better command of his tools and knows more about his birds. Even the beginner should soon learn to depend upon his own imagination for the pose- and action-positions of his carvings. His aim should be to carve original models so that they will appear fresh and stimulating to the observer. The advantage of using a live model is in promoting greater originality, both in concept and skills, in addition to affording authentic details of markings, color and form.

Only last spring (1967) I experienced the inadequacy of book information. I was using a very poor edition of Audubon's *Birds of America.* I had carved a life-size Great Blue Heron wading in water. The work was scaled from the picture and the color patches painted on accordingly. When the carving was completed and the colors brushed in, there was a noticeable lack of authenticity in the general appearance of the bird. Something was wrong. The heron did not seem natural, for I could observe these birds wading in the creek just beyond my backyard. The birds are not sociable, so a close view is seldom possible, but their regal, statuesque poise and general characteristics may be observed with field glasses. About this time some friends from the city visited our farm. When the wife saw the carved heron, she exclaimed, "Why we saw one of these birds as we crossed over the bridge at Church Hill." Being familiar with the location, the author replied, "Well, if you did it is a dead 'pigeon' for it will never be able to take off without flying over the highway and it will not be high enough to clear the traffic."

No more was said concerning the matter for the moment. Later my wife and I accompanied our friends on a drive in the country. When we returned, we saw the heron spread out on the pavement before crossing the bridge. The bird had been killed instantly by a passing automobile. Our driver stopped the car and I stepped out and picked up the bleeding heron. It had just been hit. I held it out of the car window until we reached home. The next day, after carefully observing the dead bird, measuring vital parts, and studying the color markings, I skinned the creature for future reference. I learned that my carving was indeed imperfect in several details—perhaps not entirely the fault of the book. For example, the heron's neck was as long as its body; the thighs were burnt sienna in color, and the bill was longer and different than the carved model both in shape and color. Eight full inches were added to the neck and the bill was entirely recarved. The bill terminated in a sharp, black point, and there were streaks of yellow on both mandibles. Underneath them the concave section was lined with white downy feathers. The feathers of the neck were long and droopy, showing white flecks all the way down to the necktie. There were also flashes of burnt sienna on the wing shoulders. The belly was almost white and the remainder of the bird was slate blue, the color from which the heron gets its descriptive name. Many of the features just enumerated could not have been illustrated by the artist even if he had been faithfully reproduced, but the picture was poor and the pose was not the best for reference in carving the bird.

My carved heron was inaccurate in several important details which is the danger when carving solely from pictures. I had, to the best of my ability, followed the contours shown in the book illustration, but failed to achieve the desired results. But in this particular case there was still another factor, a corrective one, which was the result of my familiarity with the bird. I knew that the poise was not precisely "heron," and the general appearance was not realistic. Yet, it was enough like the live bird for my friends to recognize it. It could easily have passed for a good model to the layman, but the discriminating eyes of an artist would know better.

The imaginative phase of beginning a carving must take in many aspects of the bird's characteristics. His creative planning goes for nought if accuracy of detail is not achieved. Most, if not all, carvers make mistakes in their work—sometimes unpardonable ones. Minor mistakes will probably go unnoticed except by the most thoroughly informed individuals, but major errors stand out like sore thumbs. Gross faults mark the inadequacy of a carver and he will never be recognized as a master even though his work shows the magic touch of a chisel. In the case of bird carving, the artist must be precise in both form and color. He must be either abstract, stylized, or realistic in his models. He cannot exercise the liberties allowed in the former two techniques if he desires to please collectors.

While writing this chapter, a friend called my attention to a featured article appearing in one of our larger metropolitan newspapers. It concerned an able craftsman who had turned his woodworking experience and talents to the carving of birds. The main illustration was of a duck in flight, expertly streamlined with the *regular bill of a duck*. The caption "Merganser" was unfortunate, for anyone familiar with ducks knew that the title and the picture did not match. The carver had not done his preliminary work thoroughly. Those who are familiar with wildlife know that the bill of the Merganser is somewhat like that of the tube-nosed birds; it is long and slender. The biting edges (lamellae) are serrated like a fine-toothed saw with the points in the direction of the head. In fact, the colloquial names, sawbill, tweezers and several others, have reference to its uncommon bill.

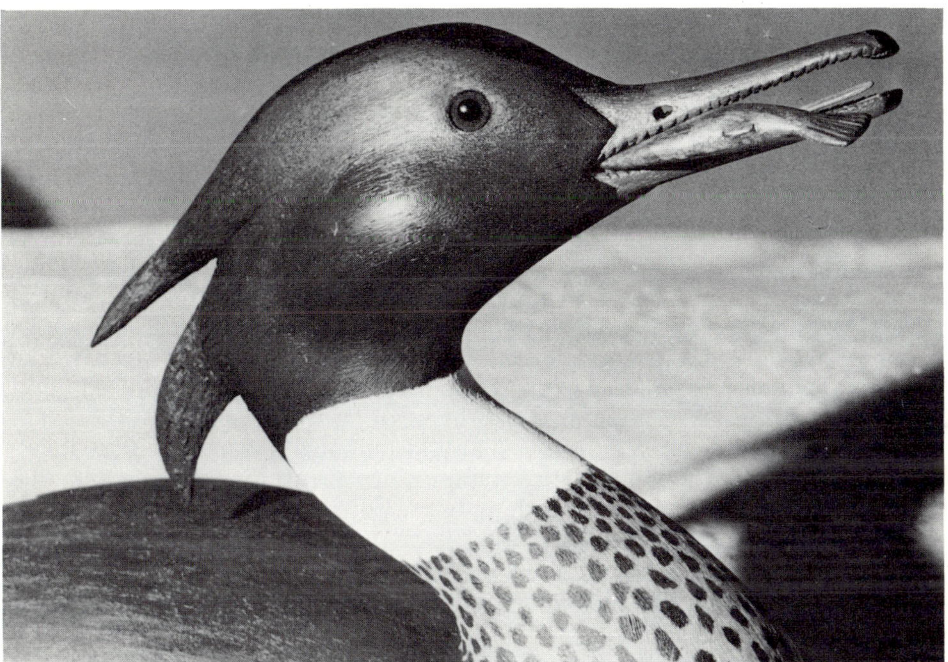

Figure 10. Head of male American Merganser. Head and upper neck, metallic greenish black. Crown feathers elongated but not forming noticeable crest. Carving by Bill Birk, Remington Arms Co.

Figure 10 shows the head of a carved Merganser by Bill Birk of the Remington Arms Co.* Mr. Birk knows his birds, but apparently neither the proofreader nor the carver of the featured article knew their Mergansers. Notice that the *nail* of the upper mandible hooks over the lower, a design common with the tube-nosed birds but very uncommon in ducks.

The two illustrations in the preceding paragraphs are narrated to indicate the danger of using books and pictures alone for related information. The carver must have some familiarity with the birds he carves. If he is not familiar with the species, he should visit a zoo, game reservations—any

* The head of the Merganser shown in the photograph is that of a decoy duck carved by Mr. Birk and now owned by the son of the former Governor of Maryland and Mayor of Baltimore, Theodore R. McKeldin.

place where a live (or stuffed) specimen may be found. Otherwise, in all likelihood, he will carve inaccurate feet, bills, or some other important part of his subject. His study of F. H. Kortright's book (*see* Appendix) might save him from an embarrassing moment, but no book can take the place of the live or stuffed specimen. Yet books are the carver's best friends. They are an easy and convenient source of reference, and the best of them are authentic; that is, they are as accurate as a picture can be. Reproductions can never be the same as real birds because of the problems of the technique, with regard to both perspective and color. A foreshortened member in a picture, or the off-color of feather markings, can play havoc with a carving involving these features. Even painting a picture is not the same as painting a carving—there is a strange difference. Even so, the wildlife painter achieves amazing results and his pictures are invaluable if the foregoing discussion is seriously considered.

Most wood-carvers of my acquaintance have little to guide them in the way of drawings, especially detailed drafts. Most of them depend upon a design vividly engraved in their respective minds resulting from their organized related information and familiarity with their subject. All, more or less, use books for references; some make use of zoos and game reservations. Carvers living near larger cities study stuffed models in museums of natural history. A few others carve from memory alone. These are the individuals who have studied wildfowl all of their lives. They have spent many of their waking hours roaming the fields, marshes, and beaches. They are as familiar with the forms, markings, and other characteristics of the birds they carve as they are with the appearance of their closest friends. But most carvers, including the author, depend heavily upon artists like Peterson, Singer, Weber, and other recognized painters, for both form and color, and still other book references for vital statistics.

When I decide to carve a figure of any kind—bird, animal, or figurine—I spend many, many hours in contemplation, mentally working out the details such as size, pose, and perch or base. I do this at night while in bed, before sleep overtakes me. Many times during this period I continue to muse upon my subject into the wee hours of the morning. The whole composition is first crystallized in my thinking before the wood is selected. This power of visualization is invaluable to the creative artist. The gift varies, no doubt, both in intensity and vividness among individuals, but all carvers must possess some talent in this respect, for the mental image is a highly important aspect throughout the entire carving procedure. Upon this power rests, in no small degree, a feeling of and for the concrete shapes the carving is to assume; of form flowing behind the chisel, so that the fillets and angles of direction seem to take their respective places naturally in the block, as if following a grooved template. In a manner of speaking, this is so, for the strange phenomenon is but the directing impulse of the preconceived image. The solid block that looked so formidable and impossible at the beginning takes on new meaning. As the form begins to emerge, the task becomes easier and more exciting. The chips fly as with a magic rhythm guided by skilled fingers that know the way. Verily, the great Creator must have had a chisel and mallet in his hands when he carved out the universe.

After the thought processes have jelled—after the bird has been carved in the imagination—a template of the pose along the central axis is drawn on sheet metal or a piece of tracing cloth. When cut out, the sheet metal template may be used from either side and the tracing cloth also can be used from both surfaces. The template becomes the anchor holding all of the parts in their respective positions. The outline is never lost. It constitutes the center line of both the back and the breast. Whenever it is cut away it is redrawn, for even a casual observer can tell when a carving deviates from the central plane.

The block is carefully outlined with the template and a profile cut of proper thickness. The importance of an accurate profile cannot be overemphasized. It establishes to a high degree the length and depth dimensions, leaving only the third, breadth, for the carver to consider while chipping out the rough figure. The vital statistics of breadth, height, wingspan, and other dimensions are already in the carver's mind, or close by on a notepad. So, the rough carving from here on out is merely removing unwanted material beyond the divider or caliper marks.

When one of his observers inquired, "How do you do it?" Michelangelo is reported to have said, "O, there is nothing much to sculpturing—you merely knock off the marble you don't want."

A more modern professional has phrased the thought differently: "If you are carving an elephant, chip away all material that is not elephant."

These facetious statements are, of course, an oversimplification of the problem. Yet, they contain much food for thought, especially for the beginner. They are basically true. The real difficulty is in knowing what marble to knock off and what is not elephant. In the case of the author's technique, a good start has already been made in comprehending the problem. The mental image of the carving already conceived and the more tangible silhouette likeness (template) will help show the way to differentiating between the subject and the material in which it is encased.

Later on in this text some instruction will be provided in the use of tools in the carving process, and more specific directions for chipping off wood that is not a part of the bird. In the meantime, think upon these things: the background material, the mental image and the template. Coordinate them! These procedures, before the carving begins, will be of invaluable assistance to you.

Chapter 4

PROJECT NO. 1

COSTUME JEWELRY

Ever since this book on bird carving was conceived, I had been casting about for a suitable project for the first lesson. Quite by accident, the matter was decided for me by a young lady. She had broken off the wing of her mallard duck, a piece of costume jewelry made of rosewood. She asked me to repair it since she valued it highly for sentimental reasons. It was a beautiful little pin about 3½″ in its greatest dimension. The head was painted green and the collarband was white. The rest of the duck was plain except for the main markings, which were lightly incised. While repairing the pin, the project was conceived. Miniature birds seemed to be the answer to all of my inquiring thoughts.

Birds are probably the most interesting creatures on earth. They are easy to carve. Even a poor effort has a pleasing result. Birds not only offer a challenge; they have intrinsic value, even when inexpertly carved. Children with varying degrees of skill whittle them successfully. Certainly costume jewelry would not be too difficult for the beginning carver; yet it would have the potential of consuming interest. It would provide some elementary exercise with the carving tools, especially the knife, V-tool, coping saw and files. The small Japanese carving set would be satisfactory for these small carvings.

Women like costume jewelry and the lesson would give them, their husbands, or friends, an opportunity to carve their own bird motifs. Also, the pins would be an ideal dinner gift for the hostess and for many other occasions. These were my thoughts and sufficient reasons to make the project appealing to carvers of either sex.

The carving material is inexpensive. If scrap wood is available it will do for the beginner. A fellow carver in Florida recently sent me such a carving made of yellow pine—a gazelle on a circular background. A visit to the lumberyard or cabinetmaker might result in a number of pieces of beautiful woods for which the proprietor has no further use. While the cost is little or nothing, the intrinsic value of the finished pin is very favorable, especially if the work is cleverly done. Carving a bird or duck in the flat requires little skill as compared to carving it in the round. A whittler can perform such jobs and have something to show for his efforts. The more skilled carvers, too, should like the project if they have not advanced from high relief to the third dimension. This lesson, therefore, should be highly productive of initial enthusiasm and lead naturally to more insight and appreciation of the carver's art.

As stated previously, only a few tools are necessary for this project. In fact, the operations may be performed on the kitchen table, but why run the risk of getting off to a poor start by aggravating the little woman, or mother, and perhaps snuffing out all further interest by cutting off a finger? While a machinist's vise is not entirely necessary in this project, it is highly desirable because of convenience, speed, and safety. The lesson will proceed with the assumption that a vise is available, leaving the unfortunate carver without one to struggle with his handicap. From the beginning the neophyte should be safety conscious. He should learn to keep his fingers *back* of the cutting edge of his tools. He should not think of the Band-Aid kit as his most important facility. A bloody finger is a nuisance; it is usually painful and is always an impediment to the carving efforts. Furthermore, the vise will provide greater control of the tools as the carver can use both hands to manipulate them.

As indicated earlier, the wood for the beginner should be inexpensive and easy to carve. It should be well seasoned and clear of knots, contrary grain and other faults. An experienced carver may desire to use more expensive

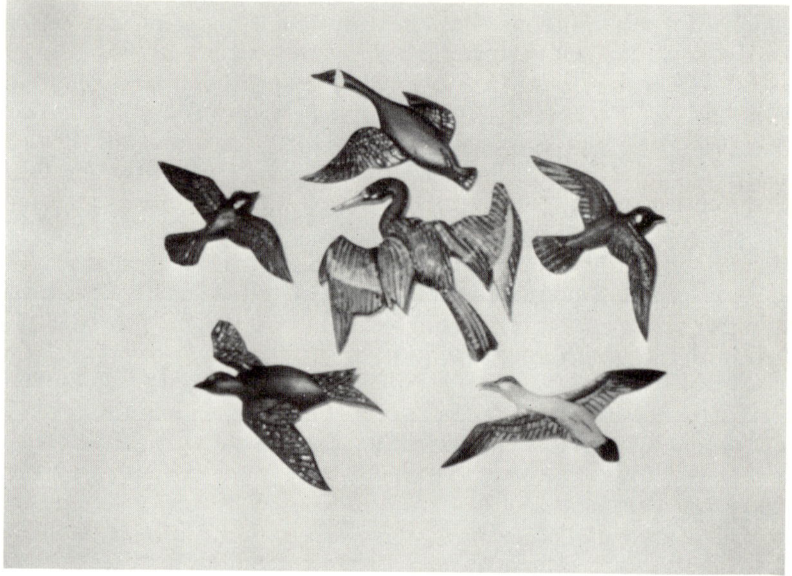

Figure 11. Costume jewelry.

woods to achieve more pleasing effects. In fact, the birds shown in Figure 11 were carved from rosewood and holly. But the beginner should be content with less expensive wood until he is able to carve interesting pieces of jewelry. Irrespective of the kind of wood from which the pins are fashioned, they will be attractive if skillfully carved and finished to a professional gloss. A pin nicely done will bring $5.00 in almost any market.

The material for the pins should be ¼″ thick with both surfaces dressed. It should be cut in blocks or squares large enough to include the entire outline of the bird with a little waste wood to spare. A piece of standard veneer (1/28″ thick) should be bonded to one surface, the grain running crosswise.* Bonding the veneer crosswise will strengthen the weaker sections of the carving. Several of these blocks may be prepared and clamped in the vise to set overnight (Figure 12).

When the laminated blocks have set long enough, remove from the vise. Draw the outline of the desired birds or ducks on the ¼″ side, or surface,

* If contact cement is available (the kind used to bond veneers), it may be used with excellent results. Follow the directions on the can.

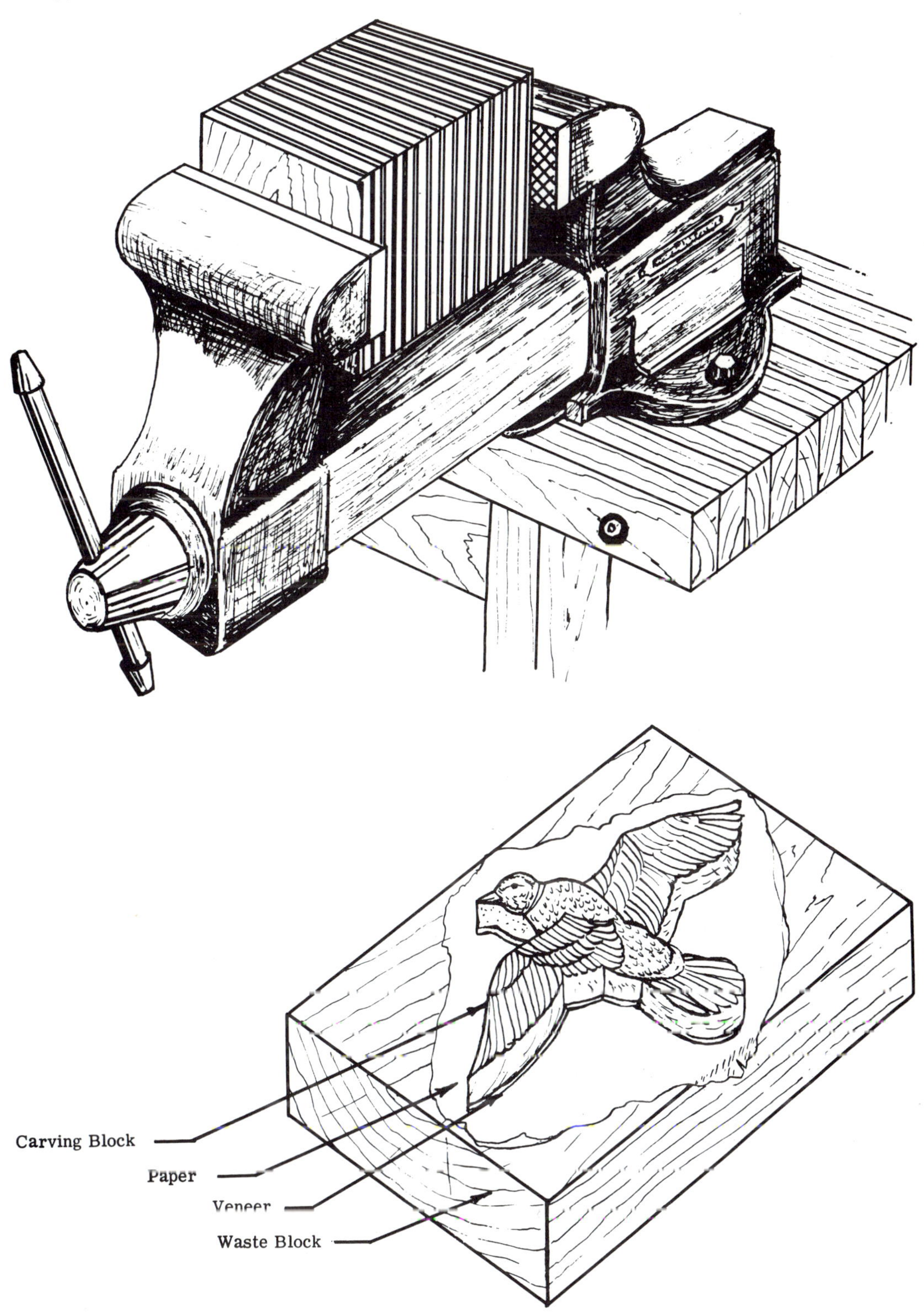

Figure 12. Preparing blocks for costume jewelry.

with the grain running with the length of the bird, usually (but sometimes with the wings, depending upon the structure of the design). (*See* Figure 13.) Saw along the outer edge of the outline with a coping saw. Remember that the teeth of a coping saw point toward the handle and that the cut is made, Chinese fashion, with the pull stroke. Saw slowly and carefully, following the outline; the resulting silhouette or profile should not appear as if it had been chewed out by a beaver. The kerf should be clean and crisp. The finished surface of the block showing the outline of the bird may be protected from vise marks by inserting a piece of soft wood or leather between the vise jaws and the block.

When the outline has been cut out, smooth the edges with a sharp knife, or rifler file, where necessary. Next, cut some blocks of ¾″ waste wood large enough to receive the bird. Glue the profile to the block (veneer down) with a piece of brown paper placed between the two surfaces. Mucilage or rubber cement should be used for this operation as the bird must be lifted off of the block when carved. The paper will facilitate the separation of the two parts. As in the case of the laminated blocks, several or all of them may be clamped together in the vise at one time.

When the cement has set, remove the blocks and clamp one of them in the vise with the bird side up. Carving may now begin. There are several contours to consider. The advancing edge of the wing is thicker than the trailing edge. Some wings have camber on one side, some on the other. None of the edges should be carved down to the waste block; the feathered edge is too weak. Carve down to about 1/16″ in the low places and when the bird is removed from the waste block, chamfer from the other side with a steep angle. The back wing is set lower on the body than the other as the view is usually from above. When viewed from below, as in the case of the Canada Goose, the technique is not much different. Strive for a realistic effect. Imagine how the bird would look when viewed from the perspective indicated (Figures 11 and 13). The feather and wing markings can usually be scored in with a small V-tool, but a sharp knife might be handy as well. Both chisel and knife are best operated while the bird is clamped in the vise. Control the depth of the cuts to a minimum. Carve the feathers lightly; deep cuts weaken the carving and it will be no more effective. The V-tool may be pushed gently with the hands in many places, and in all spots only a light tap of a small mallet is necessary.

After the bird has been carved, locate the eyehole with a prick punch or small nail. But before installing the eye, be sure that the carving is smooth as a result of either very fine sandpaper operations or keen tool cuts. A carver with some experience might not use sandpaper at all; the raw chipped surfare is more effective. Always sand with the grain.

The eyes may be formed in various ways. The best eyes are made of glass and may be purchased small enough for the birds of this lesson (2 mm). Rhinestones may be effectively used and marquise jewels, especially, point up the carving in its jeweled aspects. An eye may be made of a small escutcheon pin, polishing the brass to a high luster. But escutcheon pins split the wood easily, so a small hole should be bored for them. To keep them from falling out, they may be slightly burred from the other side. If a small drill bit is not available, a small brad with the head removed will serve equally as well for such small holes. A common method for small birds is to form the eyes with a sharp nail set (deeply countersunk) of the proper size. Practice this operation on a waste piece of material until the proper effect is achieved. Do not install the glass or jeweled eyes until after

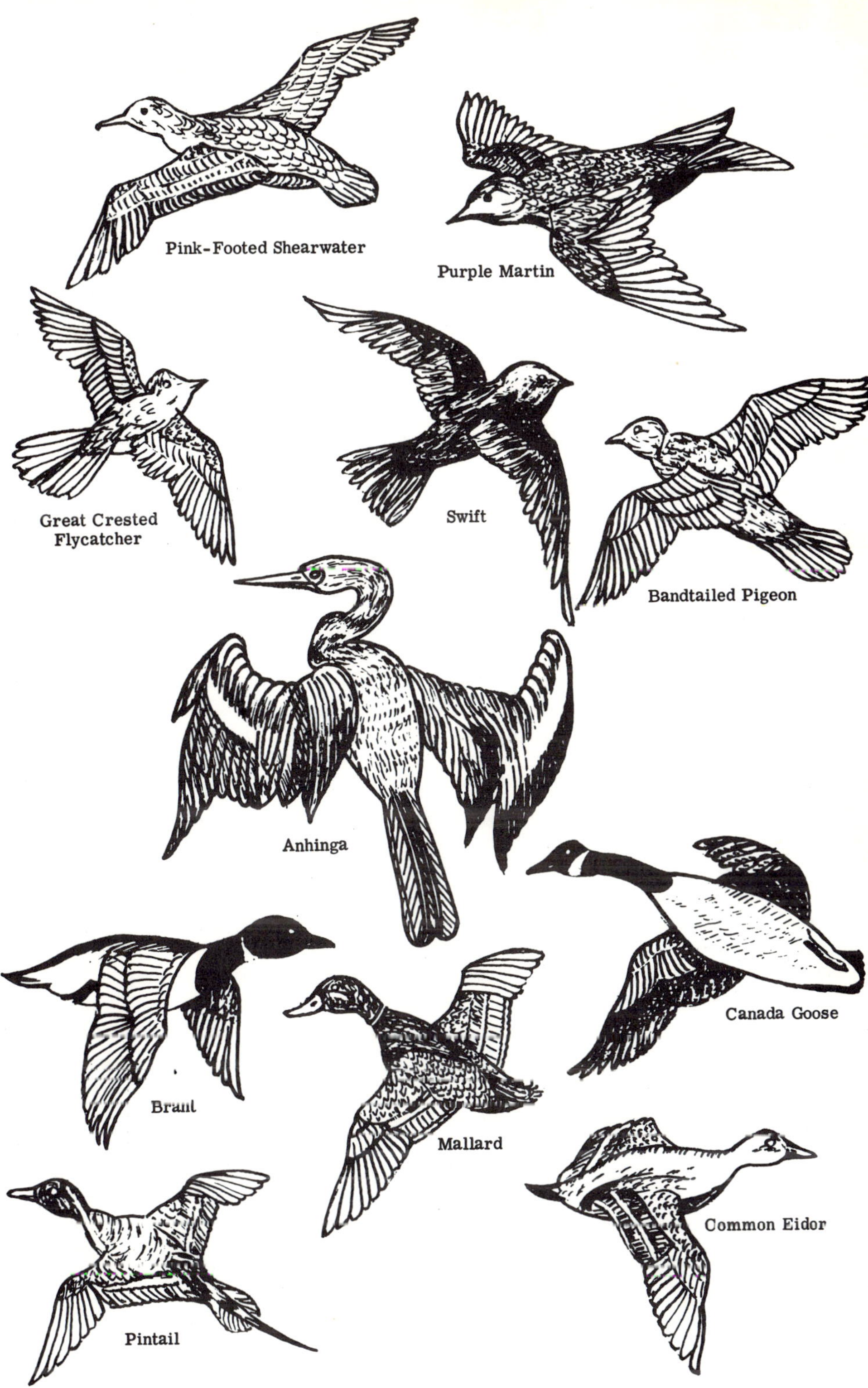

Figure 13. Motifs for costume jewelry made of wood.

the finishing operations. The glass scratches easily and varnish dulls them. The eyes may be stuck in place with the varnish used in the finishing process. Of course the varnish should be clear. Lacquer may also be used. Glass eyes usually are attached to fine wire. Insert the eye and wind the wire around the bird's neck until the varnish sets. For glass eyes, consult the chart in Chapter 14.

Give the bird a coat of sealer before removing from the waste block. Firzite or Beauty-Lok are satisfactory sealers. Even a coat of clear varnish or lacquer may be applied before the bird is removed from the block. It is less likely to be soiled by the fingers.

When the initial finish has dried thoroughly the bird may be removed from the waste block. Start with a very thin chisel where the grain runs with the lifting action. Trying to lift the carving off by prying under the grain at right angles will probably result in a splitting effect. The carving should not be difficult to remove, but if it should be contrary cut into the waste wood and shave off the surplus material with a knife. While holding the carving in the hand cut the chamfers referred to earlier and make the outline crisp. Join all of the undercuts in an artistic contour.

The next operation should be installing the safety-bar pin. These findings are available at most jewelry stores. The general catalogs of such materials listed in the Appendix carry them. The pins are fastened to the back with contact cement. Coat both the pin and the back where the pin is to be located with a good coat of the cement. Allow to set up for at least twenty minutes before bonding. Be sure you place the pin in the right position on the first trial. The bonding is instantaneous. To further strengthen the pin, coat the surface of the joint with contact cement. The pin will serve as a holding device while applying the remaining finish. Read Chapter 13 before attempting to finish any carvings described in this book.

Before applying the finish the typical markings of the bird concerned should be painted in with enamel. Do not overdo the painting of colors. The natural wood is highly effective and the colors are used only to give special emphasis, to identify the species. The mallard duck that I repaired had a green head with a white collarband. The rest of the surface was natural wood. In this case the speculum might have been painted, but the artistic taste of the carver decided against it. Be sure each coat of varnish is hard before rubbing down with fine steel wool. The last coat may be rubbed down with rottenstone and linseed oil.

The illustrations shown in Figure 13 are supplied for the beginner who lacks drawing experience. They represent a small fraction of many designs possible. The ambitious creative carver will design equally effective ones.

As these lines are being written there is no way of knowing how large the reproduction of the birds will be, so a suitable size should be suggested. The birds illustrated averaged about 3½″ in their longest direction. In all probability the drawings will have to be enlarged. This task will present no serious problem. On a piece of tracing cloth or transparent paper prepare a grid of lines ¼″ apart. Place the grid over the desired bird and carefully trace in the design. If the bird is to be enlarged, prepare another grid with the lines farther apart to produce the desired enlargement. A ⅜″ grid will increase the illustration one-half its size; ½″ apart will double the size of the picture (Figure 14). Obviously, the principle may be used in reverse to reduce the size of the birds.

Accompanying each wildfowl illustrated is a description of its outstanding markings. These markings may be painted on the carving with regular commercial enamel paint of the desired color or paint from the tube with a drop or so of dryer. A brush full of color will usually do the job, so do not waste your paint. The colors and the incised feathers will identify the species of the bird the carving represents. This latter phase of the lesson will challenge the artistic taste of the carver as well as his ability to carve a beautiful bird.

Shearwater. This is a tube-nosed bird with pink feet. The beak is yellow with a black tip. The wing bars may be tipped lightly with the same yellow. Under the neck and small portion of the belly show a bluish white. Beak and wing bars will provide sufficient color emphasis.

Purple Martin. A dark wood is preferable for this carving. A soft wood dyed dark purple would be desirable. No further color should be necessary except for the eye which should be a light color for contrast.

Pintail. This duck is the most popular of all wildfowl among professional carvers. There are few indeed who have not carved its likeness in one form or another. The chief markings are the white stripes from the breast continuing up the neck and almost meeting just above and in back of the eyes. The tail feathers of the drake fan out conspicuously (white) and two or more long feathers continue some distance beyond and usually terminate in a point. The long pointed tail is the marking which gives the duck its name—or rather *his* tail, for only the male has this marking.

Common Eider. Orange brown bill which rises higher on the head than in most ducks. Wing bars are white; primary and secondary feathers are greenish black. The head, front portion of the back, and belly are white. Female is brown instead of the foregoing drake markings. The bill and primary feathers should give enough color emphasis.

Great Crested Flycatcher. Paint primary and tail feathers a brick red, tipped with burnt sienna. Leave the rest of the wood natural.

Black Swift. Ebony would be ideal for this bird. Beginners should use soft wood dyed with India ink. A little white may be indicated on the forehead with a streak across the eye.

Bandtail Pigeon. This is a beautiful bird. Yellow bill, small white neckband. Back may be brushed lightly with emerald green. Taper color to blend with natural wood. The main distinguishing marks are the gray tail feathers and dark brown (reddish) band.

Anhinga. Very long bill, top mandible yellow; lower orange. Blue mask over eyes. Wings are stark white with black plume feathers hanging over them. Ash, holly or any white wood is suitable for this bird with the plume feathers inked in.

Brant. This goose is very familiar; somewhat like the Canada goose except the neck is shorter and has a neckband (white) instead of cheek markings. Neck should be black.

Canada Goose. White cheeks, long black neck. Black tail feathers and slate-black legs and feet. Leave the rest of the goose natural.

Mallard. Most familiar duck. May be found on most farms. Emerald green head, yellow bill, and ultramarine speculum. Blue bronze powder may be lightly brushed over blue to produce a sheen. Green neck and white collarband with the speculum (perhaps) afford enough color emphasis.

The carvings shown in Figure 11 were made by the author to test out the descriptive matter of this chapter. The color arrangement was not always followed for in order to kill two birds with one stone, rosewood and native holly were used instead of the soft woods recommended for the beginner.

ASSIGNMENT: Carve all of the birds illustrated. Design another pin, using any motif desired.

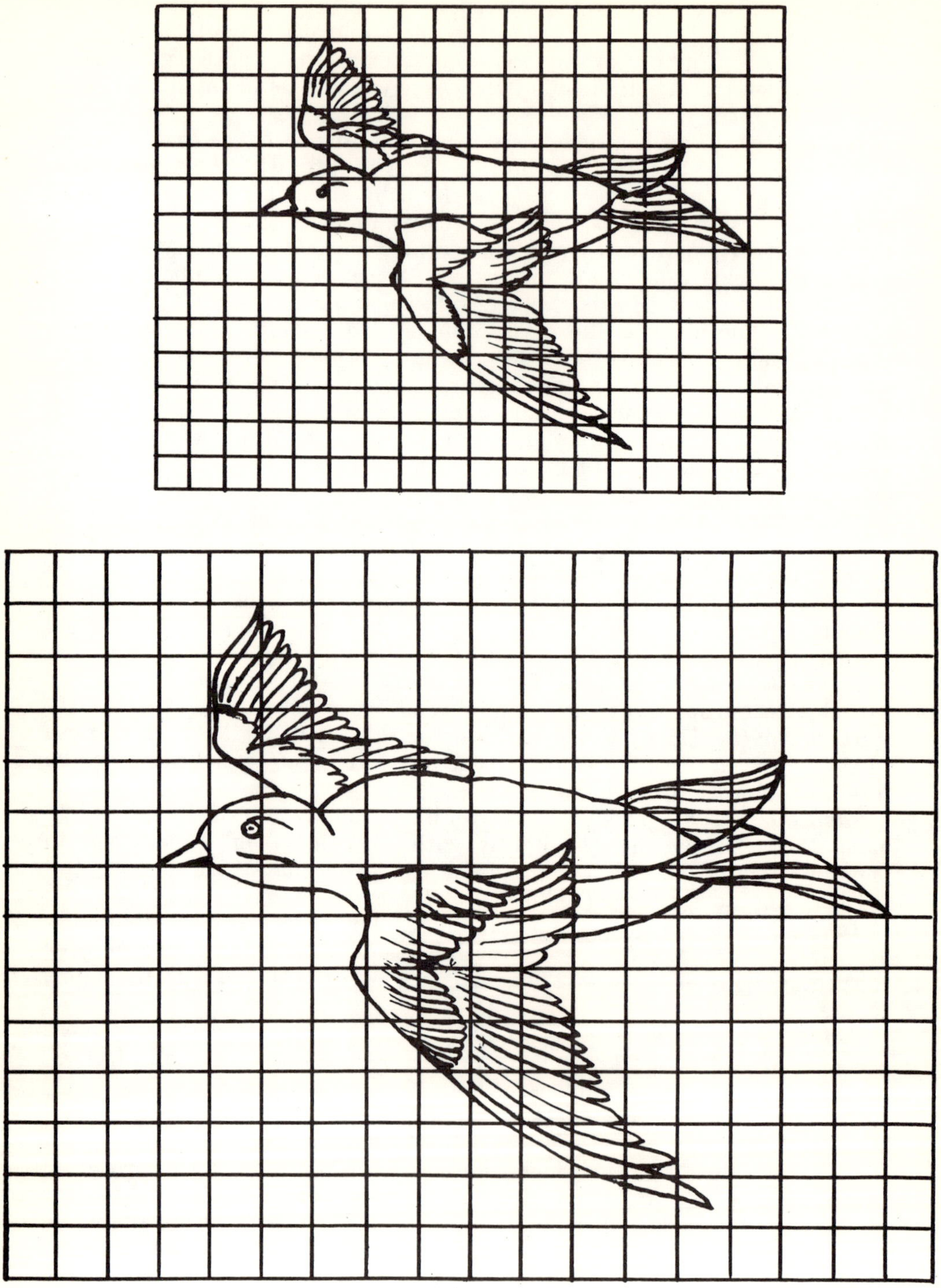

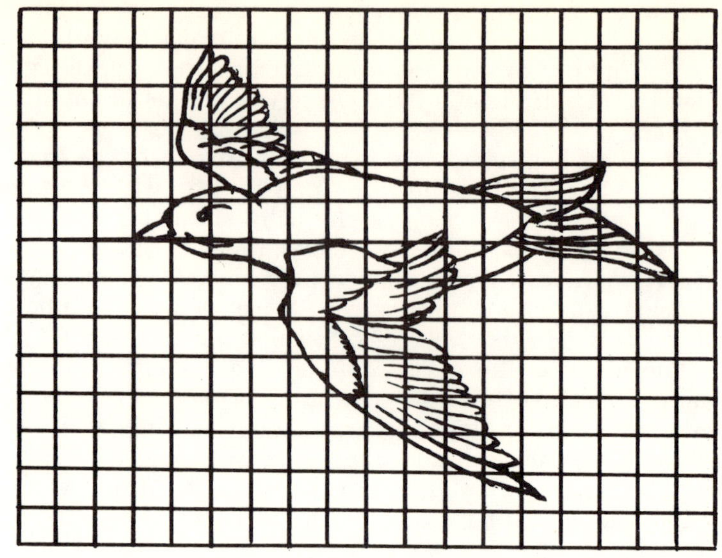

Figure 14. Method of enlargement

Chapter 5

PROJECT NO. 2

A SKEIN OF GEESE

While casting about for a suitable project for the second lesson, which logically should begin where the Costume Jewelry left off, and lead naturally to a more difficult effort, I observed a Canada goose stranded on the ice just off our waterfront. My first impulse was to launch the rowboat and rescue the unfortunate, wounded creature. But it seemed in no immediate danger and the day was cold and stormy; the hour was late and although the mind was willing, the flesh was weak. Therefore, rationalizing the situation, I believed that the goose could take care of itself until morning. In any event, it would violently resist any effort to bring it ashore. I gave no further thought to the matter for the moment. But during the night the wounded bird kept drifting into my thoughts. Early the next morning I rushed down to the waterfront to rescue the goose, irrespective of its wishes in the venture. But the altruistic thought had not been taken at the flood and now the rescue would be only an empty gesture. During the night the noble bird had perished.

While bringing the goose ashore, the thought of using it for some worthy cause or purpose entered my mind. I mourned the sad death of the pathetic creature that had died forsaken, frozen on the ice. Only a few brief days ago it could keep its place in the skein and fly as majestically as any other in the flock. While it suffered on the ice its fellows were feeding happily on the wildlife reservation at Bombay Hook or some other nearby place of refuge. With such depressing thoughts in mind the idea of using the goose for the second lesson was tentatively conceived. The idea jelled after I had read the morning paper. In the pictorial section was an excellent photograph of Canada geese in flight by Chuck McGowen of the *Wilmington Morning News* staff. "Canada Geese on the Wing" (Figure 15) carved in high relief against a flat surface, as a wall, would not only help to develop the carving skills but would provide an interesting objective to drive the efforts. The skein of geese would be comparatively easy to carve and when finished in their natural colors would be a unique decor for the home—a decorative work of art. What an impressive picture for the wall leading up the stairway, opposite but higher than the banister rail! The drawings might have to be reversed in some instances for the geese should be flying up, and not down, the staircase.

So the second lesson will be a skein of geese. They should be carved as realistically as possible on the facing side and mostly flat on the other with the outline undercut on a steep angle to project the birds from the wall. After the geese are carved and arranged against the wall they should give the appearance of the picture they represent, almost as realistic as McGowen's photograph.

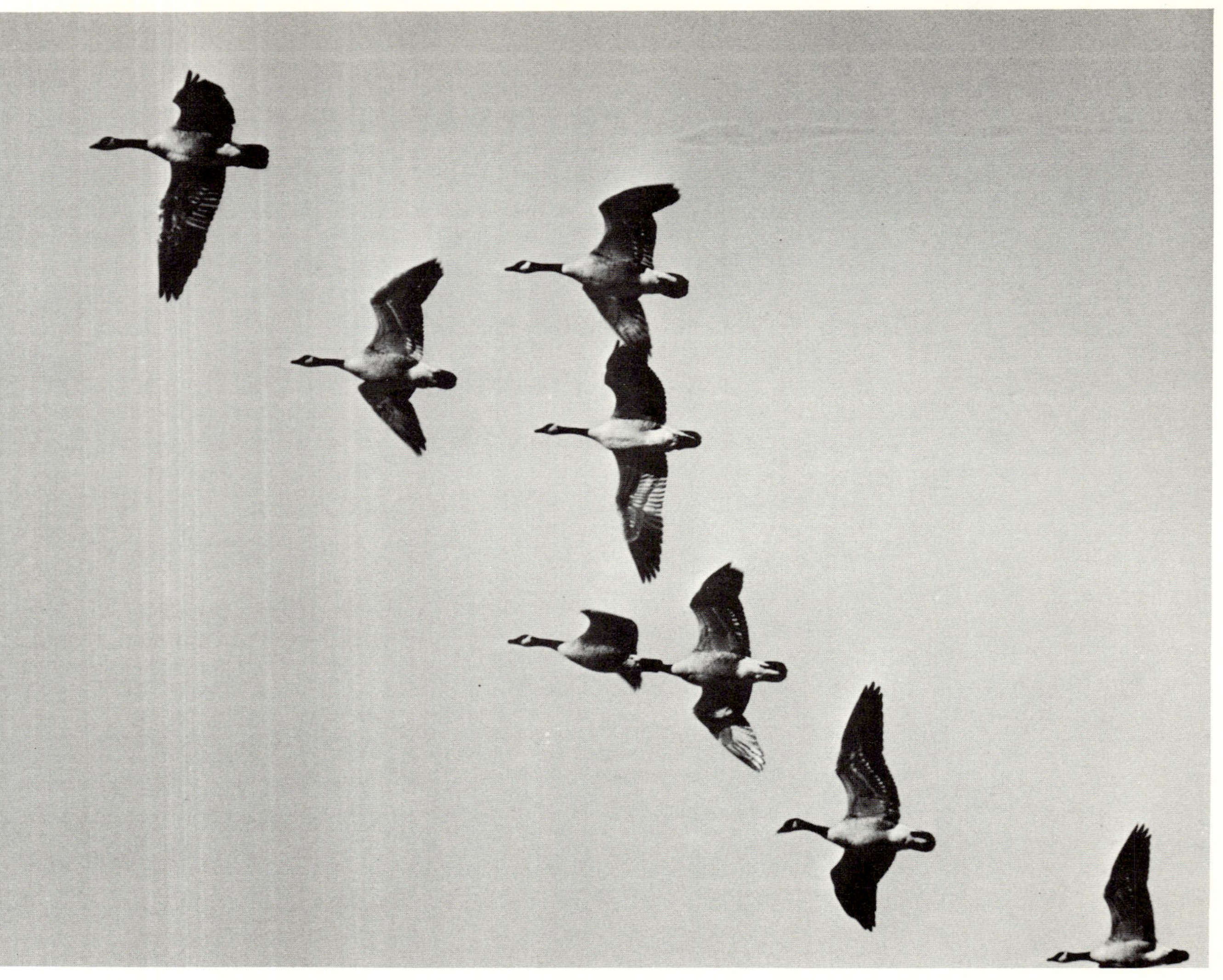

Figure 15. Canada geese on the wing. Photo: Chuck McGowen. *Courtesy* News-Journal Co.

As usual, the first task is to draw a template, one for each bird. The drawings in Figures 16–18 inclusive show the proper profiles. The carving

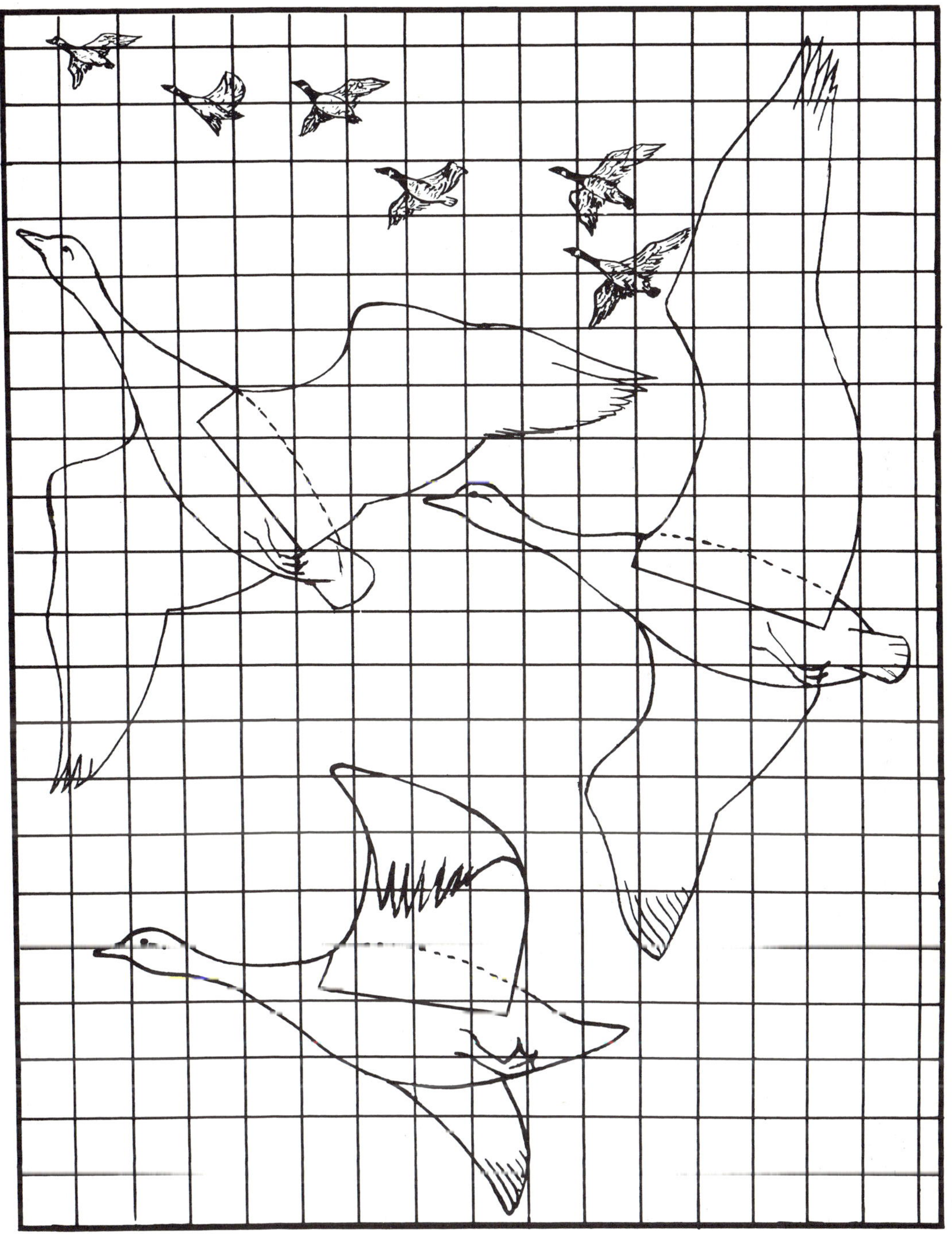

Figure 16. Template outlines (½″ squares).

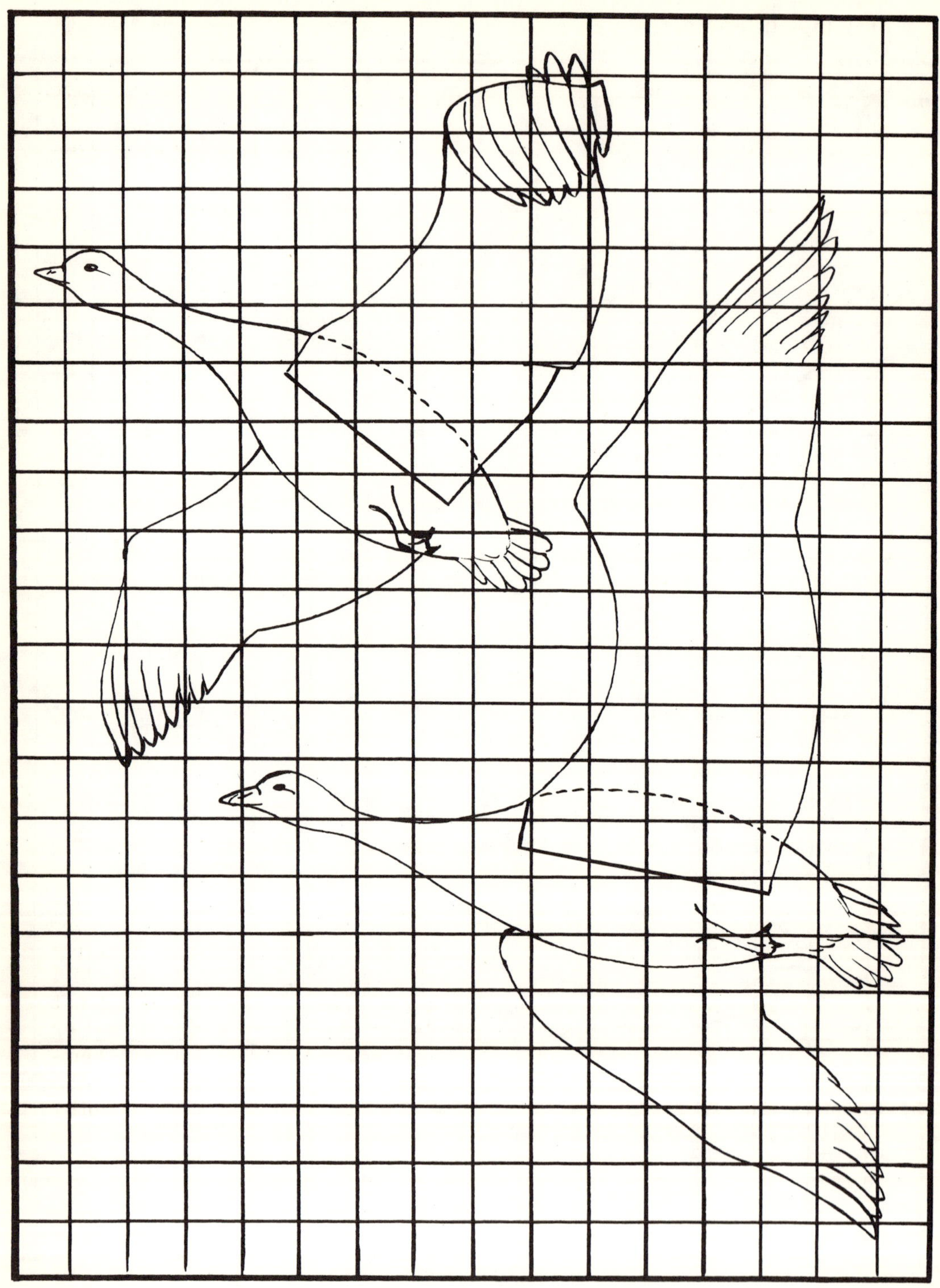

Figure 17. Template outlines (continued).

material should be white pine or one of its substitutes, especially for beginners. (Experienced carvers who might be inspired by the idea may desire to carve their geese in expensive woods and give them a natural finish.) The bodies of the birds are carved from 1″ stock and the wings are 5/8″ thick. After they have been drawn on tracing cloth and *enlarged,* the profiles should be used to guide the carver in shaping the wings and the body. Figure 19 shows the method of construction. Note that the grain runs with the length of the body and the wings also. Obviously, these birds should not be carved from a single block; first, because of the grain problem, and second, because of the extra work required. Learn to do the joinery work with precision. In the present case the premium is not on this phase of the work, however, as the geese will be painted. Any inaccuracies may be filled with a plastic filler. The gluing job should be done skillfully for the strength of the profiles is only as strong as the joints. In the naturally finished birds, the seams must be expertly joined or the carver's ears will be subjected to many unfavorable remarks by critical observers. Precision in this case is just as important as any other aspect of the carving.

Before gluing the wings in place, prepare a block of waste wood 1″ × 2″ × 4″. Glue the wings in place and the block on the wall side of the wing. Clamp the whole assembly in the vise and let set overnight.

After the wings have set firmly, remove from the vise and reclamp the waste block between the jaws. The profile is now ready to be carved. The first operation is planing off the uneven surface. Study Figure 20 showing the wing shape, method of laying out, and cutting the feather markings. First, shape the wings as illustrated. Remember that the leading edge is heavy, considerably thicker than the trailing edge. Do not taper the wings to a feathered edge but leave at least 1/8″ material at the lowest spots to be tapered from the under side on a steep angle. A feathered edge will break off. In all carving procedures watch the strength factor; carving is a time-consuming activity, so do not ruin many hours of work by weakening certain sections of your birds. The wings also taper toward the first primary feather, but, again, do not carve the wings too thin. Depend on the under-cutting from the wall side to sharpen your edge. Note that the tips curve slightly in the opposite direction from the concave shape. As in the case of the costume jewelry, the lower wing sets below the body, the breast and belly being rounded to it.

When shaping the feathers notice that they are carved in a step-like series, beginning with the plane of the primary and secondary feathers and continuing up the wing to the shoulders. The risers of these steps are not more than 1/16″ in any place, the feathers of one section ending 1/16″ or less below the feather tips of the following one. Next, the feathers themselves may be laid out and carved. Remember the edge of one slips under the adjacent feather in a shingled fashion, the lower edge about 1/32″ (depth) below the other. During the sanding operation these elevations may be controlled to give the desired effect.

Most of the wing carving can be done with the V-tool and small flat chisel, but a sharp knife will be useful from time to time. Whatever tools are used, the chips should be sharp and crisp. Do not produce a "hairy" effect. Most of the carving should be done while the profile is held firmly in the vise; you have more control of your tools when both hands are free to use them. The wall edges of the carving are probably best carved while it is held in one hand and the knife in the other. The neck and head should be carved also without the benefit of the vise.

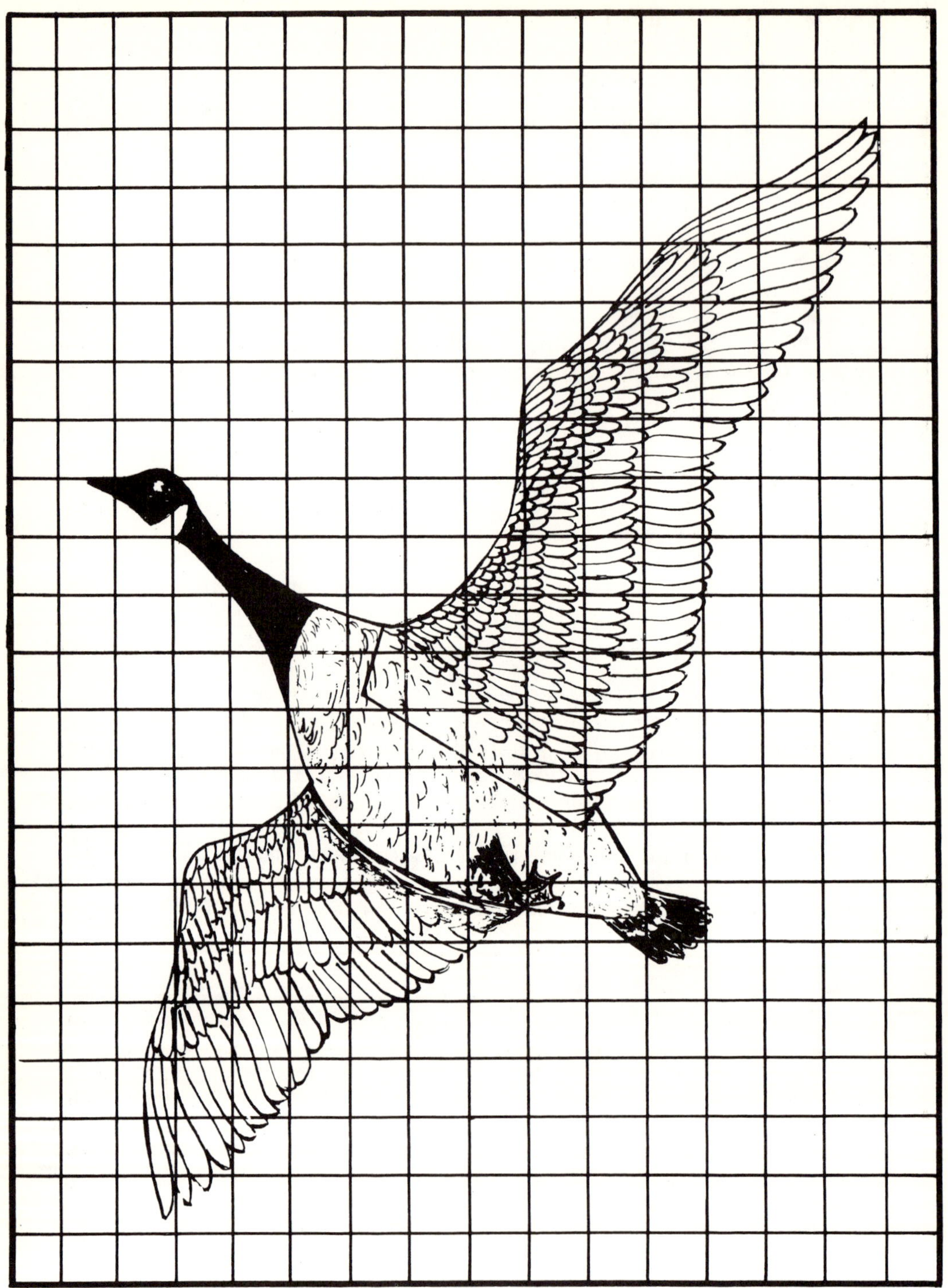

Figure 18. Outline showing markings of Canada goose (½″ squares).

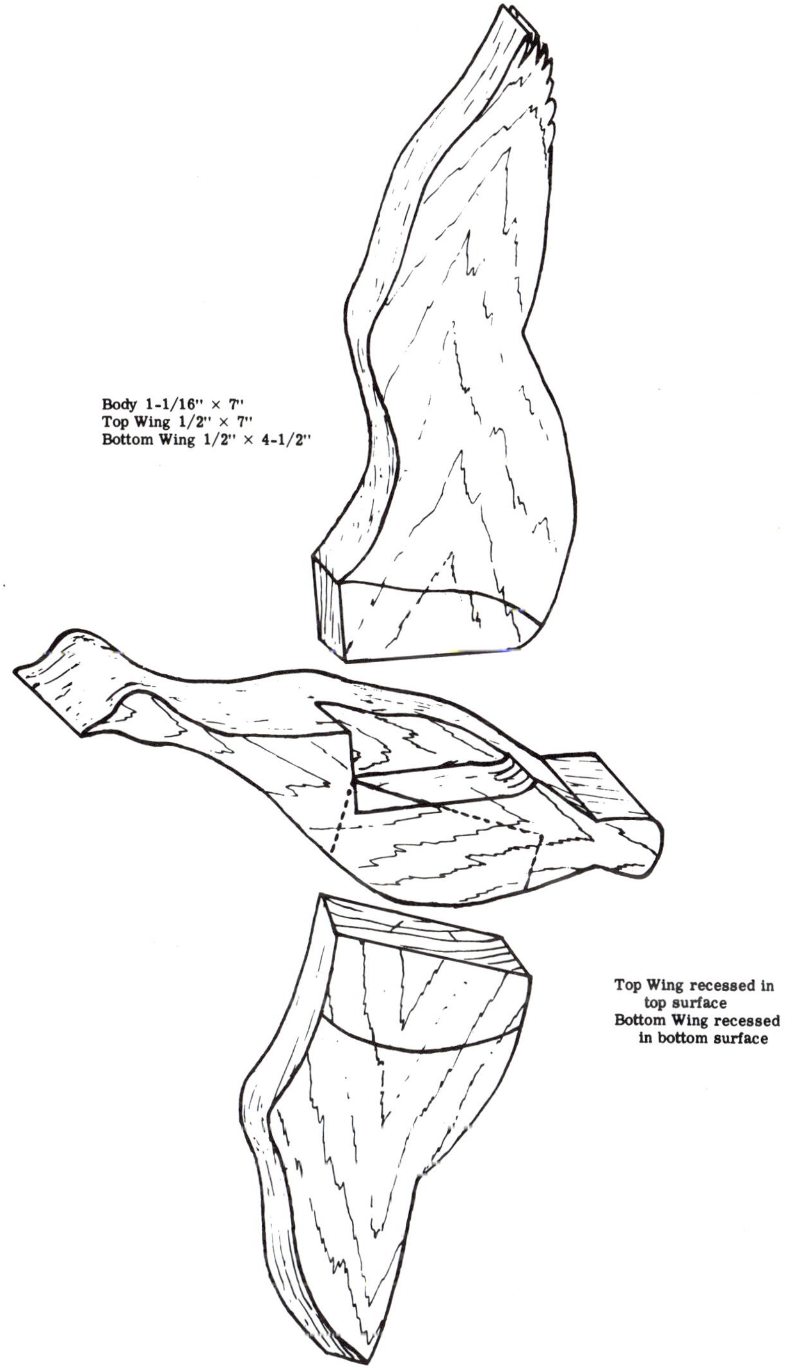

Figure 19. Flying goose construction.

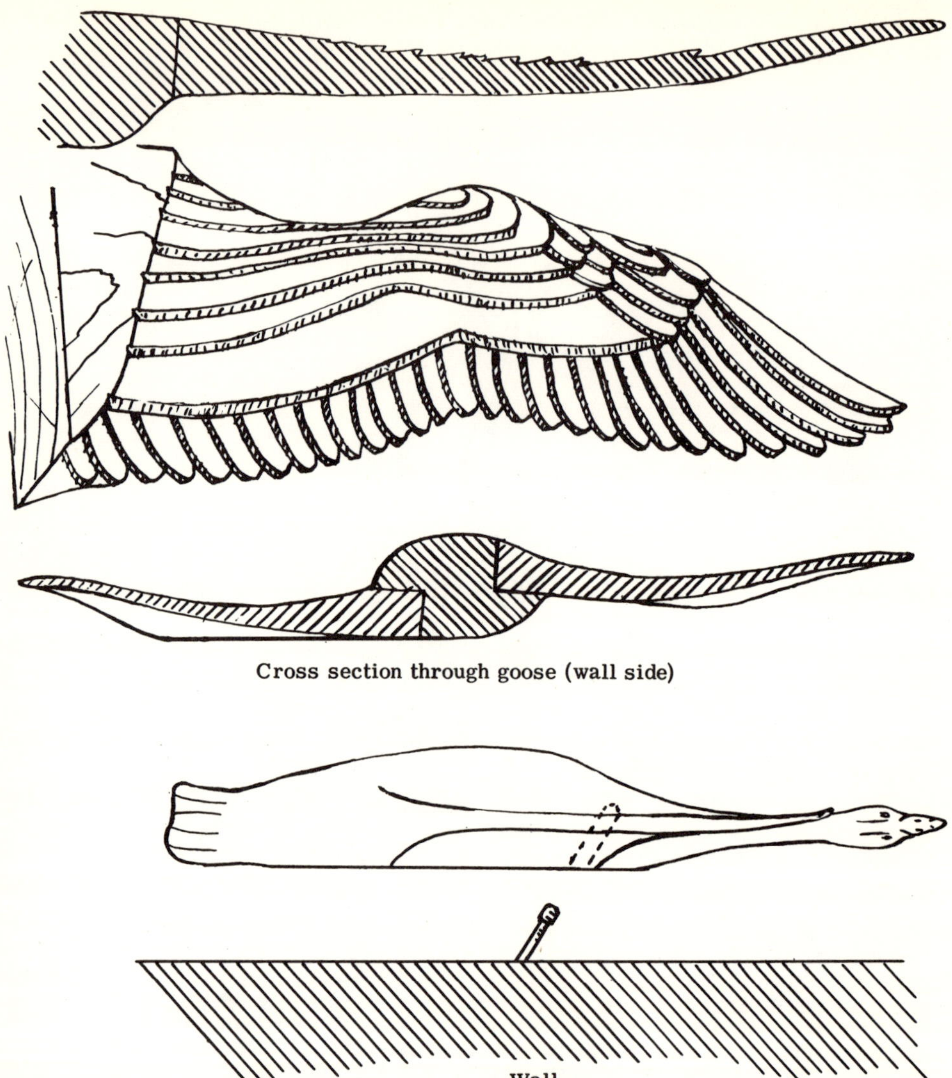

Figure 20. Method of carving feathers and hanging carving on the wall.

Locate the neck and head in the middle of the block or body profile. Carve it from both sides with a sharp knife, watching the grain very closely. A false cut here could ruin your work or cause extra time in repairing the split-off section. The head lifted from the wall will give a more realistic effect and will allow some variation in neck direction too. Carving the neck and head are delicate operations, especially the head. Remember that the bill of a goose is rather short and heavy and that the thickest part of the head is just behind the eye and under it. The cheek is the highest elevation and molds gently into the eye cavity. The crown of the head in a flying goose is not very pronounced as it is stretched forward to streamline the bird. Locate the eye with a prick punch or small nail so that it may be seen through several coats of paint.

Generally speaking, the breast and belly are rounded from the top wing to the bottom with a clean curve, the most abrupt appearing near the bottom where it joins the bottom wing. There is nearly ½″ of space between the two elevations (Figures 18 and 19). Only one leg with foot shows; the other is out of view.

Never feather the wing down to a sharp angle, as previously stated. Taper from the under-side with a steep angle of about 45°. Viewed from the carved, feathered side, the edge will look as if lifted from the wall and will give a better effect than the weaker design which is so easily broken.

At this point take a good look at your carving. All of the rough work has been done so the profile should look very much as the finished bird will appear. Are all of the cuts "goose"? If any corrections seem necessary, make them while the raw wood is still available. Does the feather effect please you? If you are satisfied, ripple the breast slightly—just enough to kill the smooth surface and give a soft feathery effect. Be careful in this delicate operation; too much carving on the belly and breast is much worse than none at all. Sand all other parts of the goose and prepare it for the sealing coat of finish. Figure 21 shows one of the geese before the finishing coat has been applied.

Before the finishing process is undertaken, the waste block must be removed. Probably the best way to do this is by splitting the block next to the carving. Place the block in the vise, end up, and tighten the screw. Carefully split the block with a wide chisel and mallet. Do not let the carving fall to the floor as some of the outline could be damaged. Dress off the waste wood with a knife or place the carving on a sandbag and after it is slightly embedded, chip off the waste-block remains with a chisel and mallet. The advantage of a sandbag holding device is that both hands may be used in tooling the object.

Carve the chamfers on the under side with a sharp knife, joining all of the back curves in a clean contour.

Next, drill the hole for hanging the carving. The hole should be drilled at the center of gravity to allow the bird to hang naturally. Determine this point by trial and error. Drive in a small brad where you think the hole should be located (about center of carving from back to breast). Loop a piece of string around the brad and hang against the wall. In all probability the goose will tip in one direction or another. Remove the brad and repeat the experiment until the desired spot has been located. Drill the hole at an angle as shown in the drawing (Figure 20) pointing toward the top of the carving, and about ½″ deep. This hole may be used to provide a handle for finishing the bird; sharpen the end of a stick and force into the hole for this purpose.

The finishing directions in Chapter 13 should be read carefully and studied before finishing any of the birds. Turn to this chapter and finish your geese. Be sure your markings are the right shape and in the right place. Be sure of your colors also.

After the finish has been applied and thoroughly dried, drill the eyehole. Glass eyes are preferred, but any of the methods described for making eyes in Chapter 14 may be used. Commercial eyes save time and will give "zip" to your carvings. Drill the eyehole to fit the eye and deep enough to allow about ⅓ of it to protrude. Drill the hole for the wire as small as possible. Cement the eye in place. Any quick-drying tube cement will be suitable. Just a drop into the hole will be sufficient. Insert the wire and pull the eye into position (glass eye). Use the surplus wire to hold the eye in place by wrapping it around the neck of the bird. After the cement has set hard, the wire may be filed off flush with the surface.

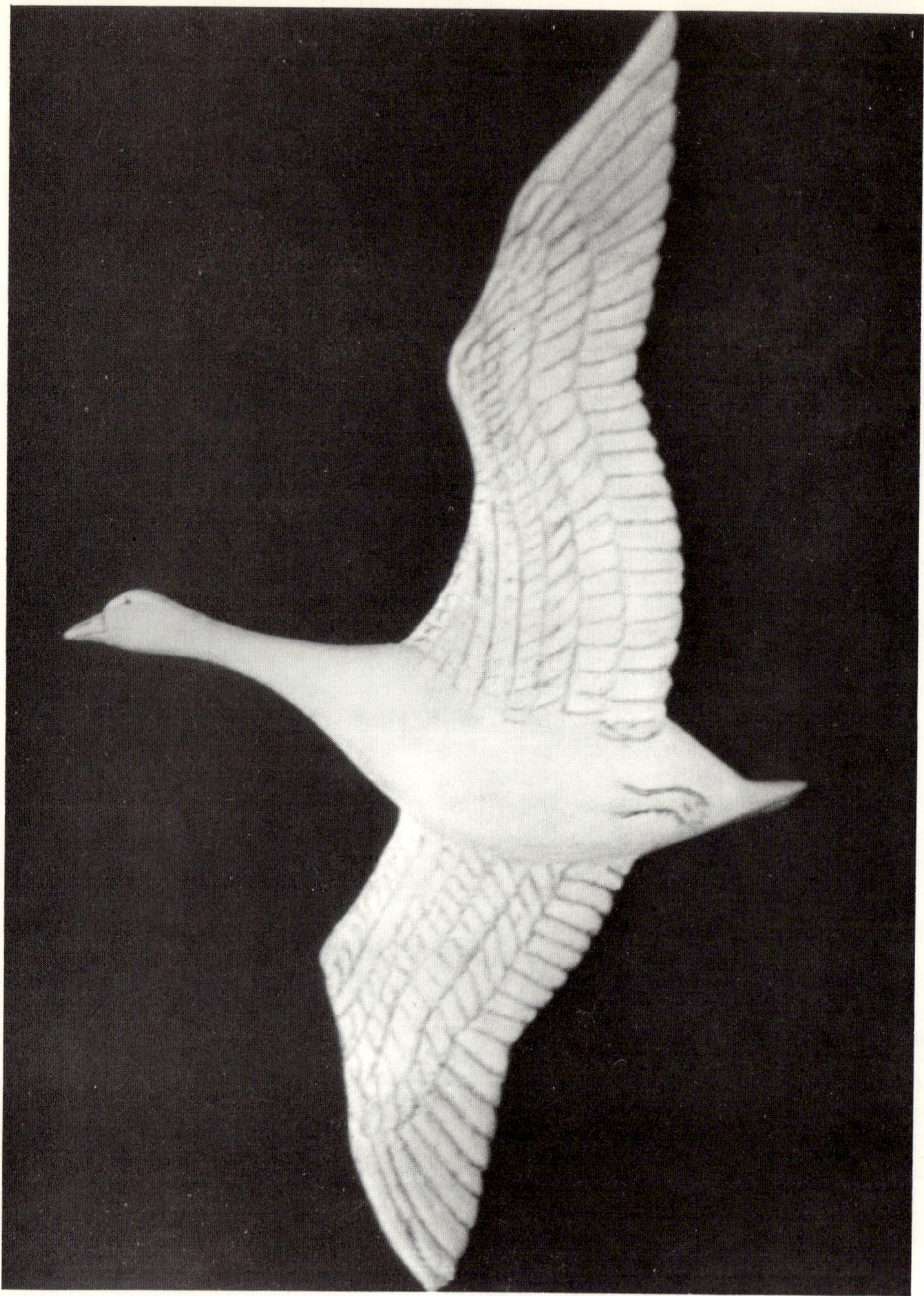

Figure 21. A carved Canada goose before the finish is applied.

ASSIGNMENT: Carve at least six geese—more will have a better effect. Carve a large duck, using the technique described in this lesson. You may not be able to use it yet, but later on it will be suitable for a plaque, or it may be used immediately over the doorway. Study Ted Hanks' plaques shown in Chapter 17 (Figure 82). Do not depend entirely, however, on the brainchildren of other carvers. Learn to conceive and design your own motifs. Try some spectacular wing arrangements showing action on your duck relief carving.

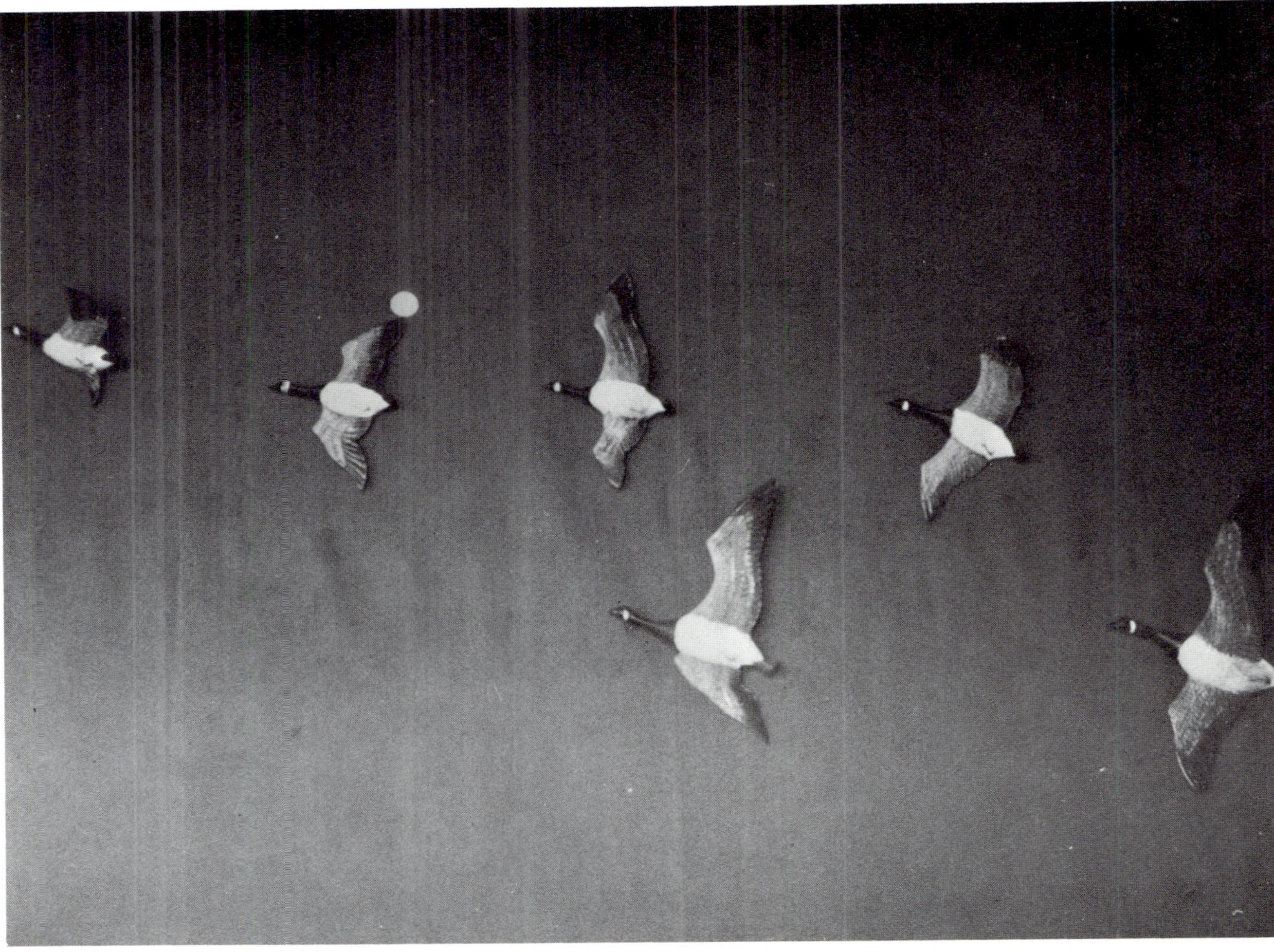

Figure 22. Completed skein of geese hanging on the wall.

Chapter 6

PROJECT NO. 3

LET'S CARVE A DECOY DUCK

A thing of beauty in every trace,
  In shape and form and classic grace,—
Embodiment of highest art,—
  Wood endowed with soul and heart.

W. L. Breyfogle
(From *Sense and Satire*)

The subject of this lesson is a drake mallard decoy duck. The drake mallard is one of the most beautiful models to carve. The hen of the species is not so colorful or varied, and is marked quite like a black duck but with lighter colors. There is little wonder that she is attracted to her mate instinctively, and with unusual affection. Because of this fact, their "tribe" increases, and they become probably the most plentiful of all wild ducks. They have been domesticated and there are few barnyards where ducks are raised which do not have a flock of mallards.

Why some individuals get pleasure in killing these elegant creatures is difficult to understand. To lure them within range of their guns with decoys is still more difficult to conceive by an experienced carver. But this is the human race for you in one of its paradoxical aspects. The slaughterhouse is revolting enough but perhaps this "carnivorous" pursuit of food is necessary, for man, like all other meat-eating creatures, must kill to survive. He has polished up his tooth and claw techniques somewhat, but he is still, nonetheless, a predatory animal.

The reader is warned before pursuing this text further that wildlife carving does not mix with the kind of sportsmanship indicated in the foregoing paragraph. I have known many addicted gunners who have turned carvers only to lose all interest in killing game fowl. "How I ever got any pleasure in killing birds and ducks I shall never know," said a nationally known wood-carver in my presence recently. Indeed, when an individual has been nurtured for a time on a diet of study and observation of wildlife, there is instilled in his nervous organism a sympathy and an understanding of life, and how precious it is to all living creatures. The creative spirit in its more sensitive aspects plays havoc with the more brutal concepts of living, and makes a person more aware of the mystery and wonder of nature in all of its myriad forms. Their civilizing regeneration has prepared them to assume the mantle of potential carvers. They, with diligence and industry, will become creators in their own rights, and many of them will become famous in their own time.

With these thoughts in mind the critical reader is probably wondering why a decoy duck was chosen as a worthy subject for this lesson. Be assured, it was not ill-conceived, for as a decoy *per se* it has no significance so far as this lesson is concerned. It is more like a sign of the times when

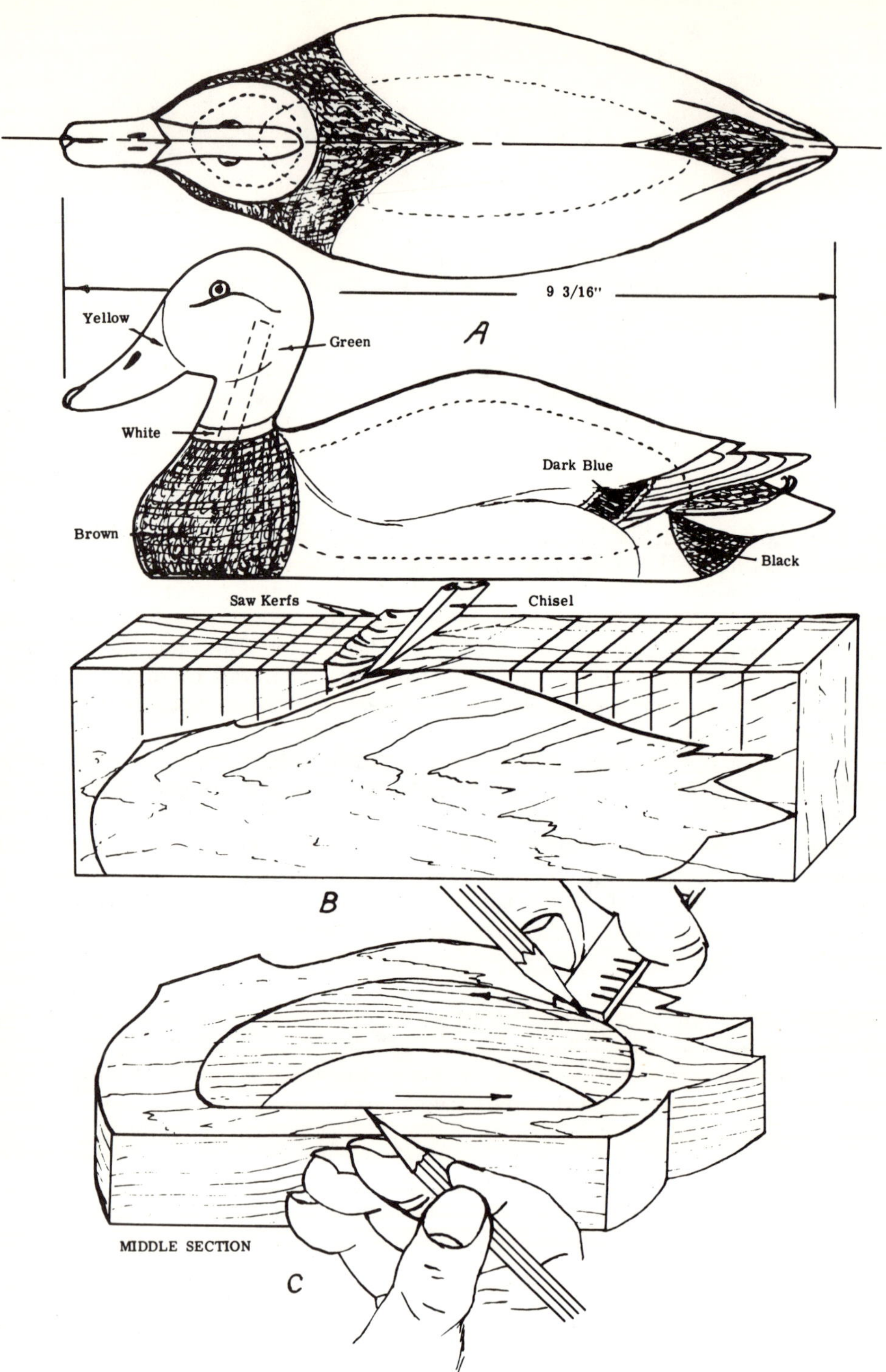

Figure 23. (A) Mallard decoy duck; (B) cutting out the profiles; (C) laying out the middle section.

no respectable home can afford to be without a decoy duck or two to tell of a past "glory" when every man was a Nimrod of sorts. But there are still pagans among us who have not been "converted" and they have a keen sense and interest in such carvings. They, too, should be served until they have seen the light. Also, the most sensitive of artists may have a shrunken head hanging by its hair in his studio, a skull, or any number of such sanguine trophies that have become symbols of a gory past. But by no stretch of the imagination can these persons be considered brutal beings, glorying in the primitive acts which have given their collection significance.

The more decorative decoy is the objective of this lesson, but the more sportive of our readers may carve many ducks, full size, according to the plans given here, and paint them male and female to satisfy their instinctive yearnings for hunting.* But give these individuals time. They will learn the better course of direction. They will eventually use their decoys as museum pieces, and their love of hunting will be sublimated in more altruistic instincts.

Preparing the Block. First draw the template. The drawings in Figure 23 are obviously intended to serve several purposes. It is the profile, or outline, with which we are now concerned. The drawing is of a decoy duck, half size. If a full size carving is desired the dimensions should be doubled. As was stated earlier, the template should be made of either tracing cloth or sheet metal. Usually sheet metal is preferred because it can be used over and over again. After serving the present purpose the template may be hung on a nail through the eyehole and stored for future use. The metal for this profile may be cut from a large fruit can; this provides the first use for your tin snips.

After the template has been formed, cut three pieces of 5/4″ white pine, wide and long enough to include the template. These boards will actually measure about 1 1/16″ thick if regular stock is used, making a combined thickness of over 3¼″. Apply the template to one of these boards and transfer the outline upon it. Repeat this operation for each of the other two boards.

Next, cut along the outside edges of these outlines making three separate profiles or silhouettes. The coping saw is used to cut all cross-grained portions and the angular sections of the tail ends. The parts which run with the grain may be cut off with a sharp 1″ chisel. Before using the chisel, the profiles should be prepared as shown in Figure 23 to simplify the job. Prepare all three boards in this manner. Remember this technique when removing waste wood in the absence of a band saw. When working down to a finished line always cut well above it for the first chip in order to determine the direction of the grain. If the direction is away from the line, the chisel may be used closer without splitting into the design. If the grain indicates a contrary direction, the chipping process must be reversed. After the profiles have been accurately formed, select one of them for the middle section. Scribe another outline within the block ½″ from the outer edge. The bottom edge may be ¼″ as there will be no more wood removed from this part of the carving. The outline is drawn as shown in Figure 23. This is another good trick to remember. If the space is too great to be scribed with the fingers, use a rule as a gauge and draw the line parallel to the contour. The latter method is similar to using a marking gauge. In fact,

* Before these decoys may be used in a practical manner they must be weighted with lead or steel to which the anchor line may be attached. Also, a waterproof glue should be used, such as weldwood.

both methods are based on the same principle and the marking gauge may be used instead. But the finger method of drawing parallel lines should be learned so that they may be drawn in the twinkle of an eye.

Cut out the inner wood with a coping caw. If a band saw is available, start at some point in the bottom where the kerf will not show and saw out the inner material. The coping saw, of course, may be started with a hole bored in the waste wood.

After forming the other two profiles, each in turn may be dished out to a depth of 1/4" following the outline of the middle section. Use your large gouge or fishtail for this operation. When finished, glue the three profiles together and clamp in a vise or by the use of two C-clamps until the glue starts to ooze. Never squeeze out all of the glue from a joint. A "starved" joint will not hold.

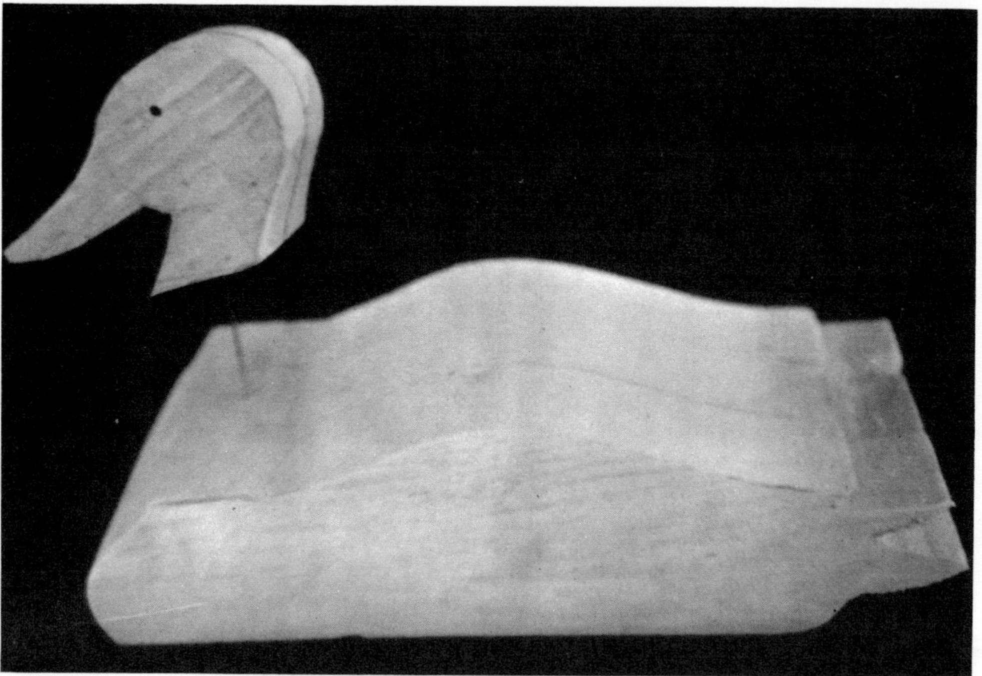

Figure 24. Decoy profile ready to carve.

Carving the Head. While the body block is setting up, the head may be laid out and carved. Draw the head carefully, allowing the lower edge of the collarband to be used as the point of contact with the body of the duck. First, cut the material to the proper thickness; about 1 1/2" thick. The lines of the head are critical. The least misguided contour may result in a spoiled carving. Be sure the bill (mandibles) is drawn *with the grain.* Again, the cross-grained sections should be cut out with a coping saw. The other parts may be gouged out roughly. Finally, all of the head may be roughly rasped out with the improved rasp.

Draw the top view of the head according to the drawing (front and top views, Figure 23). Note the size of the bill and how it welds with the crown lines. The crown is much thinner than the cheeks, both coming together in a concave to form the eye cavity, with the brow protecting the eye from above and the cheek from below. The holes for the eyes are still lower in the head block. Commercial eyes are recommended, but other designs may be used. Before carving the contours, locate the eyes and drill a 1/16″ hole through the block, perpendicularly. The hole will eliminate guesswork after the head is formed. Figure 24 shows the profiles ready to carve.

The head is not really difficult to carve if caution is taken in preserving the main contour lines. Examine your carving frequently. Do not continue to carve without thought of direction; make every chip count. Cut away all material that is not duck head. Use the rasp for the rough cuts and your knife for the final work. A good picture will help you; have one handy while you carve. Note the nail carving on the bill. This requires some fancy knifework because it extends beyond and above the surface of the bill as though it were an afterthought of the Almighty when it became necessary to reenforce the original design. Carefully locate the nostrils and cut them with a sharp knife or small gouge. Remember that the neck is not a perfect circle. The windpipe is located in front of the neck, causing a sharper curve in this section. The cross-sectional shape more closely resembles an egg contour. Make the final chips with a sharp knife while holding the head in your hand. Fine sandpaper may be used to finish the job if tool effects are not desired.

Carving the Body. When the body has been clamped for several hours, the C-clamps may be removed and the third dimension lines drawn. Remove all waste wood, using the hand saw for the greater operations. The finer work may be done with chisels, gouges, and rasp. The improved rasp is ideal for shaping decoys. As the duck begins to take shape, view your work frequently. More haste may result in less speed—an old adage which a clever carver appreciates. Visualize the shape of the duck and studiously observe the picture which should be nearby. Remember that the back does not come to a point in cross section but is comparatively flat, sometimes actually concave in the center. Remember, too, that the greatest width is at the position of the wing shoulders; that the tail sets in slightly from the wing feathers. Carve both sides as you proceed. Repeat on one side what you did on the other. The seams where the boards come together will help you keep your carving in balance. Do not carve where the head joins the body. Leave plenty of wood here and avoid destroying the slightly elevated plane. After the rasping job, dress down with a sharp spokeshave or another sharp tool where the spokeshave will not work. A sharp knife and several carving tools will be useful from time to time, especially the fishtail gouge. When the body is completed, dress down thoroughly with fine sandpaper. Carefully examine your work from various angles. If there are some places where the removal of more material seems desirable, take it off—take it all off. If by chance there are some low spots where too much wood has been removed, wipe away the tears in your eyes and proceed to fill in the low places with one of the plastic fillers, such as Pay Day.* Allow the filler to set firmly before recarving the surface. This patchwork will be permitted this time, for the decoy is merely practice exercise to acquaint you with the tools and how to use them.

After the corrections have been made (if necessary), the feather markings may be penciled in and then incised with the V-tool. Use your vise as much as possible for all carving operations for greater control of your

* See Chapter 14 for information on fillers, especially the polyester material which blends easily and quickly with its catalyst requiring about fifteen minutes' gel time.

tools. Placing leather or soft wood between the jaws and the carving will protect it from vise marks.

The drawings in Figure 23 indicate the feather markings required. Carve them in lightly. The lower wing feathers may be carved deeper than the others. Note that the back end (under tail coverts) of the duck is nearly pointed below the tail feathers. Watch this section of your carving carefully and consult your picture or pictures frequently. Do not depend too much on your imagination at this stage of your carving skills.

Assembly. Next, attach the head to the body. Carve the joint skillfully. When completed, glue the contacting surfaces together, adjusting the head in the desired position, to one side or the other, to give the carving more eye appeal. (To simplify the drawing, the head is shown in line with the body, Figure 23). Clamp the head in position if necessary. After the glue has set for several hours, start from the bottom of the duck and bore a 1/4″ hole up through the center of the neck as indicated in the plans. The hole should not come through the crown of the head; completely through the neck section will suffice. The dowel pin should be cut about 1/8″ shorter than the hole is deep. Usually the pin will fit snugly, but if it is too tight, sand it down by holding the dowel pin in one hand and the sandpaper in the other. If the pin fits too loosely, coat the surfaces with glue and force the dowel pin in place. If it fits, merely forcing the dowel pin into the hole will be sufficient. The safest way to force the pin in place is with the vise. Place the top of the head and the lower end of the pin (after it has been started) between the vise jaws and tighten. As the jaws of the vise come together the dowel pin will enter the hole. Do not force the pin below the surface. Leave some of it projecting as the end should be dressed off flush with the decoy's bottom. Next, skillfully carve the fillet connecting the neck with the body. If you have not left enough wood to do this operation successfully, fill in with a plastic filler.

The curly feathers at the tail, so unique in drake mallards, cannot be carved from wood satisfactorily. Bird-carvers use several methods for this type of work. Some use sheet metal, others use leather, but Wendell Gilley uses lead—sheet lead hammered to look like feathers. This is the method suggested here. Cut out the shape for the feathers from 1/16″ sheet lead, allowing about 3/4″ to penetrate the decoy's rump. Flatten the edges and otherwise form the shape to look like feathers. Lead is easily worked with steel tools and may be readily cut and stamped. Saw a kerf in the rump of the duck where the feathers are to be located. Insert the feathers and lock them in place by driving a brad through from the surface above into the wood below. Smooth out the joint so that the feathers look natural curling from the duck's rump. The decoy is now ready for the final touch-up operations. Make any corrections necessary and sand the surfaces smooth with fine sandpaper. Figure 25 shows the decoy before the finish has been applied.

The decoy is now ready to paint. Consult Chapter 13 for more detailed information concerning this difficult operation. Before starting the painting glue a piece of waste wood to the bottom of the carving for a holding device. This holding device may be designed to suit the painter. The decoy may be held in a vise while being painted or the device may be drilled for steel rods to hold the decoy so it may be revolved in any angle.

The color scheme is as follows: The bill is cadmium yellow; the head a dark green, highlighted with a lighter color. The collarband is white; the breast a reddish brown. This latter color follows the triangular patch on the back. A triangular patch of black is located near the tail; the wing feathers (primaries) are black, as well as the tail coverts. The speculum is dark blue. The rest of the duck is white which might be cleverly shaded with flashes of very light grey. Be sure to follow a good color picture while painting the decoy.

The first coat of finish is a good sealer, the second is the color patches, and the third coat is the feathering operation. The applied skill of an artist is required here for realistic effects, but do not fret because you cannot attain this high degree of workmanship. This is really your first job of painting in feathers. Time and experience are necessary to do a realistic job. Follow the painting directions described in Chapter 13.

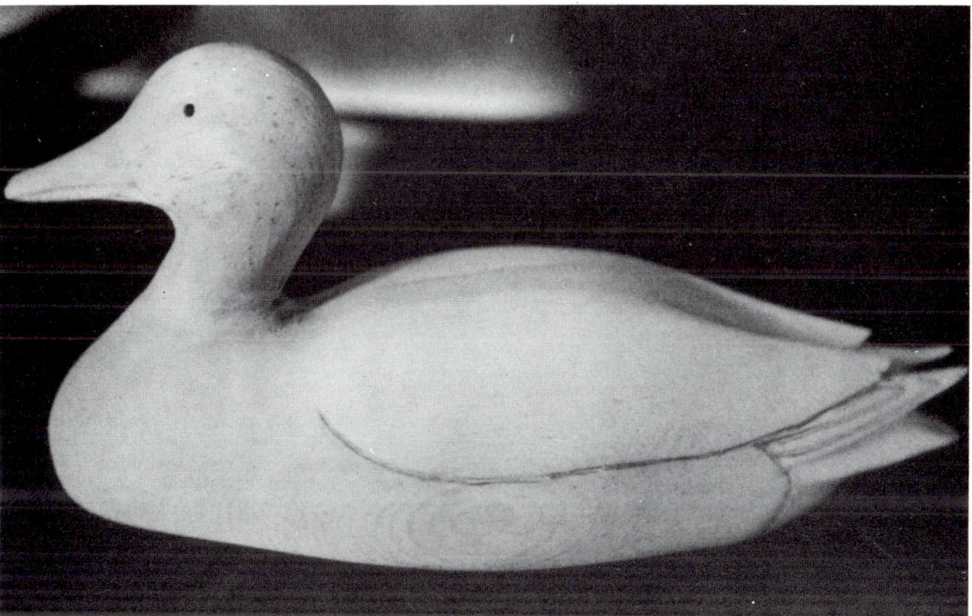

Figure 25. The decoy duck before the finish was applied.

The eyes are inserted last. These directions are for commercial eyes. Drill a hole (following the 1/16″ hole already drilled) to receive the eye so that it will protrude about one-third of its depth. Cut the wire to 3/4″ long and turn up the last 1/4″ to form a barb. Fill the small hole with glue and the large hole with plastic wood. Force the eye in place. The surplus plastic wood will be forced out and the barb will be surrounded by the glue in the small hole. The barb should hold the eye in place. Repeat this operation on the other side of the head. Be careful not to soil your paint job in these operations. Your duck should look clean and sharp. The eyes should look natural, requiring little if any touch-up work.

ASSIGNMENT: Lay out a design for a pair of full-size mallards or another species of duck. This extra work will help you to get the feel of your tools and acquire a further appreciation of the shape of ducks. Shape and form are of utmost importance, so familiarity with this aspect of carving must be achieved.

Chapter 7

PROJECT NO. 4

BELTED KINGFISHER

Our next lesson is concerned with a unique and clever bird. It is the only *small* bird that dives for fish headlong into the water. It is a lonely creature like the heron—seldom seen, even in pairs, except during the mating season. It likes the salt- and fresh-water streams and ponds where small fish abound. Again, unlike most other birds, the female is the most colorfully marked. She has brown flanks and breastband, while the male is mostly a two-colored bird, slate blue and white, except for the tips of the primary feathers which are nearly black.

Figure 26 illustrates the general topography of the Kingfisher, but a good picture should be obtained for the colors represented. Try to obtain a picture painted by either Peterson or Singer for they both do an excellent job.

The length of an adult Kingfisher is 12″ from the tip of its bill to the last tail feather. Your template should not be greater than this size. Enlarge the illustration as directed in Chapter 4 to the desired size.

Transfer your drawing to three white pine boards 1″ thick and 12″ long, and wide enough to include the template. The legs and the bill (beyond line CD) need not be included, nor the crest beyond the crown of the head. Cut out these profiles as described in the preceding chapter. The middle board, or profile should be hollowed out, leaving a margin of at least ¾″ to avoid the possibility of later carving through the solid wood. Removing the center of a carving is good practice in laminated stock as there is less danger of its checking or splitting in a dry hot room. In laminated stock removing the center is relatively simple, as has already been seen. Paul Nock, Chapter 17 (Figure 75), carves his ducks from solid blocks of wood. After they are finished he saws them in half and dishes out the center material until only ½″ remains. He then glues the two halves together again making his birds light and check proof. In the present instance neither of the side boards need to be gouged out as in the duck project. However, if the carver wishes, about ¼″ of material may be dished out to conform to the center recess without danger of penetrating the solid wood during the carving operation. Carving through the block into the cavity is a headache to be avoided.

Glue the boards together as in the duck decoy and allow to set overnight.

After removing the C-clamps from the silhouette block, mark off the center line. Turn the head at an angle of about 30° and lay out the center line for it. Draw two parallel lines 1″ on either side of the center line making the thickness of the head 2″. When finished, the head should be about 1⅞″ thick just below and beyond the eyes. Saw out the head and square the plane where the bill is to be inserted. There should be ample room in which to bore a ¾″ hole for the dowel pin from which the bill is carved (Figure 27).

Prepare a piece of tough stock (old growth poplar, birch or gum) ½″ × 2½″ × 3″. This stock is to form the crest. The grain of the block

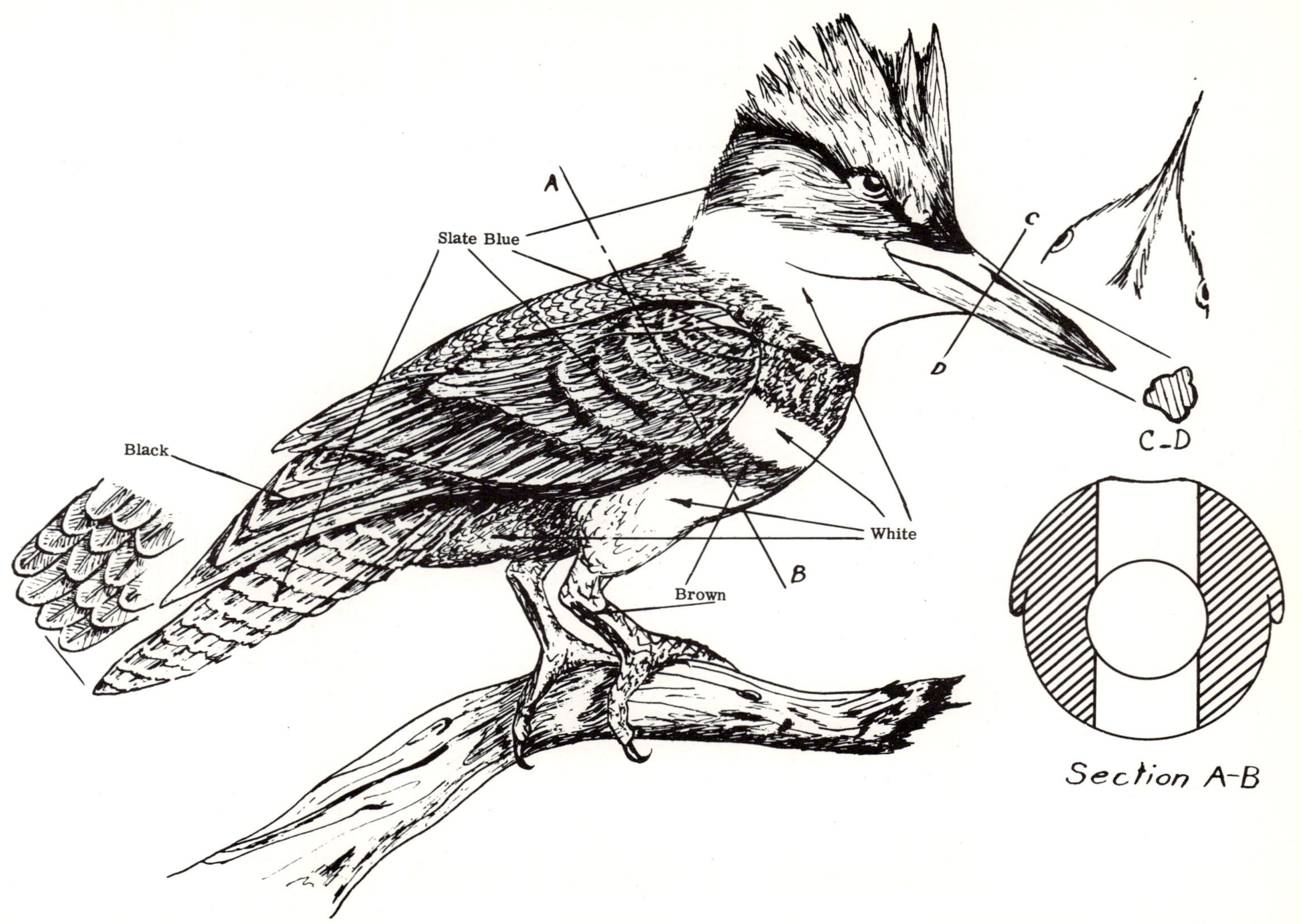

Figure 26. Belted Kingfisher

runs in the wrong direction for carving the crest, so an insert is necessary. Even though the grain should run in the right direction, white pine is entirely too soft for such fragile carving. On either side of the center line, on the crown of the head, scribe a line 1/4″ from and parallel to it, marking the space to be recessed for the crest inserts. Cut out the recess accurately and deep (about 1 1/2″). Most of the recess may be removed by boring 1/2″ holes in tandem to the proper depth. The holes will guide you for width when chiseling out the triangular waste wood. The crest sections should fit in the recess snugly requiring no clamps when glued in place. The inserts are made up of several wedge-shaped pieces with the grain running radially to the general crescent curve; that is, no portion of the insert should be cross-grained to the cuts which form the feathers. After the crest inserts

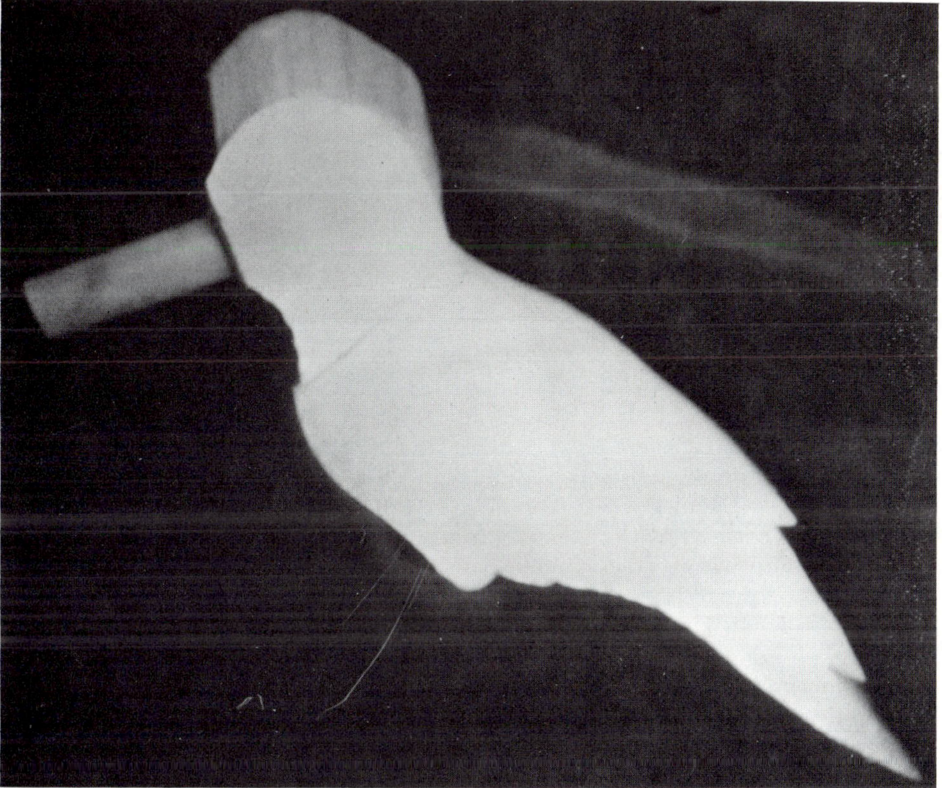

Figure 27. Kingfisher profile with inserted dowel for bill.

have set for several hours, the hole for the bill may be bored. Locate the proper point and drill 1/8″ center hole to guide the spur of the auger. Otherwise the head might split. Be sure the drill is held in the proper direction, in a plane parallel with the center of the head, and at the proper pitch for the bill. The 3/4″ hole could not be bored satisfactorily until the crest inserts had been glued in place as the 3/4″ dowel pin penetrates the lower section of them. Bore the hole about 1 1/2″ deep. Figure 27 shows the profile block with the dowel inserted. The dowel pin should fit snugly. If it does not, shave it down (before cutting from the rod) until it does. Perhaps rotating the rod with the right hand while holding a piece of coarse sandpaper in the other will reduce the diameter sufficiently. Otherwise the pin must be planed to the proper size. The fit is important, as in the carving process the head will taper to a feathered edge along the bill. If the fit is poor, an unsightly seam will result. The dowel pin should be glued securely in place. Before inserting the pin it may be shortened to 3½″.

The crest may now be shaped and carved roughly; that is, the irregular contour of the top may be formed with the coping saw and beveled to a blunt edge. Taper as shown in Figure 26. In cutting away the surplus stock of the crown to fillet with the crest, first bevel the head to it, carving each side alternately. After the bevels have been carved the fillets may be gouged in. Do this carving in easy stages and be sure both sides match. The head should be carved first, roughly, as it is at an angle to the body. It is easier to conform the body with the head than vice versa. Do not remove too much material but do not hesitate to cut into the body where necessary. Do not remove too much material at any one time without inspecting your work. You will learn that roughing out the bird is the most difficult and important procedure, for as it takes shape the carving becomes easier. When forming the bill, watch the grain of the dowel pin. A safe method is to saw it to shape with the coping saw. Files may be used to smooth out the contour. Files are useful carving tools for the beginner, although some sculptors frown on their use. Remember you are still roughing out the bird. Determine the point where the head is the thickest. The highlight of the drawing should be of some help. Also note the eye cavity which is more or less a rounded trench. The V-cut which forms the lower part of the head is less conspicuous, but pronounced nonetheless. Neither of these cuts is merely a line depression made with a V-tool, but a rounded shape giving the "kingfisher" look to your carving.

Start the body contours. Study the cross-sectional view (Figure 26). Shape the bird at the location where the body is the thickest—approximately where the wings are attached. The body tapers toward the tail which at its extremity measures 1¼″ (horizontally), and tapers vertically to the thickness of the last tail feathers. Do not carve this thin section until later. The wings do not meet over the rump but are separated about ⅜″ and rise approximately ½″ above it. Do not carve this feature until later either when there is less danger of breaking the wing tips. Note the pelvic shape beneath, which joins the tail in a Gothic arch shape. Carefully carve the thighs. They are not exactly alike. They drop below the body lines and the V-shaped breastbone terminates between them.

After the body and head have been roughed out, begin the detail carving. Score the shape of the wings. Be sure the wing shoulders are close enough to the neckline. The neckline and the shoulders should be nearly together in point of location. The wings of the kingfisher are different from those of most other birds, being smaller in area and rather unique in shape. Carve the tail very carefully, but leave the feather markings until you are ready to score the feathers of the wings. Again, you are cautioned to carve the whole bird, not just one part after another on the same side. If the bill has not been carved, do this operation next as it will help to guide you in carving other parts. Use the V-tool to cut the lips.

Examine your bird from every angle. Do not be satisfied until you are sure the carving cannot be improved.

The thighs are critical parts of the bird. While the carver was not cautioned before forming these shapes, the holes for the legs could have been drilled before the finishing chips were cut. This precaution might have prevented some chipping around the hole. But with care and a sharp drill the hole may be drilled after the thighs have been completed. Center-punch the location of the holes with a sharp prick punch. The angle should be the same for both thighs. This foresight will allow the legs to be removed without much effort after they have been fastened to the perch. If the holes chip at the beginning, do not fret. This part of the bird is easily repaired. In fact, various parts of the legs will be filled with plastic material to give realistic effects to the legs and toes. A polyester filler will work well for these parts.

Next, make the legs and feet members. Select two pieces of 3/16″ rod and several pieces of ⅛″ wire. This smaller wire is bent to form the toes. The back toe is bent to follow the leg pattern as shown in the drawing (Figure 28). The other toes are formed so that they will taper into the 3/16″ rod to form the bulge for the feet. A jig should be made to hold the toes in place while being brazed together.

Make a form as shown in Figure 28 and fill it with plaster of Paris mixed to a very thin consistency with water. When the plaster has set, drill a hole 3/16″ diameter to receive the leg extension. Cut trenches for the toes. Before using the jig, bake it to remove all moisture; otherwise, it might flake off and injure your mechanic who performs the brazing work. When you have the wires cut and formed, consult your mechanic and have him braze the legs and toes under your direction. Do not braze excessively at the joints because the toes must be bent around the perch, but braze strongly at the critical locations. Braze the back-toe wire up the leg to hold it in place. Your mechanic may think you are out of your mind as mine did when I presented him with the long legs of a whooping crane to be brazed. Help him to understand your problem.

After the legs have been brazed they may be further prepared to look natural. Two ways will be discussed. The first method is not as effective as the second but gives satisfactory results. Whip thread (coarse cotton) around the legs as shown in the illustration. First, the thread is wound upon itself for about ½″ down the leg. Wind the thread closely together. When you are almost all the way down the leg, thread a needle at the end of the thread and force it up under the windings for about ½″ and pull the needle through with the thread. Tighten the thread, blinding the end. This technique is known by sailors as "whipping" and is much used aboard sailing vessels. When the thread has been cut off, both ends have been made secure without showing. The toes may be wound with thread, too, and the feet smoothed out with plastic filler.

The second method, when cleverly done, gives a much more realistic effect. The polyester filler is carefully smoothed onto the clean metal parts (the metal must be free of rust, rolling scale, grease—filed down to the clean bare metal) and molded to shape. Surplus filler is carved off and the legs are further carved for the scale markings. The claws are left bare, of course.

The 3/16″ rods should be chamfered at both ends to make entry into the holes less difficult. An easy fit is desirable as the legs may have to be removed several times to achieve a proper pose, or position.

When the skin markings have all been carved, sand the bird with fine sandpaper, being careful not to remove any pertinent contour. Crevices should be smoothed out with rifler files. After sanding thoroughly, again inspect your bird. Do not hesitate to make corrections even at this late stage of development. As the bird nears completion, unnatural areas will be more conspicuous.

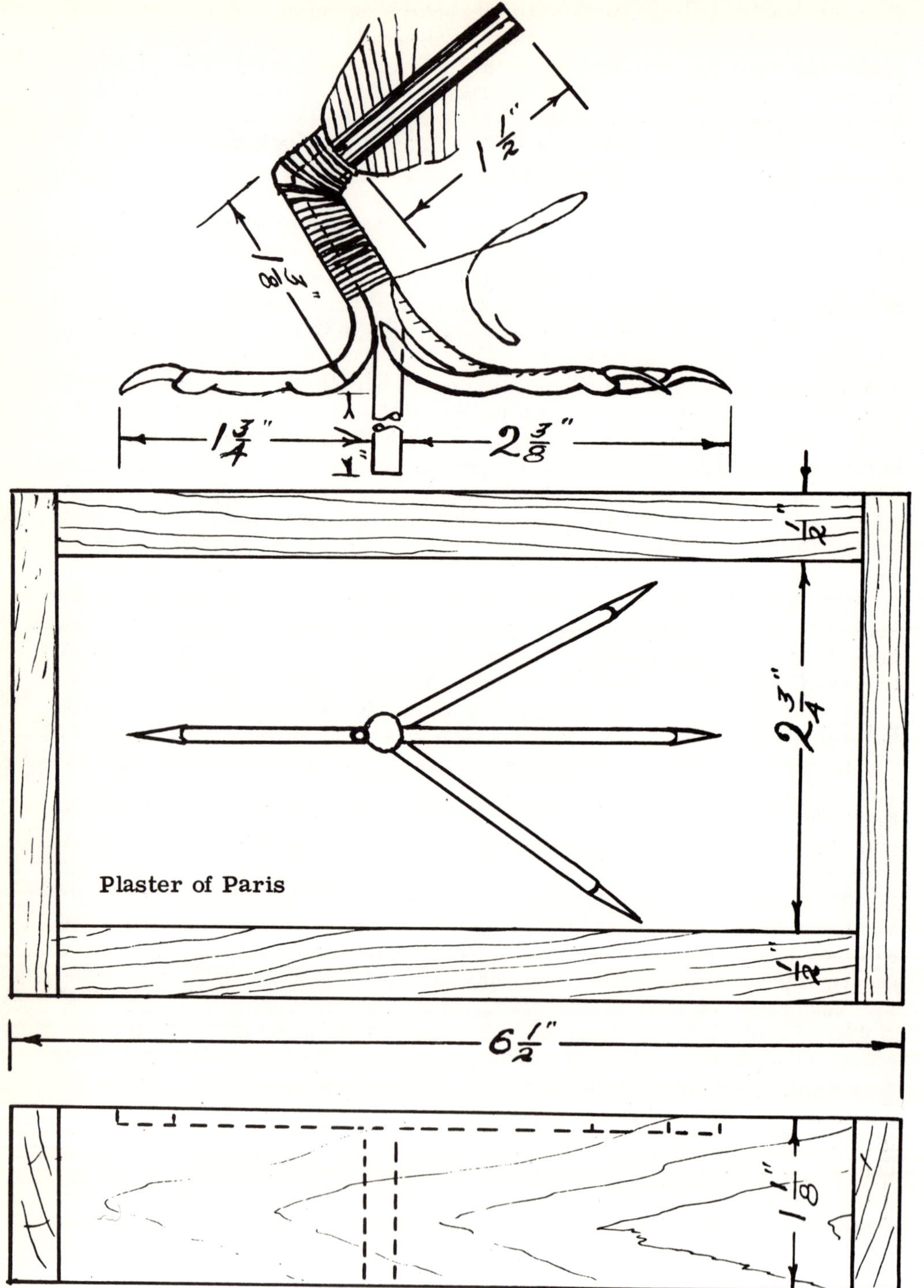

Figure 28. Leg construction.

Locate the eyes carefully. The first eye may be positioned by sight; that is, your eye locates a point which appears to be just right. Prick-punch the hole. Determine the location of the eye on the other side by triangulation, using the end of the bill for one point of reference and a point on the crest for the other. If both eyes measure the same from these points, they are similarly located on the head of the bird. If commercial eyes are used, at each eye location bore a hole the same diameter as the glass eye and deep enough to receive two-thirds of it. Drill a 1/8″ hole to receive the barb. The eye cavity of a kingfisher is very definite and the carving around the eye should be skillfully done. The eyes may be inserted at any time, but preferably after the finish has dried. Install the eyes as described in Chapter 14.

Your carving should now have a definite "kingfisher" look. Lay out the feather markings on the tail and wings. The bird should be held in the vise during most of the feathering operations. The sandbag might be used for some contrary spots, but, in any event, have both hands free to work, guiding the chisel with one hand and using the mallet in the other. Incising the feathers may be mostly done with the V-tool. Do not use the chisel with one hand while holding the bird with the other. This is a sure-fire way to cut yourself. Perhaps the back, breast, thighs, and most of the head should not be carved for feathers. Soft feathers are not usually carved but painted on. They are just as effective if the painting is skillfully done.

Construct the perch out of driftwood or a limb, as shown in Figure 26. Experienced carvers may desire a perch or another design. The perch illustrated will require a base; it could be either rustic or formal. The kind of perch is left to the fancy of the carver. Here is an opportunity to test your own ingenuity in designing a suitable perch and base or a composite arrangement.

The perch, if separate, is screwed to the base with oval-headed screws, long enough to hold it securely. Of course, the size of the holes for the shanks of the screws should be large enough for the screws to slip in freely and drilled entirely through the first member. The threaded end is the holding feature, acting as a nut on a threaded bolt; the only difference is that the wood screw cuts its own threads. The hole for the threaded section is slightly smaller than the core of the screw around which the threads wrap. Countersink for the oval head. Be careful and do not mar the head of the screw with your screwdriver.

Next, locate the bird on the perch. At the selected area, drill two 3/16″ holes the same distance apart as those in the thighs. Determine the angle accurately as the rods are not easily bent by hand. When the pose has been determined and the holes drilled, insert the lower extension of the legs. Place the bird on its legs and inspect your work. In all probability some adjustment will be required to achieve a natural pose. Make these adjustments carefully until the right effect is accomplished. After the proper position of the legs has been determined, bend the toes around the limb, or in any manner to conform with the selected perch. Notice that the toes do not wrap around the limb entirely—only enough for the desired clamping effect. The toes do, however, follow through with a clean curve.

The plastic that may have been applied earlier should be further carved or more added to give the desired effect. Do not fillet the feet or the toes to the limb. Undercut them slightly to simulate the toes of a real bird. When the legs have been satisfactorily formed and fastened, they are ready for the finish to be applied after the bird has again been placed in position.

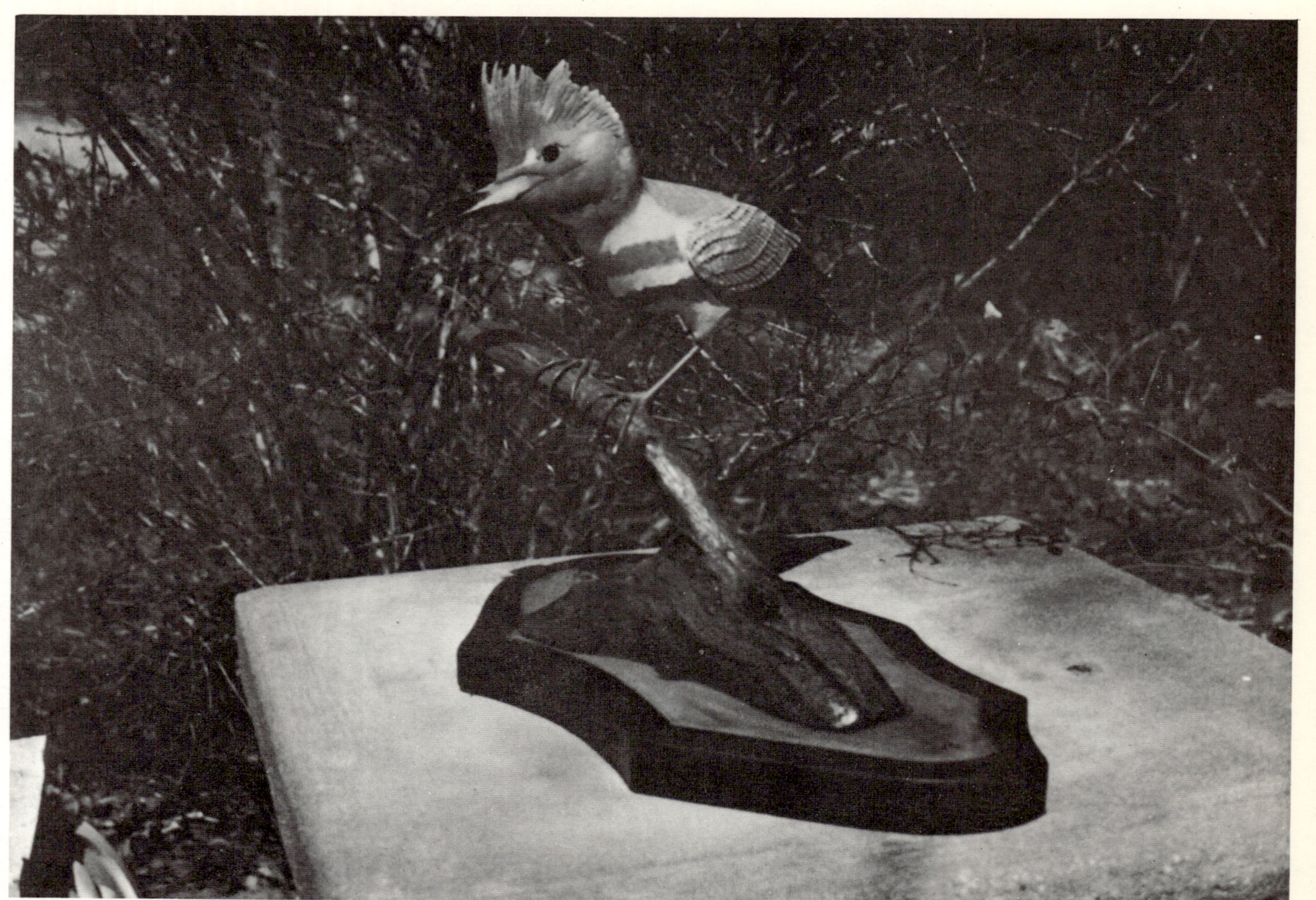

Figure 29. Belted Kingfisher.

To paint the bird, two pieces of 3/16″ rods should be suitably bent so that when placed in the leg holes and the block used to hold the bird while being painted, the bird will be in the desired position. Holes drilled at different angles and in pairs will hold the bird in almost any position. When ready for the finishing operations, inspect your bird and be sure it is clean. Apply a sealer coat, followed by the color patches when it has dried. The last coat is the feathering process. Now the fun begins! Turn to Chapter 13 and closely follow the instructions for painting polychromed birds.

Now, the finishing touches are in your own hands. Irrespective of any direction the author may advise, the final performance of your work concerned with this project depends upon your artistic taste, your familiarity with your subject, and your manual dexterity. Do your work with feeling and skill. If you have followed the initial steps faithfully and performed your finishing operations carefully, you will have a beautiful bird. Consult your picture frequently during the finishing operations. But if you are not satisfied when the last brush stroke has been made, do not be discouraged. You are still a tyro and progress may come slowly, the slower the better, perhaps, for anything attained easily is not usually appreciated. Remember that the tortoise won the race and not the hare. Figure 29 shows the author's bird.

ASSIGNMENT: Carve a Blue Jay from a good color picture. Carve any other bird which suits your fancy. A flicker pecking against a tree should stir your imagination. Pileated and Ivory-billed woodpeckers are two other suggestions. Be sure, however, to follow up this lesson with another carving of similar demands on your talents.

Chapter 8

PROJECT NO. 5

THE GREAT BLUE HERON

The stately Great Blue Heron has been discussed in two previous chapters. It is of the ornithological order *Ciconiiformes,* which comprises an ancient group dating back 100 million years or more to Cretaceous times. They (herons in general) have impressed observers over the ages in all parts of the world and are still considered one of the most interesting birds of the tidewater regions and inland shallow lakes where they feed. They have been carved by most wood-carvers, four examples being used in this text alone, including the author's bird.

Before the carving begins, a determination should be made concerning the finish the carving will assume. A polychromed bird will require different techniques than the naturally finished models; the latter, for example, require more expert workmanship in making the joints. The naturally finished birds should be carved mainly from a log or a solid block without laminations. The grain is an important feature of naturally finished carvings, so a grained or figured wood should be selected. Black walnut would be ideal for such a carving. Study the superb heron by Charles Chase in Chapter 17 (Figure 67). Here is a target for you to shoot at in your carving techniques. Also in the same chapter are pictures of polychromed herons by Captain Riggs and General de Gavre, illustrating the difference in appearance. The author's bird, pictured in Figure 57, has feathers painted on. These latter examples require less manual dexterity as minor errors may be corrected with a plastic filler. The polychromed models may be made of laminated blocks of soft wood and have much of the inside material removed; that is, the birds can easily be made hollow, as in the duck decoy project.

In either type of finish the neck and head may be carved separately, preferably of three pieces of stock with the grain running in the appropriate direction. Each joint should be doweled together as shown in Figure 30. Be sure the grain runs with the length of the bill. Also, in both types the legs must be reinforced with steel rods to achieve the desired slimness on the one hand and the required strength on the other. The method of carving legs is explained in Chapter 14. Some further directions will be given here to simplify matters.

An ash log would make a very beautiful carving if a light colored wood is desired (natural finish). Red cedar is also suggested, but be prepared for some patchwork as imperfections usually run throughout the entire tree. Open-grained woods should be filled with a good filler specifically made for this purpose. Be sure the surplus is rubbed off clean. In fact, the filling operation may be followed by scraping with a cabinet scraper or with sandpaper to bring the solid grain back to the natural color of the wood. If soft wood like white pine or basswood is selected for natural finished birds, an oil-penetrating dye may be used to advantage. Be sure your joinery is skillful, however.

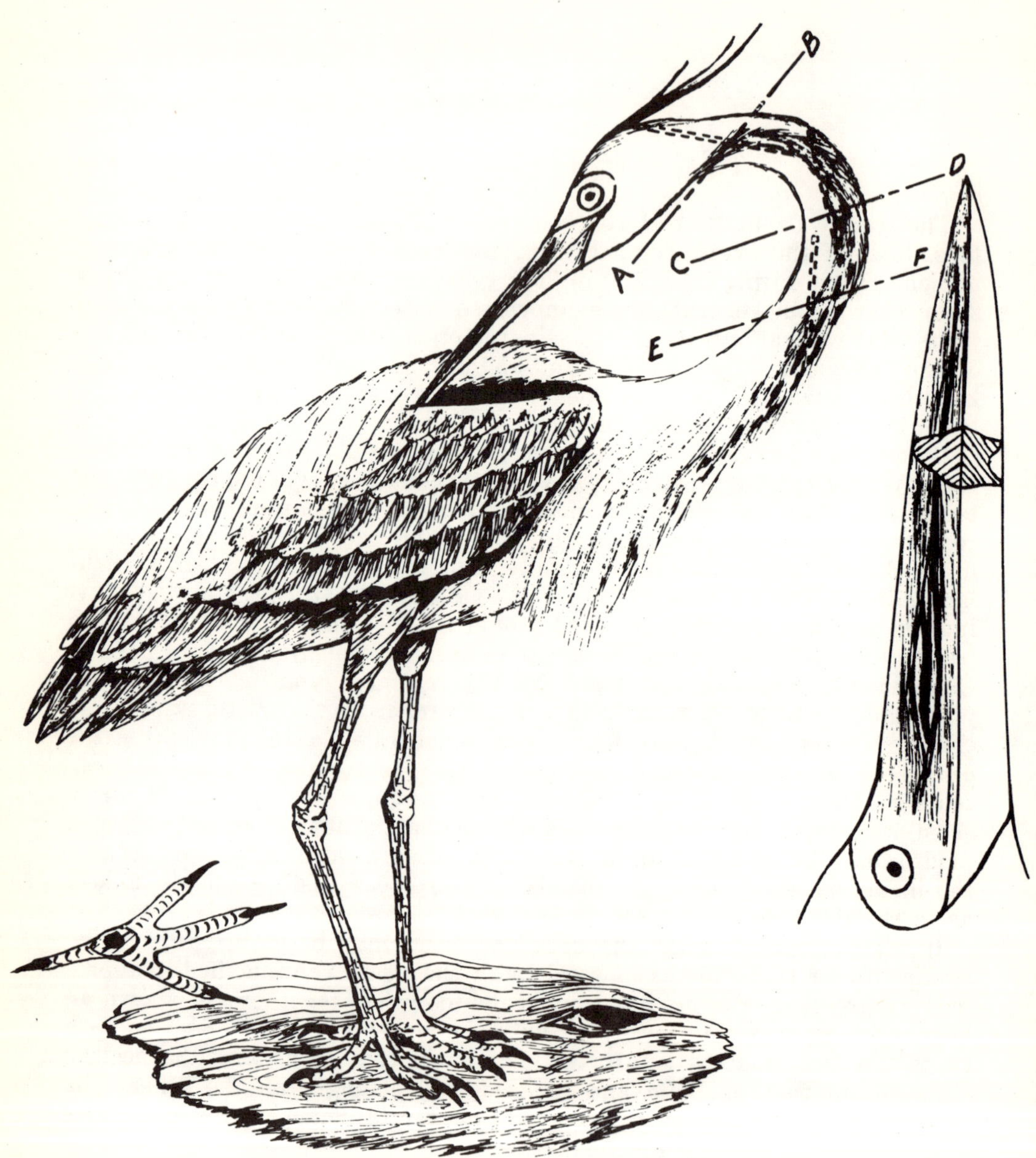

Figure 30. Great Blue Heron.

Of course, the polychromed models will be made of soft wood, boards glued together after the silhouettes have been formed. Almost any type of construction may be used providing there are no weak sections, but the neck construction is best if done according to the above directions. The advantage of carving from laminated stock is the ease with which such carvings can be hollowed out and made light in weight and almost checkproof.

A suggested design is included in this lesson, as usual (Figure 30). In drawing the template include the whole bird except the legs; they are carved separately and attached to the bird after it has been completed. The profile block (either polychromed or natural finish) should include the neck to section line, C-D. The section between C-D and A-B should be carved with the grain of the wood following the general direction of the neck. The grain in the head section should follow the length of the bill. While the rough carving is in process, the joints should be made, glued together, and when set, bored for ½″ dowel pins (full-scale models). Study the drawing for this procedure. So far as I know, this particular pose has never been carved. It was selected to provide the beginner with some exercise in fastening together different members of birds; in strengthening a particular type of shape which runs perpendicular to the grain of the block. While the topography of the heron is supplied, providing a nucleus around which to design the whole project, a more authentic picture should be studied and be available when scoring in the feather markings and painting on the colors. Arthur Singer has painted this bird in a pose suitable for this carving and Frederick Kent Truslow of the *National Geographic* staff has an excellent picture in *Water, Prey, and Game Birds of North America.*

The vital statistics for a full-scale model are as follows: length, 42-52 inches; width (greatest section), 6-7 inches; legs, 8 inches, each section, the top including the thighs and the bottom including the feet; toes (middle), 5 inches, (side), 4 inches, (back), 3 inches (claws included); bill, 1¼ × 6 inches; neck, 14-16 inches (not counting head and bill); body about as long as the neck and head.

Note that the eye seems to be located in the back part of the bill, probably farther forward than that of any other bird. Note also the willowy feathers over the back and wings.

The loose feathers of the neck start under the cheeks and terminate in a necktie on the front of the breast. The neck should be recessed along its entire length for a series of inserts from which to carve these feathers. Start under the cheeks and spiral your design around the neck until the inserts are hanging vertically. The recess should be ½″ wide and 1″ deep. The inserts should be made of tough wood, the grain running perpendicular to the neck, and made up of sections about three inches wide. The neck should be roughly carved before performing this operation, remembering that the windpipe is on the front side of the neck, making the cross section almost egg-shaped. Both types of birds should have this insert construction, remembering that the natural finished birds should be carved with greater skill than the polychromed models.

Locate the thighs properly for the position of the legs. After they are carved and bored for the legs (watch direction here), a dowel pin may be temporarily inserted to strengthen the cross-grained parts. Leave at least 1″ extending beyond the hole to facilitate removing when the legs are ready. If the dowel pins are made longer, they may be used as holding devices during the painting operations.

The method of making legs is described in Chapter 14, but some further directions are given here. Either type of bird may have steel rod legs covered with one of the polyester fillers. This filler is not easy to apply. After the metal has been properly bent, with the toes welded or brazed in position, it should be cleaned with a file until the bright metal shows. Cut a piece of wax paper wide enough to wrap around the legs with 1/8″ space between and as long as the leg section. Prepare enough "Pay Day" to form an 1/8″ layer over the wax paper. Next place the leg section in the middle and wrap both ends around the rod until they meet. Press the seam together and allow the filler to set. Prepare the other section in a like manner and when it has set, remove the wax paper and patch up the cracks and spaces, including the bulge for the foot. Repeat the foregoing procedure in preparing the other leg. The toes should be covered with the filler also and thoroughly welded into the feet. After the whole leg has set, it may be sanded and carved for the leg scales.

The legs of natural finished birds may be made of the same wood as the bird, laminated around the steel rod (*see* Chapter 14). When the polyester method is used, the legs should be darkened with a suitable paint color. The actual color of a heron's legs are a greenish slate black, predominantly slate black.

The mount for the bird should be either a sanded surface or a rather flat rustic perch. It should be weathered to a driftwood sheen. Observe the perches used by the professional carvers represented in this book.

This lesson should have been an exciting one for the beginner. Such birds are always carved by experienced craftsmen with excitement and great expectations. You have a lot of bird for your efforts and, if done skillfully, a beautiful carving that will win the admiration of your friends. This project should point up your skills and otherwise indicate the progress you have made. If you have done a good job, your bird will be a good showpiece. Place it in a competitive exhibit and win the highly prized honor of having the best bird in the show.

ASSIGNMENT: Carve another bird. A Canada goose will be a good project and give you a chance to make some lead feet if you do not want to carve them as shown in Chapter 14. A goose is a long-necked bird and will give you further exercise in neck construction. Carve any kind of bird, but carve, carve, carve.

Chapter 9

BIRD MODELS OF POLYESTER FILLER

The main difficulty in making carved birds and ducks popular with the public is the fabulous price which an individual must pay for a good example of the wood-carver's art. Recently at a wildlife carving show I was invited to see the superb work of an artist friend—a pair of Passenger pigeons.

"If you let these carvings go for less than a thousand dollars, you ought to have your head examined," I said.

The artist smiled. "These birds are not for sale, but I would consider a commission to carve another pair for *two* thousand dollars."

She probably will get her commission. I know of another recent case of this sort. The carver received seventeen hundred dollars for his beautifully carved bird which had been given a natural finish. In order for the carver to receive even the Federal minimum wage for his work such prices are necessary. Carving birds to meet the high standards set by such carvers as the Ward Brothers consumes more time than the layman realizes, to say nothing about his skill and the expense of his materials. Therefore, the carvings of the better known artists are priced beyond the means of all except the more affluent enthusiast. A fiberglas or polyester duplicate of the original polychromed carving is an exact replica of the original and may be sold at a much lower price. Of course, such duplicates do not have the intrinsic worth of the carved wooden models and a connoisseur will settle for nothing less than the original carving from the carver's own hands. But the technique of duplicating the original bird carving realistically does bring the price within range of the average pocketbook, and at the same time provides another, entirely different approach to the carver's art and sales volume.

So far as I am concerned, the technique offers still another advantage. Instead of the laborious work necessary to create a wooden subject, the carver may mold his bird of modeling clay (common potter's clay, or the more practical Plastilina which does not harden) and when formed to meet his exacting standards, cast negative molds about it, from which accurate squeezed duplicates may be made. Also, this method offsets the rising cost of suitable carving woods which are, irrespective of the expense, becoming more difficult to obtain. The clay models require no elaborate equipment; only the clay, plaster, a few modeling tools, and the skilled supple hands of the artist are necessary.

Fiberglas may be used as the squeeze material for forming the birds of this chapter. But, due to the carving which must follow squeezed models, a denser material was found more desirable. Any of the polyester fillers used by automobile body and fender mechanics to fill dents may be used in the projects which will be discussed. The material is manufactured by several companies under a legion of trade names (*see* Appendix). The material is comparatively inexpensive considering the work it does. It has been mentioned several times in this text. In painted birds and ducks, the filler is nearly as important as the wood from which the subject is carved. The method offers an economical process for duplicating carvings. In fact, the technique seems to be the answer to a busy carver's prayer.

The process of making polyester duplicates consists mainly of two operations. The first is quite difficult for beginners who have had no experience casting plaster forms, but the second is merely kindergarten play. The idea is to cast a many-piece mold of the subject, so that the polyester filler may be squeezed over the negative surface in exactly the same manner a child fills the wooden molds of simple forms with plastic modeling clay. Casting the negative forms is the rub! The novice must learn to do this effectively, and he should experiment with the process until he becomes proficient in the activity. A ball or a cylinder makes an excellent beginning model. Most subjects will require at least two molds, the line or plane of separation being the highest elevation of the subject. The parting plane is always indicated by a parting line drawn directly on the model to be duplicated. In the case of the ball, this line of separation is located at the "equator"; in the cylinder, along its radial axis. One-half of the ball is pressed down in moist sand (bank sand) until the parting line is flush with the sand surface. The surface of the sand should be smooth and sharp around the ball (Figure 31).

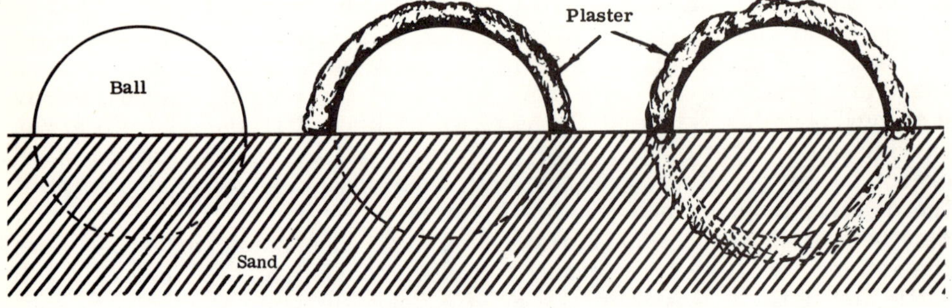

Figure 31. Ball and cylinder casting.

Plaster is mixed in the manner discussed later and flipped upon the exposed surface of the model until it is covered. Then, the remaining thickness may be built up by troweling on the heavier plaster with a spatula. The wall should be about 3/4″ thick. In less than an hour the plaster will set (depending upon the atmospheric conditions) if it is good—"live" and not "dead." Dead plaster is worthless for it will not set up properly. Assuming that the plaster is satisfactory, the ball may be removed from the sand after the plaster has set. Thoroughly clean the parting surface and the uncovered surface of the ball with green soap and water. Key the parting surface in at least two places. A keyhole is merely a depression cut into the parting surface. A coin will cut this depression handily. Brush the ball and parting surface with olive oil or paste wax to form a nonbonding film. Bury the cast in the sand to hold it in the proper position for the next operation.

Flip plaster onto the surface of the ball, as before, until it is covered and then build up to a proper thickness with a spatula. Allow the cast to set for a few hours before trying to pry the two halves apart. The separation of the forms in this instance is simple, but in some of the more difficult cases, the operation can become quite exacting. Prepare two thin hardwood wedges and insert in the parting seam at opposite locations. Tap the wedges lightly and alternately with a small hammer until the shells separate. Both negative impressions of the ball should be clean and accurate.

The casting of the negative forms for the cylinder is performed in the same manner as in the case of the ball. The ends of the cylinder should not be undercut but slightly inclined away from the center.

For the purpose of this lesson, the process of casting negative forms will be illustrated by using the Mallard duck decoy, Project No. 3, Chapter 6, as a model. With little improvising the duck may be imprinted in a two-piece mold. The section between the wing tips is negative; that is, it is undercut and would lock the plaster cast if allowed to remain. The space, therefore, must be positively shaped. This is done by molding plastic clay into the space and modeling it until the surface is suitably formed for casting. The hollow space under the bill should be likewise treated. With all undercuts eliminated, the duck may be prepared for the negative molds. First, draw a parting line along the central plane of the duck, noting that the plane turns with the head. Coat the surface with a nonbonding material (olive oil or paste wax) to prevent the plaster from sticking to the model. A box of moist sand is prepared into which the duck is pressed until the parting line is flush with the sand surface. Next, cut a piece of sheet metal about 3½″ wide and long enough to encompass the duck, allowing for a space of 1″ all around it. Bend the sheet metal to conform to the general shape of the duck and press down into the sand until the top edge is about 1″ above the highest contour of the model. The flat side of the sheet metal is pressed against the bottom of the duck as this particular section will be cast hollow (Figure 32).

At this point some knowledge of foundry practice will be of great help in understanding the theory and method of casting. For those readers who are already familiar with the techniques, the following paragraphs may be skipped and the process of casting the negative forms continued. But for the novice, the more he knows about the process of casting, the more likely he is to succeed in his work. He should be patient with my digression from the subject to allow him to form a clear mental picture of the process. The know-how is highly important and should be achieved before any attempt is made to exercise the physical aspects. The *World Book Encyclopedia* has a brief article under "Cast and Casting" concerning green sand molding. The Bibliography (*see* Appendix) lists several books on the subject which are adequately illustrated. Any good city library will have them and the beginner will do well to study them if he is seriously inclined toward his work.

No attempt will be made here to describe the process of green sand molding in detail. But a brief sketch of the operations involved should really be sufficient for an individual clever enough to carve the likeness of wildlife of the marshes and fields around him. Foundrymen use a special molding sand which does not concern us at this time. His tools are few: a flask is made up of two parts—the bottom section is called a "drag," the top section a "cope"; a rammer, one end round (the butt) and the other wedge-shaped (the peen); a number of trowels, slicks, and other molding gadgets. A pattern, the exact replica of the subject to be cast, is essential. It is usually split and the two parts are held together with short dowel pins.

The drag of the flask is placed, top part down, on a bottom board and the flat section of the pattern located in the central area. A fine dusting powder is blown over the pattern followed by fine riddled sand over the whole surface. Properly tempered molding sand is then shoveled into the drag from the sandpile and peened around the pattern in several stages until the drag is filled and running over. The surplus sand is struck off with a straightedge and more sand is riddled onto the surface. A molding board is then seated on the drag and the whole assembly is carefully turned over to expose the half-pattern embedded in the sand. Next, the doweled section of the pattern is placed over its "mate" and the cope section of the flask is dropped in place. The pattern is again dusted to facilitate withdrawal from the mold. Fine seashore sand is riddled over the entire surface of the cope to form a parting plane. The sand will allow the cope to be lifted off with a clean separation. Molding sand is riddled over the surface as in the first instance and peened tightly around the pattern. Before the sand is shoveled into the cope, however, a sprue pin is located near the pattern and molded into the sand. The sprue pin forms the sprue hole into which the metal is poured. When the cope has been rammed tightly the top is struck off as before and a depression is cut around the sprue pin to form a well and to enlarge the pouring space. A steel wire (about No. 10 gauge) is thrust down over the pattern area but not deep enough to touch the pattern. This operation is performed several times to provide escape vents for the hot gases formed by the molten metal. This procedure prevents the casting from "blowing."

After the sprue pin is withdrawn, the cope is carefully lifted off the drag and placed nearby on its side. If the cope-half of the pattern is withdrawn also, so much the better. Then only the drag-half needs to be removed, a procedure which is sometimes tricky. The pattern is gently rapped to loosen it from the sand and then carefully lifted out. Some repairs are usually necessary and they should be made at this time. The spoon trowel and slicks are the tools used for this purpose. A gate is cut in the drag part of the flask leading from the pattern to the sprue hole, the depth being least near the pattern depression. This precaution allows the metal to be cast thinner at this point, permitting the gate to break off easily when the drag is "shaken out." The cope is replaced in its original position and the flask clamped together. If the casting is heavy, a metal weight is placed over the cope to prevent the sand from lifting. The mold is now ready to pour with molten iron, bronze, or any other metal.

Forming plaster casts is little different in process and none in theory. As was stated earlier, the duck is forced down into the sand until the parting line is flush with the sand surface. A sheet-metal fence is placed around the model for obvious reasons. It is used to contain the plaster in a small area and make the completed mold as light and convenient to handle as possible. Plaster is flicked upon the exposed half of the duck with the fingers until the surface is covered. This technique prevents air holes from forming to ensure a perfect registry in the plaster. When the surface has been completely covered, the remainder of the plaster may be poured in until the space has been filled. The surplus plaster may be struck off as in the green-sand method. The mold is allowed to set until the plaster is hard enough to be scratched with the thumbnail (a clean, sharp scratch).

Before mixing the plaster, a reinforcing wire should be prepared (an old coat hanger). It should be bent to conform to the shape of the mold and small enough to allow a 1″ margin around the cast. It should be placed over the duck with at least ½″ of plaster in between.

There is no set rule for mixing plaster. First, a trial test should be made to determine its condition. "Dead" plaster is worthless for form casting. If the plaster is satisfactory it will set up quickly. Fill a clean container with enough water to fill the space to be cast. Live plaster is then sifted through the fingers into the water until a mound appears at the surface. A little more plaster is sifted in and the batch allowed to set for a few moments. Gently mix the plaster with the fingers—slowly. Mixing the plaster quickly will cause it to set up quickly, allowing little time for the casting operation. In this particular instance time is not a factor, but in most cases it is. Plaster cannot be used after it has nearly set. When the mixture begins to thicken a noticeable amount of heat will be generated due to the chemical reaction taking place. But the heat will not be sufficient to harm the fingers. When the mixture assumes the thickness of sweet cream, begin to flick it on the model. After the surface has been completely covered, the rest of the thickness may be built up with a spatula, or in the present instance, poured in. If you do not have enough plaster, mix a new batch.

The cast should set in less than an hour. Allow enough time, however, for atmospheric conditions greatly affect the setting-up period. When you are sure the plaster has set, remove the sheet-metal fence and withdraw the cast from the sand. Clean thoroughly with green soap and water (your druggist will have green liquid soap). Key the surface in at least three places with a coin or a spoon and brush the surface with olive oil or paste wax—not too heavily, but just enough to form a nonbonding surface. Replace the cast in the sand, with the exposed side of the duck up, and slip the sheet metal in place, allowing it to drop over the cast about ½″. Pack sand around the sheet-metal fence to hold it firmly in place. Proceed with the same operation as before until the form has been filled. Do not forget the reinforcing wire. This time allow several hours for the cast to set; too much time is far better than too little. When the forms are ready to be pried apart, prepare several thin hardwood wedges. Insert them in the seam in various locations and tap them lightly with a hammer in a clockwise fashion until the molds separate. Figure 33 shows the forms apart with the duck still embedded in the upper half. If there is no hurry, several hours should elapse before attempting to remove the model from this section. A period of drying out will facilitate the removal operation. It should not be difficult to remove, but some prying action may be necessary.

There are times, especially in the country, when casting plaster is not available. I did not have enough plaster to pour the forms described above. I used a 50/50 mixture of white Portland cement and finely riddled sand. The setting-up process is slowed down considerably, for at least twenty-four hours should be allowed for the molds to set and harden—even longer is desirable. But when the casts have been properly formed, they are stronger and just as practical, although heavier. In small work this extra weight works no handicap, but in larger work weight can be a vital factor. These forms should be reinforced, too, but there is no particular rush necessary in pressing in the wires.

When the forms have been pried apart and thoroughly cleaned, the squeeze surfaces should be rubbed down with olive oil or paste wax to form a nonbonding film. Be sure every spot has been adequately treated. Allow the surface to dry before squeezing on the polyester filler. Too much oil

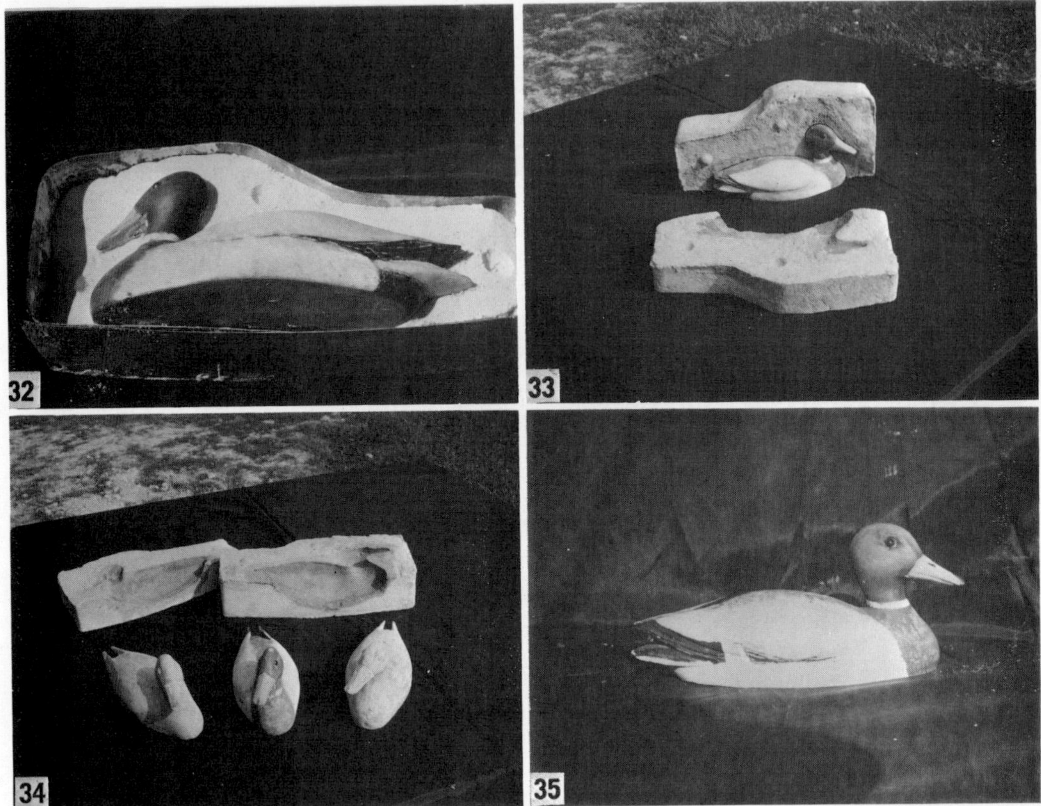

Figure 32. Duck fenced in with sheet metal. One-half of the mold has been cast.
Figure 33. The mold has been pried apart; the model is still embedded in upper half.
Figure 34. Polyester ducks formed from two-part mold. Duck in the center is the model.
Figure 35. Finished duck painted in the natural colors of a Mallard Drake.

will affect the filler and the surface next to the form is most important for satisfactory registration. In the meantime, carve a hardwood spatula to press in the filler. Oil it thoroughly and allow time for the oil to soak in. An ordinary case knife will work well, and there is no substitute for the fingers. A piece of wax paper under them will prove helpful.

Mix a batch of polyester filler according to the manufacturer's directions printed on the can.* A piece of glass makes an ideal surface upon which to mix the hardener and filler with a putty knife. Paste the polyester filler onto the negative forms and squeeze into every nook and corner. The entire surface should be covered to a thickness of ¼″. Remember that the space between the wing tips was filled with clay; so this part should have an extra thick coating to allow for the carving which must follow to restore the proper contour. (Here is an example to illustrate why polyester filler was used instead of fiberglas.) After both molds have been covered with the filler, place the two forms together and complete the squeezing from the open bottom. Be sure the keys register to ensure the forms being in

* The author used Martin Senour's "Fuse-tite" for the duck. The manufacturer calls it a polymetric body filler. It is olive green in color and sets up rapidly. The Oatey Company manufactures a number of polyester fillers which have proved to be satisfactory.

their proper position. Fasten them together with a strong cord. A bead around the bottom edge will give the work a professional touch. After the casts have set for several hours, the forms may be pried apart. Do not rush this process as the filler does not reach its maximum strength upon setting. Pry the molds apart as before. The plastic duck will remain in one form as the model did (Figure 33) but it should not be difficult to remove. In fact, it may lift out easily after setting a few more hours.

The polyester duck should be an exact duplicate of the carved model, even showing the feather markings. Figure 34 shows two of these squeezed forms with the model between them. The fins and other casting irregularities have been removed, but no particular effort has been made to prepare the surfaces for painting.

To level the bottom edge so the duck will rest evenly on a table, place a whole sheet of coarse sandpaper on a smooth, flat surface. The duck is rubbed back and forth over this abrasive surface until the bottom fits perfectly. Sand the surface of the duck until smooth. Repair any air holes that may have formed. Recarve the section between the wing tips and under the bill. A sharp file will work wonders in these tight places. Otherwise prepare the duck for the painting procedure.

Paint the ground coat white and allow to dry. The duck may then be painted according to the directions supplied in Chapters 6 and 12 (of course, the priming coat is omitted).

Figure 35 shows the duck painted with the natural colors of a Mallard drake.

Figure 36 shows a group of three Blue Jays molded according to the polyester technique described for the duck.

To round out this lesson of squeeze molding from many-piece molds, a Redtail Hawk carved by the author (Figure 37) will be used as a model. The bird will require at least ten molds, not including the mold between the legs. First, definite parting lines should be drawn on the model, outlining the various mold segments. Some of these lines are visible on the photographed model. These areas are fenced in, one at a time, with clay (Plastilina or common wet clay) and the plaster is flicked upon the surface as in the case of the duck. Figure 38 shows the leg mold already cast and a section of the belly fenced in ready for the plaster application. The molds should be 1″ thick and reinforced with wire.

A Redtail Hawk is a large bird and the model has been carved life-size. So, the casting of the molds will not be child's play. It is assumed that the individual who attempts such a project will be familiar with both the green-sand and the waste-mold procedures. The project is included in this book to illustrate the possibilities of polyester duplicates and to give the more informed and experienced carver an opportunity to try his skill in the more difficult squeeze-mold techniques.

The first operation, after outlining the various piece-molds, is to thoroughly treat the model with a nonbonding substance (olive oil or paste wax). This treatment is important, for if the plaster sticks to the bird, the carver is in trouble. To avoid this embarrassment, proper precaution should be taken. Also, there may be some undercut spots which should be filled with Plastilina or soft clay to block off the negative surfaces. These recesses may be recarved in the molded bird after the filler has set and the bird is removed from the molds. Of course, such locations should be given an extra coating of the filler, or another cause for embarrassment occurs when the

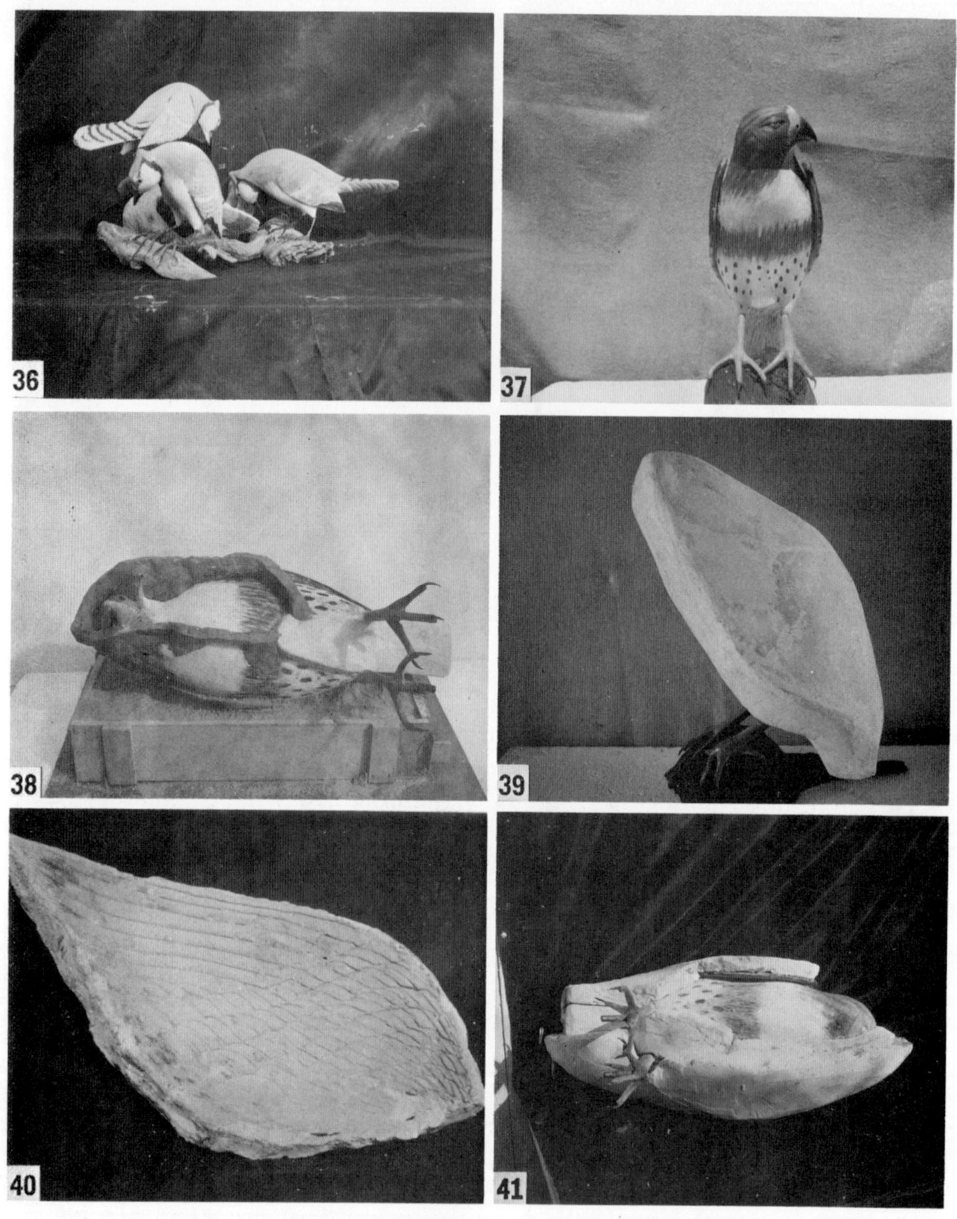

Figure 36. A group of three Blue Jays molded from polyester filler.
Figure 37. Redtail Hawk carved by the author.
Figure 38. Casting the many-piece mold. Photograph shows tail section already cast. The area of the next mold has been fenced in with clay.
Figure 39. All sections cast. The many-piece mold is now ready for the retaining shell-mold to be cast.
Figure 40. Underside of a wing section (piece-mold).
Figure 41. Top retaining shell removed; also one of the piece-molds, exposing part of the model.

chisel cuts through the thin wall. Incidentally, when such accidents do happen, cut a piece of cardboard more than sufficient to cover the hole, fasten a string in the center, and coat the cardboard with a generous supply of filler. Thrust the cardboard into the hole at its smallest dimension and

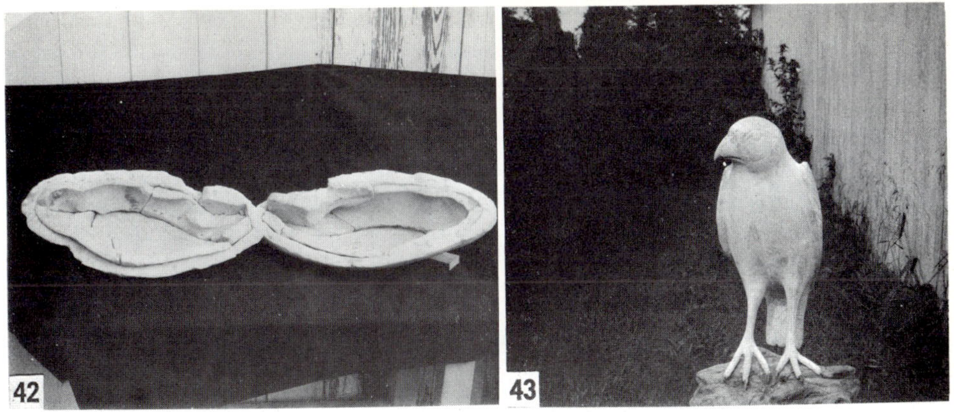

Figure 42. Piece-molds nested in their respective shells.
Figure 43. The polyester bird squeezed from the molds.

when through, pull the cardboard in place with the string and hold until the polyester filler sets sufficiently to remain in place. Watch out for such sensitive spots and avoid extra work.

Figure 38 shows the leg section already cast. Note that the surface is comparatively smooth and elevated toward the center midway between the legs. This taper will allow the retaining form to break freely from it. A thin layer of clay should be wrapped around each thigh before the cast is made to keep it from binding.

The section along the center of the belly following around to the ridge of the bill has been fenced in with clay to receive the plaster. The edges are quite irregular and will help the adjacent molds to register perfectly. The edges should be slightly inclined in a preferred direction so the molds will not lock together when being removed. Cast all sections with this thought in mind.

Figure 39 shows all of the sections cast around the bird. Note that the legs have not been covered. They should be made separately, as described in Chapter 14 (Figure 58), and installed after the polyester bird has been assembled.

A wing section can be discerned on the surface of the plastered bird. The underside of this mold is shown in Figure 40. Note that the feathers have registered satisfactorily.

The next operation is to cast a two-piece mold about the plastered bird. This mold is designed to hold the piece-molds in place while the polyester filler is being squeezed over the negative surfaces. The parting line should follow the length of the mold midway both the back and belly. If care has been exercised, the seam of the corresponding piece-molds may be followed and the seams of the two parts will coincide. They need not coincide, however, for satisfactory results.

The section between the legs is not cast in this form. The space is filled with clay 1″ thick with the greatest breadth halfway down the legs. At the legs the clay needs to be a little wider than the legs but wrapped completely around them. Fence in one-half of the plastered bird along the parting line and treat the surface with a nonbonding film. Before casting the form, several pieces of reinforcing steel should be prepared. The steel should be deformed bars used to reinforce cement. One bar should be bent to conform with the contour of the parting line and small enough to fit 1″ from the edge. This reinforcement is important. At least three other bars should be cut and formed to run at right angles with the first. Next, cast the form using the same techniques as in the previous projects. When the cast has set, remove the clay fence and cut keyholes in the parting surface. Clean thoroughly with green soap and water. Cast the other half as in the previous case.

Figure 41 shows the top retaining shell removed as well as one of the piece-molds. Part of the bird is exposed. The bottom retaining shell is still in place with all of the piece-molds firmly nested together. Remove the bottom retaining shell and carefully remove the piece-molds one at a time. Reassemble the piece-molds in their respective shells.

Figure 42 shows the piece-molds nested in place ready to receive the non-bonding film. Be sure that all parts of the mold have been thoroughly treated with olive oil or paste wax. After the surfaces have been properly treated to prevent the polyester from sticking to the molds, the squeezing process may begin. The thickness of the walls should average ¼″ thick, but heavier where post-carving will be necessary. Mix the polyester in batches about the size of the fist and squeeze over the surface with a tablespoon and putty knife. Do not mix too much of the filler at one time; it is too expensive to waste. The filler should be applied as quickly as possible as it is best when first mixed. About three quarts were required for my bird. I used Martin Senour's "Blue Moon"—more expensive than some other brands.

At this stage of development, some thought should be given to the strength of various parts of the bird. The bill, for the most part, should be solid with a properly bent wire in the center of the small cross section. The thighs should be solid because holes must be drilled in them later to receive the legs. The tail section, too, should be fairly solid. There are some other contours naturally requiring greater strength. If glass eyes are used, they may be placed in the sockets formed in the negative mold with rubber cement before applying the filler. Over this section the filler should be at least ½″ thick for the eyes may have to be relocated, requiring a hole about 7/16″ in diameter. A fold is usually located over the eye in eagles and hawks, so this fold must be formed after the bird has been removed from the mold.

After the polyester has set, a bead should be formed on one of the halves to prevent the polyester filler from dropping through the seam when the parts are assembled. The bead will act as a flange, giving greater strength to the seam.

The filler should be allowed to set up overnight before being removed from the forms. The piece-molds should then be removed one at a time, as in the case of the model. The two halves may not fit together perfectly; the accuracy will depend upon the skill of the carver in performing his groundwork. But the medium will allow for some discrepancies. If too large a seam exists, fit the parts by cutting away the higher elevations. A seam of not less than ⅛″ should be allowed for the polyester filler in cementing the halves together. When satisfied that the parts fit snugly, wire them together. Drill small holes in the thighs, the bill, the tail, and at least corresponding holes in the halves midway both the back and belly. About No. 20 gauge steel wire should be used and twisted together with a pair of pliers until the halves are firmly bound together. Of course, the polyester filler should be applied before the wires are twisted together.

Allow a few hours for the filler to set up and begin to clean the surfaces.

Do not remove the wires until the next day. Figure 43 shows the author's bird after removing the fins and other irregularities from the surface. As can be seen, the legs have also been installed and the bird mounted. The legs are much too long, unfortunately, but this error can easily be corrected with another set.

Sand the surface until all defects have been removed. Paint a ground coat of any convenient color and finish according to directions supplied in Chapter 13. The Hawk is a very effective piece of sculpture when painted cleverly. A florist mistook my bird for a live specimen and a visitor to an art show where the bird was exhibited thought it was a stuffed model. These individuals would have "flipped their lids" if the bird had been painted by Mrs. Black or Lem Ward.

In this particular case, all kinds of pose variations are possible. Both legs of the model touch the perch, but the polyester bird has only one foot on the perch while the other is raised in a clutched position. The head may be carefully sawed off and turned in another direction. With a little innovation the wings may be cast separately and attached to the bird outspread. The polyester molding technique offers unlimited possibilities to carvers. The foregoing lesson, hopefully, points the way. No clever carver should find the medium difficult or prosaic. Other materials than polyester filler should be experimented with—such as fiberglas—even a combination of the two mediums would be challenging and could lead to exciting creations in art forms.

Chapter 10

PROJECT NO. 6

THE WORKBENCH

The workbench was planned originally to be the first project. However, due to its somewhat complex construction, demanding some mechanical experience, it was considered more appropriate for a later lesson, after the beginner has had some experience with tools. This is not to say that it may not be selected as the first project by those individuals who have some carpentry experience and desire to have a good workbench to use at the very start. Others may omit the project altogether for one reason or another—mainly because of the expense and lack of confidence in doing the job satisfactorily. But a workbench of some description must be available or the neophyte will be greatly handicapped, if not thwarted altogether, in his carving efforts.

A workbench is a primary requirement of all craftsmen who seriously work at their trade or hobby. A few carvers, even in America, use their laps, but they are the exceptions to the rule. Most good carvers have a sturdy bench equipped with either a rapid-acting or machinist's vise, or both, mounted on the bench to hold their work. I have both types attached to my bench and have found both to be timesaving pieces of equipment.

The workbench described in this chapter is a rather imposing project for a beginner, especially if he has had no previous carpentry experience. However, some experience is presumed, otherwise the tyro might be wise in calling on outside help to assist him with his work. In the meantime, with the aid of a skilled mechanic, he will learn much about the tools he will use in his carving activities. If the project is thought to be too difficult, even with the help of a carpenter, he should procure a bench of some sort to tide him over the period of his incompetency. But a bench he should have, and the one suggested here will be of invaluable assistance to him while carving his birds.

The bench has been designed to be constructed with a minimum of tools and carpentry experience. I built the workbench (Figures 44 and 46) following my own plans as illustrated in this chapter. I found them complete, requiring little initiative on the part of the builder to fill in the gaps not covered by the illustrations. If the beginner can read line drawings, he will have no trouble conceiving the method of construction. Little difficulty will be experienced if he follows the plans religiously. The main problem is to study the plans until he has the idea as clearly as the person who drew them. Being familiar with the method of construction, the next faculty of importance is following it. Use the rule and try square accurately, and saw down the lines with a square cut. For a small fee a power handsaw may be rented which will perform the sawing operations skillfully, requiring only the guidance of the operator.

The bench has been designed for the beginner, but as already suggested, I assume some mechanical ability or he would not be interested in carving in the first place. The first direction is to lay out the work accurately and carefully. If using a six-foot folding rule be sure you are reading from the right side. Do not minimize the use of the try square and framing square in laying out your work and for testing. When lines are drawn they must be assumed to be correct. Therefore, do not cut them off—just divide them, leaving one-half of the line visible. It is better to saw up to the lines than to cut them off entirely. If at this point the task begins to assume difficult significance, remember this operation of sawing close to a line is the peak of

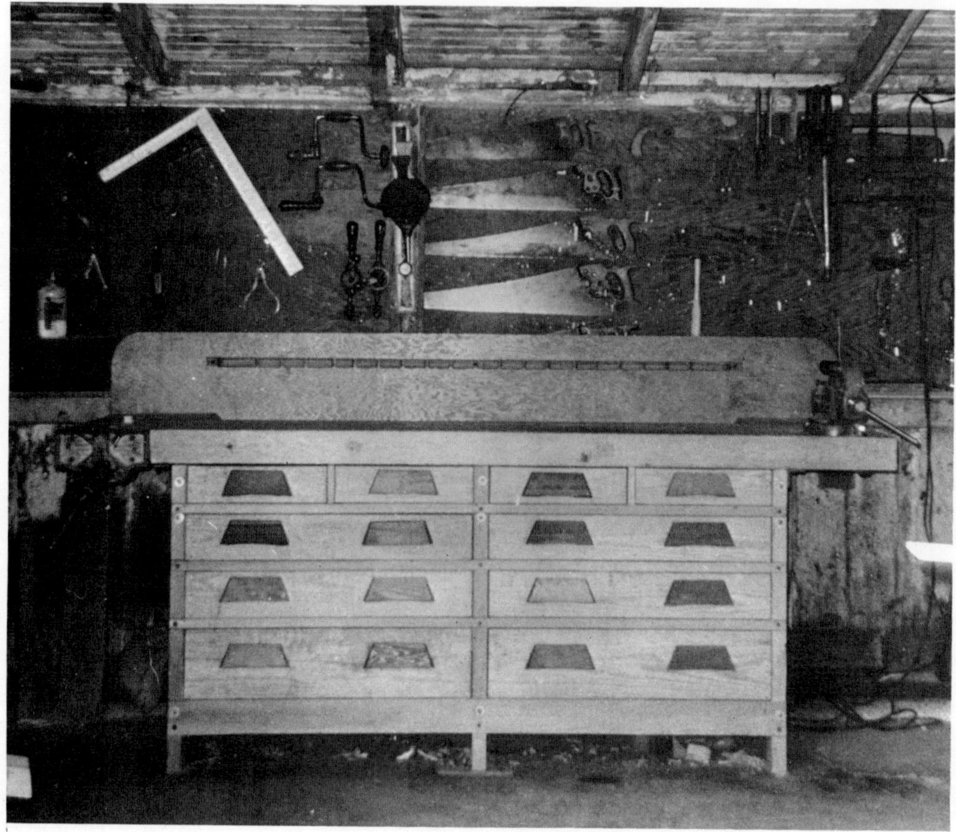

Figure 44. Workbench.

performance required. Accuracy is of the essence, and without it you will have a jerry job. Accuracy is not too much to expect from a budding carver; so now that you are up to your neck in the work, proceed with courage and determination. Here is your real opportunity to test your reserve in these two characteristics which all carvers must have. If the beginner gives up easily he will be casting into the fire most of his carving efforts. Most of the carvings in this book are not difficult, but they are not child's play, either. The workbench is a little more difficult but it, too, can be successfully constructed by an individual with little experience.

Any bench requires at least four legs for stability. The bench design in this chapter consists of three leg units, each self-contained, and when joined together with rails running lengthwise, compose a strong, sturdy understructure. A ½″ plywood back further increases the rigidity of the bench.

Figure 45A shows one-half of a top rail, grooved for two ⅜″ tie rods. These tie rods should extend beyond the rail sufficiently to go through the 2 × 4's (legs), the plywood back, and leave enough threads to take a ⅜″ U.S. Std. threaded nut on both ends (about 30½″). The tie rods should be cut to size (hacksaw) and threaded on both ends about 2″ down to allow for future tightening (the thread should be ⅜″ U.S. Std. Coarse). If the carver

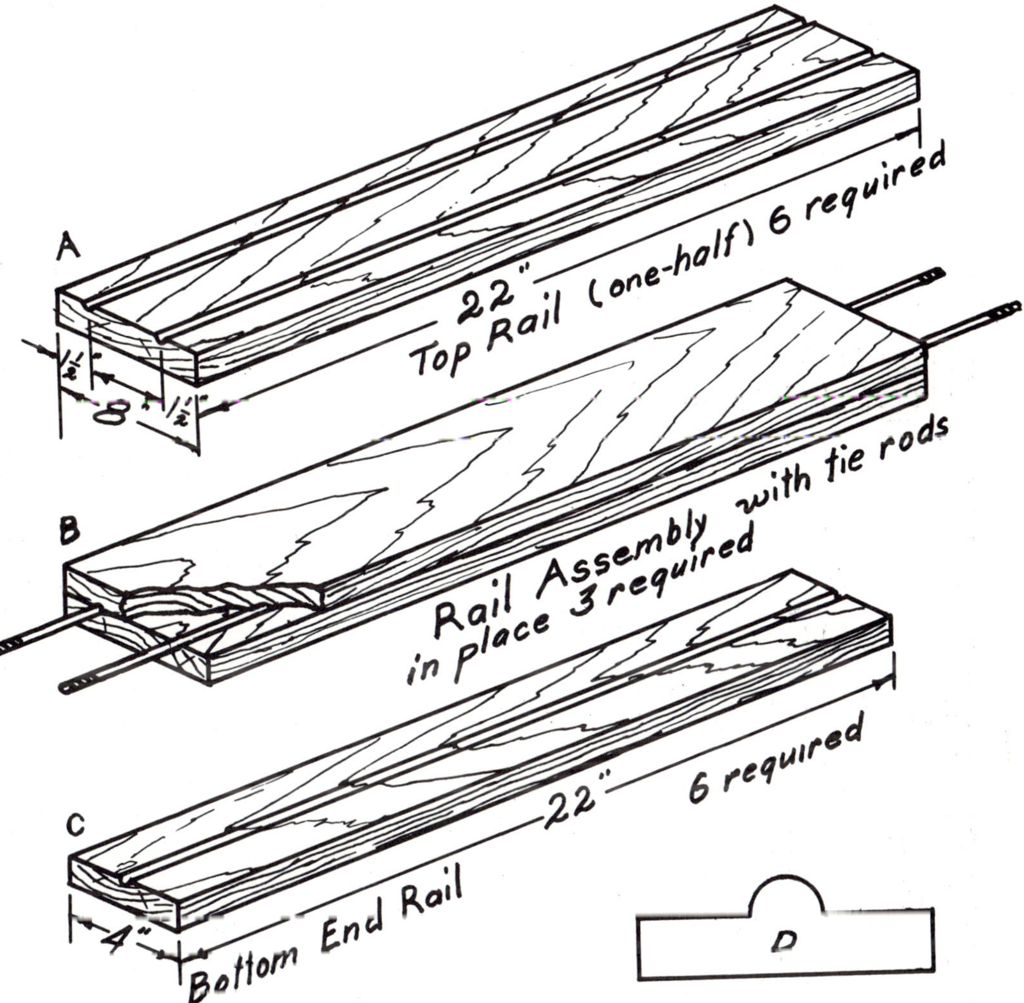

Figure 45. Construction of end rails. (D shows scraper formed to correct depth of grooves.)

cannot perform this operation, he should cut the metal to size and have his automobile mechanic perform the work for him. The grooves should be laid out accurately and carved with a gouge of suitable size and sweep. The groove should be large enough to allow a loose fit of the tie rods when the halves are glued together. (If a table saw with an adjustable head is available, these grooves may be dadoed in.) To insure the proper depth, a piece of scrap steel may be formed as shown in Figure 45D to remove the high spots.

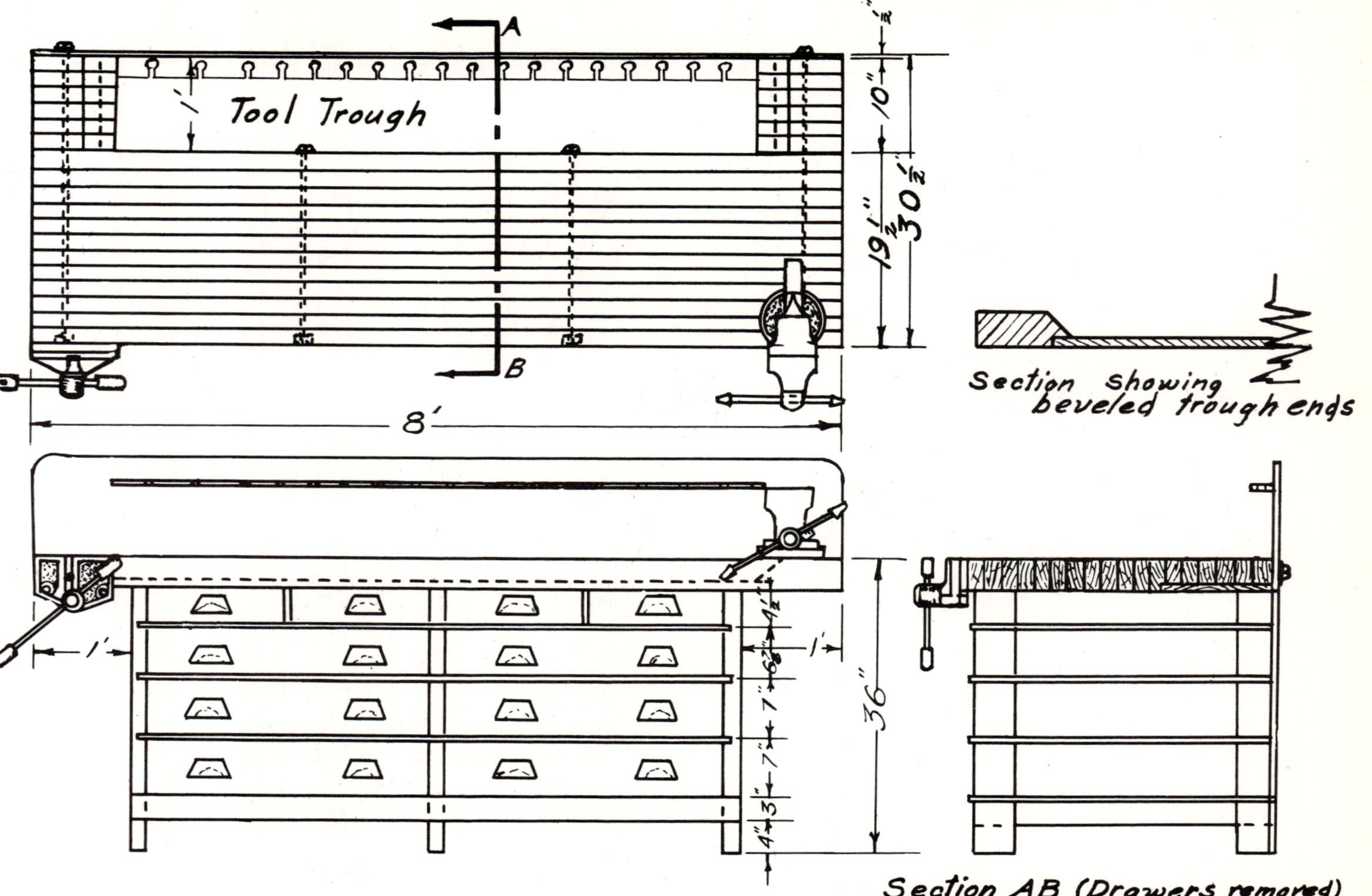

Figure 46. Top, front, and end views of workbench.

When six of these half-rails have been prepared, the tie rods may be inserted and each of the contacting surfaces coated with glue and assembled (Figure 45B). To hold the boards in place while being clamped together, four nails should be used, one in each corner, which are not long enough to penetrate both boards. When the three rails have been assembled, one should be placed upon the other and clamped together tightly with C-clamps (or short-bar bar clamps). Unless otherwise specified, U.S. Plywood White Glue is recommended for all projects discussed in this book.

The lower end rails (Figure 45C) should be prepared in the same manner as the top rails described in the foregoing paragraphs.

The 2 × 4's shown in the drawing are 32⅜″ long. The length should be governed by the height of the carver who will use the bench. He should be able to stand at his bench comfortably while working without undue bending. Enough material should be allowed to extend above the top end rail to be evenly cut off later when the leg section is squared up for size. The holes for the tie rods should be located in the 2 × 4's accurately. Locate the centers of the holes from both edges and center-punch for position. Do not depend upon the auger (⅜″) to locate itself. Start from both edges and bore perpendicularly toward the center. Even a good mechanic cannot bore through from one side to the other accurately. Boring from both edges will insure an accurate hole. *Important*: Allow about 4″ for toe room below the bottom rail.

After the 2 × 4's have been prepared, assemble the rails, forming the leg sections. When the tie rods are tightened the rails should be square with the legs. If they are not, square them. Use a bar clamp for this operation or some sort of gadget to pull the legs into position. Place the bar clamp across the leg section at an angle and tighten, pulling the frame in as far as necessary. This is a good trick to remember and is probably known only to cabinetmakers. Incidentally, if the operation does not work out for the first trial, experiment until you have learned the trick. There are many advantages in constructing your own bench; it is good preparation for your more difficult carving skills.

When the frames or leg sections have been squared up and tightened, the legs and rails should be in a smooth plane, at least one side should be a flat surface to receive the ¼″ plywood panel to be installed next. Cut a piece of ¼″ plywood the proper size for each leg section (two for the middle section). Be sure the frames are square before nailing on the plywood (Figure 47). Note that the plywood is flush with all sides except the front where the drawers are located. A ½″ inset is allowed here to provide a proper drawer front finish. (The assumption is made that drawers will be desired; otherwise, any directions including drawers may be ignored.) The ¼″ plywood should be nailed with the good side down, as the other side is the finished or visible surface. The nails should be 1″ long (the nails manufactured to nail Sheetrock in place are just right for this operation). The unfinished side of each section is up—the side to which the drawer slides are fastened (*see* Figure 47). Remember that there is a left and right end leg section; so be guided by this fact in selecting the finished surface. The plywood is nailed to both sides of the middle section as has been stated (good side out). After the plywood panels have been installed, prepare and fasten in place the drawer slides.

Before installing the drawer slides, the layout for the drawers should be studied (Figures 46, 47 and 48). Lay out the cuts for the separating rails for the drawers (Figure 47). Cut these recesses down to the plywood panels

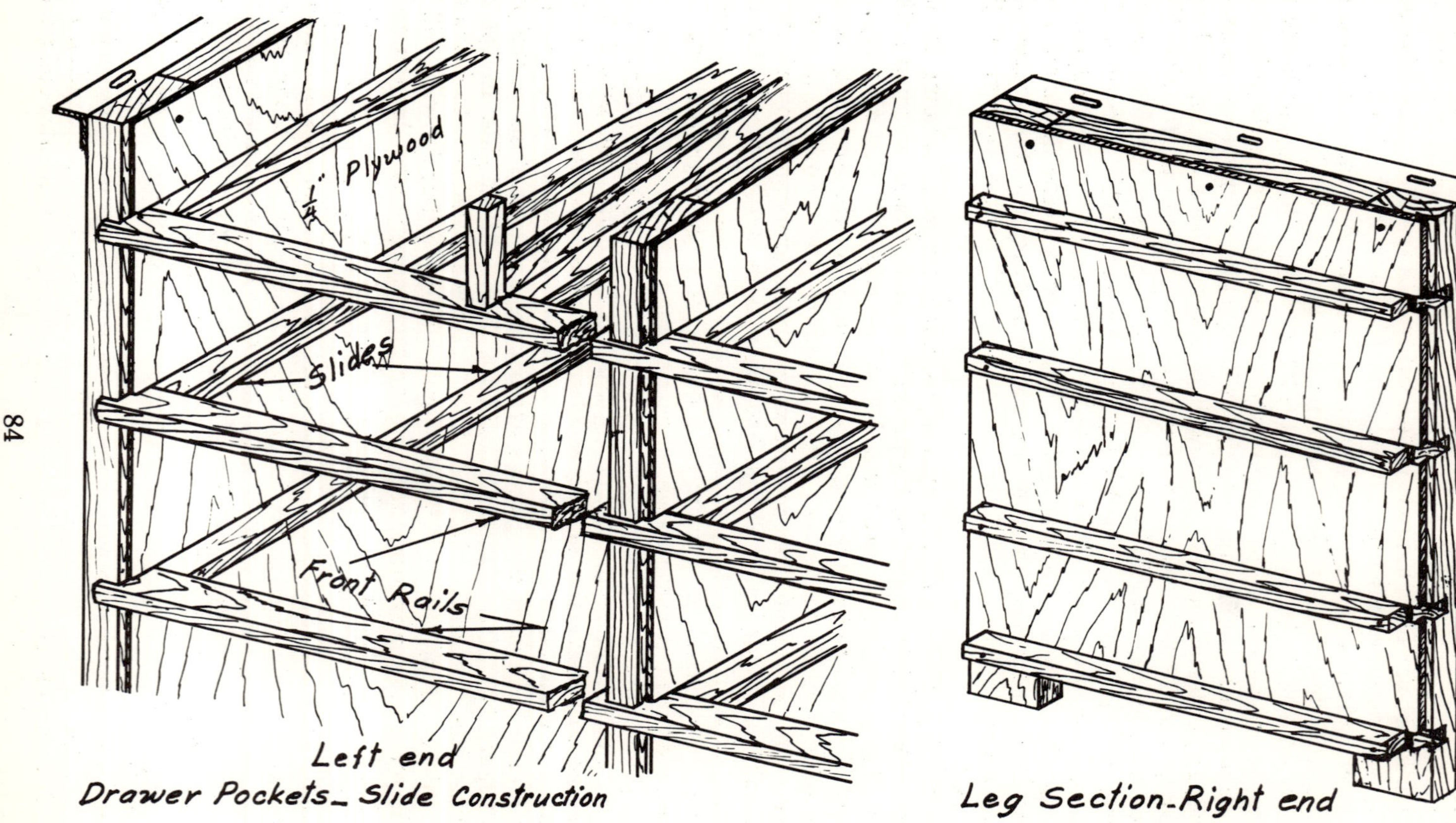

Figure 47. Understructure of workbench.

or ½″ deep, and wide enough to fit the thickness of the rails. The cuts extend to the middle of the 2 × 4's and the nosed ends of the rails extend over the seams. The cuts for the rails determine the location of the drawer slides. They should be installed next. Be sure they run parallel with the top edge of the leg sections (*see* Figure 47). They should be at right angles and flush with the separating rails. The slides are glued and nailed in place. The nails (10d. finishing) are inserted at each end so that they will have the solid 2 × 4's to hold them. The slides extend the entire width of the leg sections. Should the slides have a tendency to split while being nailed, drill a small hole in them for the nail.

Drawer Separating Rails; Bottom Rail. These members should be made accurately with respect to length, width, end and middle cuts. The ends should extend over the recesses cut for them in the 2 × 4's to blind the seam as noted in the preceding paragraph. All three rails are 1″ × 2″ × 70″.

The bottom rail is the same thickness but 4″ wide and long enough to extend completely over the legs, or about 72″. The legs should be recessed for the rail deep enough to allow about ¼″ to remain out, or about ¾″. During the assembly operations the rails may be nailed in place, leaving the center for the roundhead screws to be installed later. After the rails have been installed, the understructure should be braced securely after being squared up in its proper position.

The Back Section. The back section is made of a single piece of ½″ plywood (fir) that is good on one side. The lower portion is the same length as the understructure, but the upper section beginning at the bottom edge of the top (or the top edge of the leg sections) is the same length as the top when finished. When cut to shape and size, the back may be installed. The holes for the tie rods in the leg sections should be located accurately in the back and bored with ½″ holes, a size larger to allow for a margin of error. Unscrew the nuts in the leg sections next to the back and place it in position. Slip ⅜″ washers over the tie rods and tighten the nuts. The back is further fastened to the leg sections with common wire nails, about 6d. The understructure should now be quite rigid. The tool rack shown in Figure 46 may be installed at any time convenient to the builder.

The Top. The top is probably the most important single part of the bench. The construction involves some special features not usually found in homemade jobs. In this respect the top resembles those professionally made. The top is composed of a main section, a tool trough and trough ends. The main section is composed of twelve 2 × 4's, 8′ long, bolted together with four ½″ diameter steel rods, threaded at both ends (U.S. Std., Coarse). Two other 2 × 4's, 8′ long, will be required for the trough end sections. These ends are 14″ on their top edges and are beveled on a 45° angle to the bottom of the trough (*see* Figure 46).

One 2 × 4 of the main section should be laid out accurately for the tie rods and used as a model for all of the others. The holes should be located on both sides of the 2 × 4's as was done in the legs. Use your try square for this operation. The holes should be bored a size larger than the tie rods, or 9/16″. After the hole centers have been located, bore from both sides and meet in the middle. This work must be done with precision for twelve pieces of stock with four holes each consists of enough variables to easily make mistakes—and is costly in time and effort. The last 2 × 4 must be specially cut for the trough grounds. Study Figure 46 for this

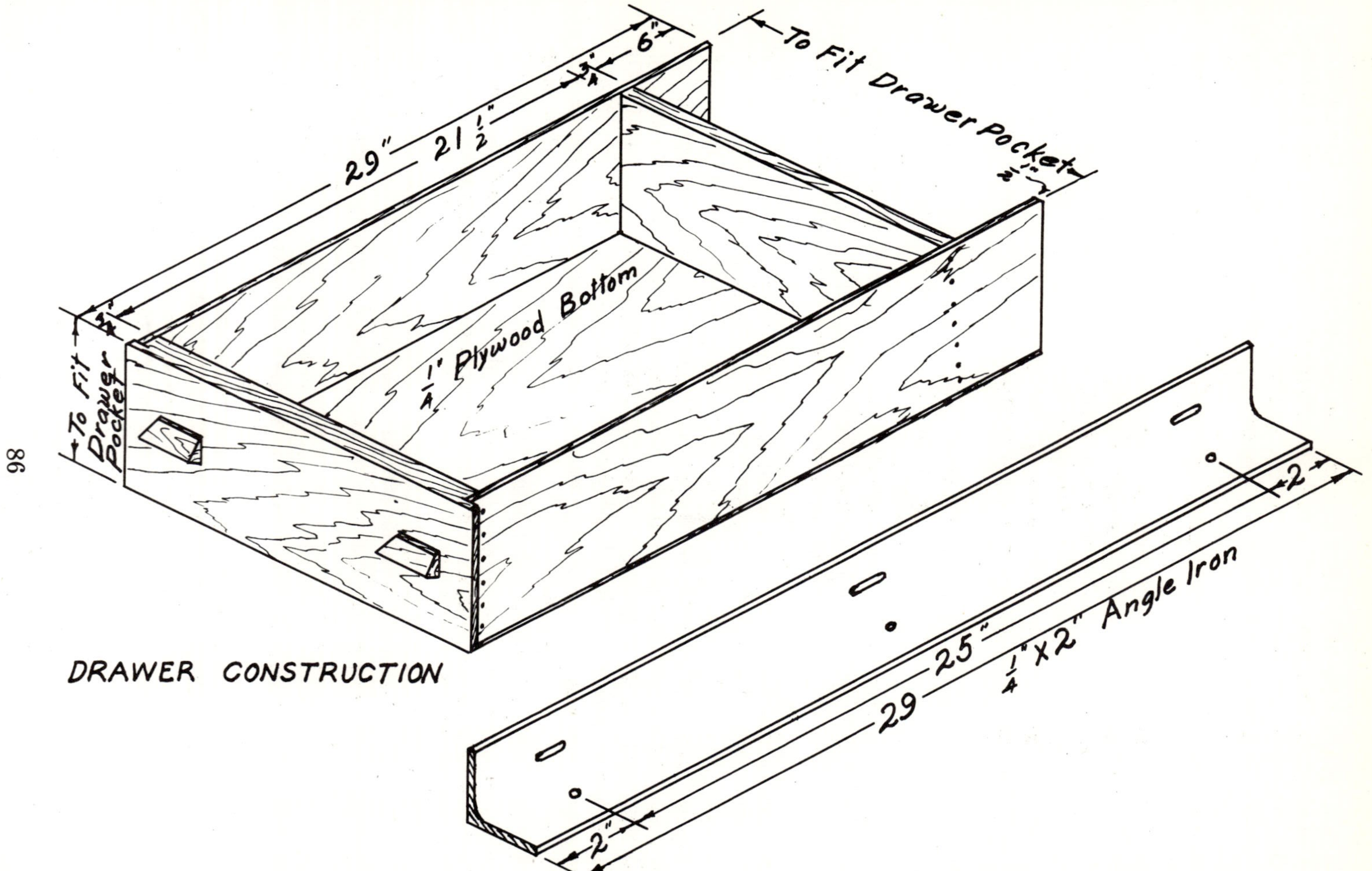

Figure 48. Drawer construction and angle iron.

construction. Note that the beveled pieces are also rabbeted to provide grounds for the ends of the trough bottom.

The holes in the front 2 × 4 are counterbored to receive a ½″ washer over which the nut of the tie rod is tightened. The nut should not be screwed down enough to allow the rod to extend. The tightening process is from the other end. The recess will be filled later with plastic wood, so the rod also should be covered. When the bench is finished, the front should be a smooth surface without protruding nuts and bolts. The counterboring is best done with an expansion bit before the 9/16″ holes are bored, but a gouge may be used to recess the holes to the proper depth.

When all of the 2 × 4's have been prepared, they may be assembled. Install the two middle tie rods first. The beveled pieces may be slipped over the end tie rods and nailed with a 10d. nail to hold them in position. Nail one member before the other is slipped on. Next, tightly bolt all of the 2 × 4's together and correct any error made in rabbeting the grounds for the trough bottom. Install the trough bottom (1″ thick stock) and fasten with heavy flatheaded screws. (The holes in the bottom board—trough bottom—should be the same size as the shanks of the screws and countersunk.) Be sure that the back edge of the trough bottom is in line with the 2 × 4's so that the top will fit tightly against the back.

NOTE: The tie rods should be prepared as in the case of the leg sections. If the builder cannot thread the rods, they should be cut to size and be threaded by a mechanic who possesses stocks and dies.

Square up the ends of the top and rest it upon the understructure.

Prepare two pieces of angle iron ¼″ × 2″ × 29″, as shown in Figure 48. If the builder does not have the proper tools for performing this job it, too, should be done by a mechanic. The slotted holes are designed to allow the top to "float" over the understructure without setting up stresses caused by the expansion or contraction of the top.

An angle iron should be installed on opposite ends of the understructure as illustrated. They are fastened with ⅜″ carriage bolts 2½″ long. The heads are countersunk on the inside to allow the drawers to slide past. Clamp the angle iron in place before boring the holes, ⅜″ diameter. Insert the carriage bolts from the inside and tighten the nuts over the angle iron. (The top may be shoved aside for the latter operation.)

Now the top may be fastened in position. Locate it properly and mark the centers of the ½″ tie rods in the plywood back. Bore these holes 9/16″, a size larger than the bolts. Shove the top in place after first removing the washers and nuts from the tie rods. Replace the washers and nuts after the top has been pushed into place. The trough bottom should be fastened to the back with 1½″ flatheaded screws.

In the center of the slotted holes in the angle iron, drill ⅜″ holes the length of the lag screw shank (lag screws ⅜″ diam., 2½″ long). Continue the hole with a ¼″ drill the remainder of the way. Before screwing in the lag screws, a washer is placed under the head to provide a slipping surface. Tighten the screws. This operation completes the bench proper, leaving only the drawers to be made and installed.

Drawers. The fronts of the drawers should be made first. They are made about ¼″ less than the opening, both in length and in width. As the fronts determine the size of the drawers in width and breadth they should have enough "play" room to keep them from sticking. Little will be said concerning the drawer construction as the simplest method has been provided in the design. Study the illustrations (Figure 48) and follow the directions carefully. The drawer fronts should be rabbeted on all edges except the top. The bottom edge should be rabbeted deeply enough to receive the plywood bottom, 1/4″. The sides should be rabbeted enough to include the sides of the drawers plus 1/8″. Note that the sides are nearly as long as the leg sections are wide, but that the bottoms are a full 6″ shorter allowing the drawers to be pulled out their entire length without spilling the contents on the floor. In other words, the drawers are 6″ shorter than the drawer pockets, so far as content space is concerned.

Drawer Pulls. The pulls are made of soft wood 1″ thick and 3″ wide. The back is recessed to receive the fingers. The pulls are tapered to 1/4″ on the top edge and otherwise shaped according to the drawing. The recessed material is removed easily with a Surform rasp. Lining up the pulls should be done with care. After their respective positions have been located, 1/4″ holes are drilled through the drawer fronts for each pull. The holes should be located to allow the screws to enter the thicker portion. A pilot hole for the screws in the pulls should be drilled after they have been located and glued in place. Small finishing nails may be used to hold the pulls while the glue is setting and the screws installed. Use roundheaded screws that are long enough to enter the pulls not more than 3/4″. In other words, the screws should not come through the surface.

A rapid-action vise should be installed on the left front end of the top of the bench, but this may be postponed to a later date. Of utmost importance, however, is a strong machinist's vise mounted on the right front end of top. The jaws should be at least 5″ wide and open about 12″. When the jaws are closed the line of their closure should clear the front edge of the bench. Otherwise no stock can be clamped that drops below the bench top. Note also where the tie rods are located in the top before boring holes to fasten the vise.

Finally, the bench should be given a coat of sealer, followed by two coats of spar varnish. Allow each coat to set thoroughly before applying the next one. The insides of the drawers should be varnished also to make them less likely to collect dirt and grease.

Now your bench is finished—complete—ready for your best carving efforts. You may not have enough money left to splurge over the weekend, but you have made a wise investment which will pay good dividends as long as you live. Do not permit the lady of the house to move it to the dining room to serve as a buffet. It is much too important for such common use. Storing the family silver and other dining doodads need not have such princely space. Only a carver's tools are worthy of such spacious and regal accommodations.

Chapter 11

PROJECT NO. 7

MARQUETRY

> What is more cheerful, now, in the fall of the year, than an open-wood fire? Do you hear those little chirps and twitters coming out of that piece of apple wood? Those are the ghosts of the robins and blue birds that sang upon a bough when it was in blossom last Spring. In Summer whole flocks of them come fluttering about the fruit trees under the window: so I have singing birds all the year round.
>
> *Miss Mehitabel's Son,*
> by Thomas Bailey Aldrich

To paraphrase Miss Mehitabel's son: what is more cheerful, now, in the fall of the year, than an open wood-fire? Do you hear those little chirps and twitters coming from those carved birds resting on the mantelpiece? Do you hear the rattle of the inlaid Kingfisher hanging above them; the Kingfisher that fished from a dead, broken limb overhanging the creek last summer? Do you see him fishing, fixed in his everlasting pose recreated with inlaid woods? Now he fishes constantly all year round.

Such a picture is not merely a ghost of last summer's bird. It is a masterpiece—a true work of art made by the steady hands of the craftsman. It appropriately hangs above the mantelpiece and satisfies the Emersonian dictum that a genuine work of art has as much reason for being as the earth and the sun.

As this book is pitched toward leisure-time activities, the contents would be incomplete without an introduction, at least, to the old, old art of marquetry. In furniture-making it was practiced by the ancient Egyptians, Grecians and Romans. Except for its waning years during the 19th century, marquetry has been used down through the ages to enhance legions of useful articles from gunstocks to paneled walls. In the beginning bits of precious metal, semiprecious stones, ivory, and wood were skillfully inlaid in the object to be decorated. This form, known as intarsia, was highly developed in Italy during the 17th century. Choir stalls, pulpits, panels, and other cathedral furniture were masterfully inlaid with different materials, producing a very beautiful decor.

The art as we know it was probably introduced and developed in Holland during the 16th century. From Holland the new technique spread throughout Europe. By the 18th century France led all other countries in creating beautiful inlaid work. Jean Mace and his descendants were considered the Masters, but the Italians, as has already been noted, had achieved world recognition by their intarsia skills. Without any apparent reason the art of marquetry waned and almost disappeared from the arts and crafts in the 19th century. Many of the masterpieces of marquetry created during the fruitful years of the Renaissance, however, were preserved. They now repose in the galleries of the Louvre in France.

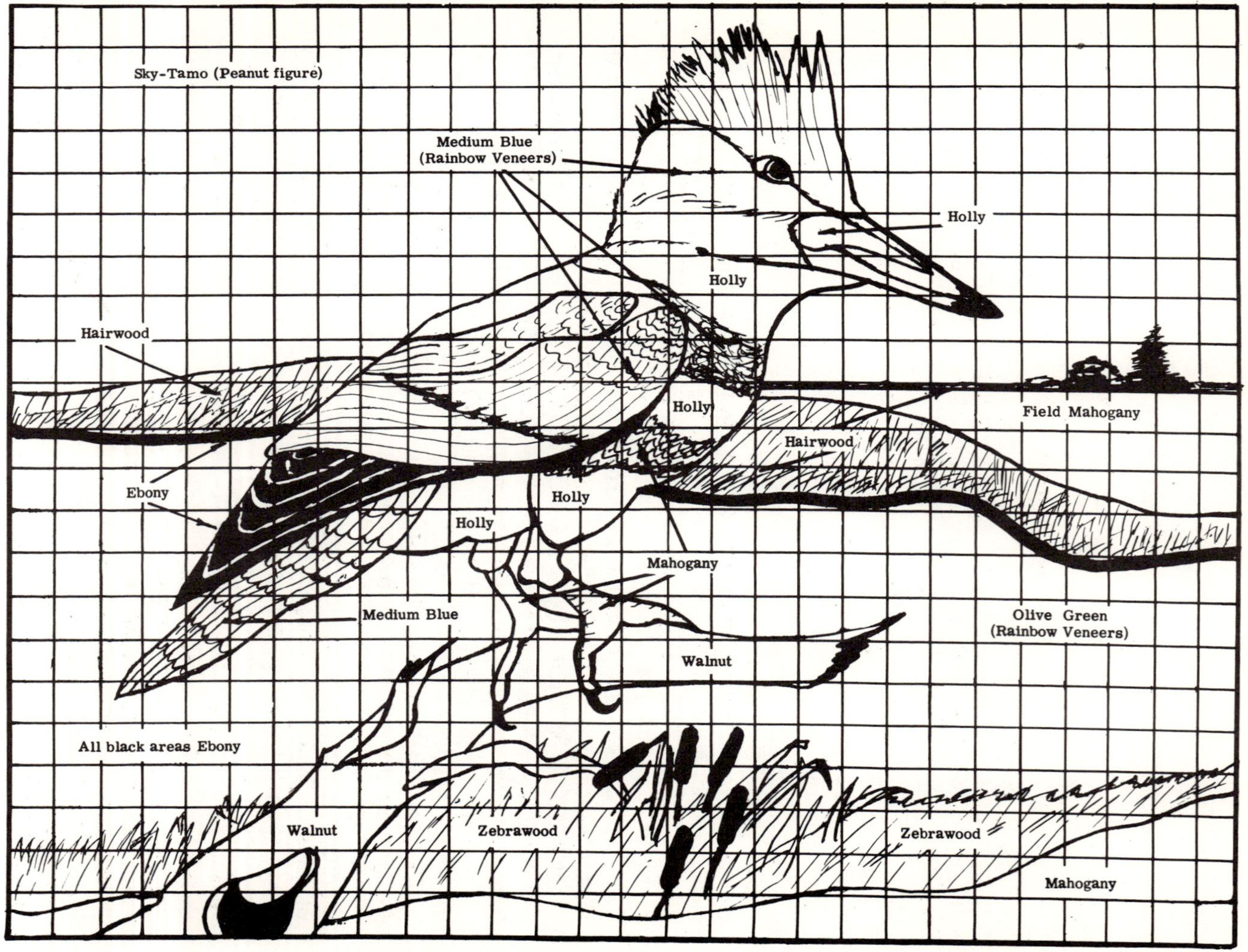

Sky-Tamo (Peanut figure)
Medium Blue (Rainbow Veneers)
Holly
Holly
Hairwood
Holly
Field Mahogany
Hairwood
Ebony
Holly
Holly
Mahogany
Medium Blue
Olive Green (Rainbow Veneers)
Walnut
All black areas Ebony
Walnut
Zebrawood
Zebrawood
Mahogany

Figure 49. Marquetry picture design (squares ½″).

Industry and culture are not bosom friends. The Industrial Revolution which meant so much to Europe in material wealth also happened in an era when the arts suffered—whether the cause was related or not. Probably the artists and craftsmen had neither the talent nor the will to pursue such an exacting art as marquetry. In our own time marquetry is becoming popular again, mainly because almost any craftsman with some artistic ability can achieve pleasing results. New materials and modern techniques have reduced the skills necessary for marquetry to simple dimensions. The craftsman can now veneer surfaces on a high level of proficiency without the use of cumbersome clamps and presses. The miracle of contact glue makes veneering child's play, comparatively speaking. This, coupled with the many exotic woods available and the ease of operating power machines, makes the craft of marquetry attractive to many craftsmen. Most companies selling veneers have kits available for less-skilled individuals. These kits of precut inlays range from a simple checkerboard to the recreation of da Vinci's *Last Supper*. Albert Constantine and Sons lists over one hundred different veneers, both domestic and imported, for the craftsman and cabinetmaker. Here is a fertile field, indeed, for the carver to explore for both pleasure and profit.

With these thoughts in mind, the last project in the book will be the construction of an inlaid picture. The main motif will be the Kingfisher of Project 4. Figure 26 has been redrawn in a habitat of reeds and water, field and sky (Figure 49). I used colored inks to tint the slate blue of the bird and the green of the water. Otherwise, the natural wood prevails. Colored veneers are now available and are stocked by most veneer companies. They are usually imported from England and are dyed throughout. These colored veneers make picture composition much easier, but the true artist still prefers the natural color and grain effects.

The picture of this project measures 12″ × 14″. Therefore, a veneer sheet, one for each color, should be cut 1″ longer and wider, or 13″ × 15″. This extra dimension is provided to allow a space for gluing the sheets together, as will be explained later.

Should some of the sheets be of insufficient width they may be easily spliced with an extra strip. First, the joining edges must fit perfectly. An easy way to do this is to overlap the edges about 1″ and cement them together with rubber cement. Rubber cement will tack the sheets sufficiently to hold them while being cut. Saw down the center of the lap with the jigsaw or split with a sharp thin knifepoint. A wavy line or kerf will not matter; in fact, the joint might be improved. When separated, remove the waste wood from both pieces; pry off with a thin-bladed knife. The material should separate easily. Fasten the edges of the veneers together with paper tape especially made for this purpose. Be sure the joint is tight. Gummed strips used for wrapping packages will also do this job satisfactorily. Do not attempt to lengthen the veneers in this fashion (butt-to-butt)—the joint will show up like a sore thumb.

The development of contact glue has been a boon to veneer users. After applying it to both surfaces to be fastened together the work is allowed to set for about twenty minutes. After this time paper will not stick to the coated surfaces. Intricate parts or inlays may be adjusted in their proper positions over paper and the paper slipped away when the proper match has been achieved. Be sure the inlay is held in place with the fingers while the paper is being removed. The bond will be instantaneous and the part cannot be successfully removed or repositioned. The first effort must be right; there is no second chance.

Before squaring the veneer sheets some thought should be given to both the direction of the grain and its texture. For example, the sky should have the grain running from left to right. A mottled texture is desirable. I used tamo from Japan for the banks of clouds on either side and zebrawood for the sky. These woods proved to be too dark. Primavera, ash, aspen, or maple would have been more desirable. The reeds and cattails should be made of a suitable veneer with the grain running perpendicularly. Lacewood was used in the sample with excellent results. Although it is a difficult wood to handle it is ideal for reed work. Some sections, such as the ebony parts, may be cut separately using a particular lamination as a model. An ebony sheet in the pile is not necessary. The black part of the tail, for example, may be cut from a small piece of ebony veneer using one of the tail laminations as a guide. The ebony and the lamination should be cemented together with rubber cement and allowed to set. When set, the two parts make the jigsaw work much easier and the ebony less likely to split. The same scheme may be used in cutting the far shoreline, the bill, and the claws. Rubber cement is used as the binding medium as it is easily broken when the parts have been cut. Many small parts are best left unsawed. The parts may be scored in later with a sharp-pointed knife blade. The scored depths may be filled with whiting or some other filler later. Also, the black and other colored parts of the picture may be made of "rainbow" colored veneers, but the results are not quite so effective.

The sheets should be squared to size by the use of a framing square and a sharp, thin-bladed knife (a veneer saw might be used). The size is 13″ × 15″ which will allow a ½″ margin all around for the gluing operation. All of the sheets are bonded in a pile, careful consideration being given to the run of the grain. Coat the margins (both sides) with veneer glue and allow them to set until untacky to the touch. Be careful in bonding the sheets together. A piece of paper, as already suggested in such cases, may be used to facilitate this operation. When all of the veneer sheets have been bonded together allow the pile to set overnight. In the meantime, however, the picture may be transferred to the top lamination which should be holly.

The backboard should next be prepared. It is made of a piece of plywood, good both sides, ¼″ thick. It should be 2″ wider and longer than the picture or 14″ × 16″. The reason for the extra inch circumscribing the picture is to hold the 1¼″ frame.

A power jigsaw is necessary in this project. A coping saw or even the power-driven type will not do. All of the cuts must be perpendicular so that the last laminations will accurately match those of the first sheet. Prepare the jigsaw for cutting out the picture. Clamp a fine fret saw blade in the reciprocating jaws and test the machine for smooth operation.* As only a small portion of the blade will be in contact with the veneer pile, this section dulls rapidly. The platen or table of the saw may be elevated by screwing a ¾″ piece of plywood to it. Clamps may be used to hold the elevated table but I have found this method unsatisfactory; the clamps are always in the way.

* A spiral jigsaw blade is now available in 25′ lengths. The blades are cut to length as needed. Two gauges are supplied, .020 and .040. The advantages of this blade should be obvious. It will cut backward as well as forward, and from left to right. The material does not have to be turned.

The iris of the eye is slightly over 1/4″ in diameter. This is a good place to begin your work. First, bore a 1/4″ hole through the veneer pile with a sharp auger. Insert the saw blade and fasten the ends in the jigsaw jaws. The eye may be repaired after the picture has been bonded to the backboard. Carefully cut the eye shape and continue down the eye cavity, around the crest, and back to the eye again. Next, saw out the bill. Cut only the gross shape as the other parts of the bill can be scored in with a sharp-pointed knife. India ink may be used to dye the black parts (if ebony is not used). Continue the bottom part of the bill into the bird's head as indicated. Back out the blade and start a new section (there are times when the saw should be stopped while this is done; backing out the blade while the saw is in motion might damage the kerf which usually should be sharp and crisp). Cut out the entire bird while your blade is still sharp. The bird is your most important concern at this time. The larger areas are easy to cut. Do not saw through the bonded edges of the pile. They act as a frame to hold the many layers of veneers in place. If your saw table is small, the picture will probably overhang in some positions. Have a box handy to collect any laminations that drop out. Do not lose a single lamination for the lost one might be the one most desired in the assembly operation.

To satisfy your curiosity and impatience, the sky section may be cut free and the upper section assembled. Remember your picture is 12″ × 14″. Cut out the background accordingly, leaving the 1/2″ margin intact. Cut the parts down to the water. The ebony shoreline may be cut separately from an ebony veneer sheet by using a lamination as a model, as explained in the case of the tail section. With luck your shoreline will be cut in one piece on either side of the bird. Ebony, lacewood, and zebrawood are difficult veneers to manage; be careful with them. Pin all of the parts cut free in their proper places on the backboard. Some of the saw kerfs may be squeezed tightly together but others must be spaced the width of the saw's gauge. Watch out for this operation for while the width of one saw kerf will not matter, doubling the space will. Do not spoil your picture by poor spacing of the inlays. After the parts have been properly positioned they may be bonded to the backboard. Work from the top downward and from left to right. Finish the picture as you progress down the backboard. Do not have any "flying buttresses" extending on your backboard for this method of working is a sure way to get your picture "out of focus." Do not start to surface your picture until it is completed. Be patient! The laminations are very thin and will not withstand many trial efforts. Complete your picture and allow the parts to set—even cut your freehand inlays before surfacing the picture.

Cut out the remaining parts and bond them in their proper locations. Be sure that you use the right lamination in every instance. By this time you have learned that there are as many pictures as there are sheets in your pile. But only certain laminations are desired in the composition; so watch out for this possible source of error. Sometimes very interesting combinations can be formed with the waste laminations, but this kind of experimentation is not in order at this time. The picture is the main point of interest. All of the waste laminations of a particular part should be collected in a box away from the unused parts. This precaution will save time by reducing the number of inlays to be considered during the assembly operation. Cut out the entire bird and tack it tentatively in place with veneer pins. When all of the parts have been cut and pinned, the bonding operation should

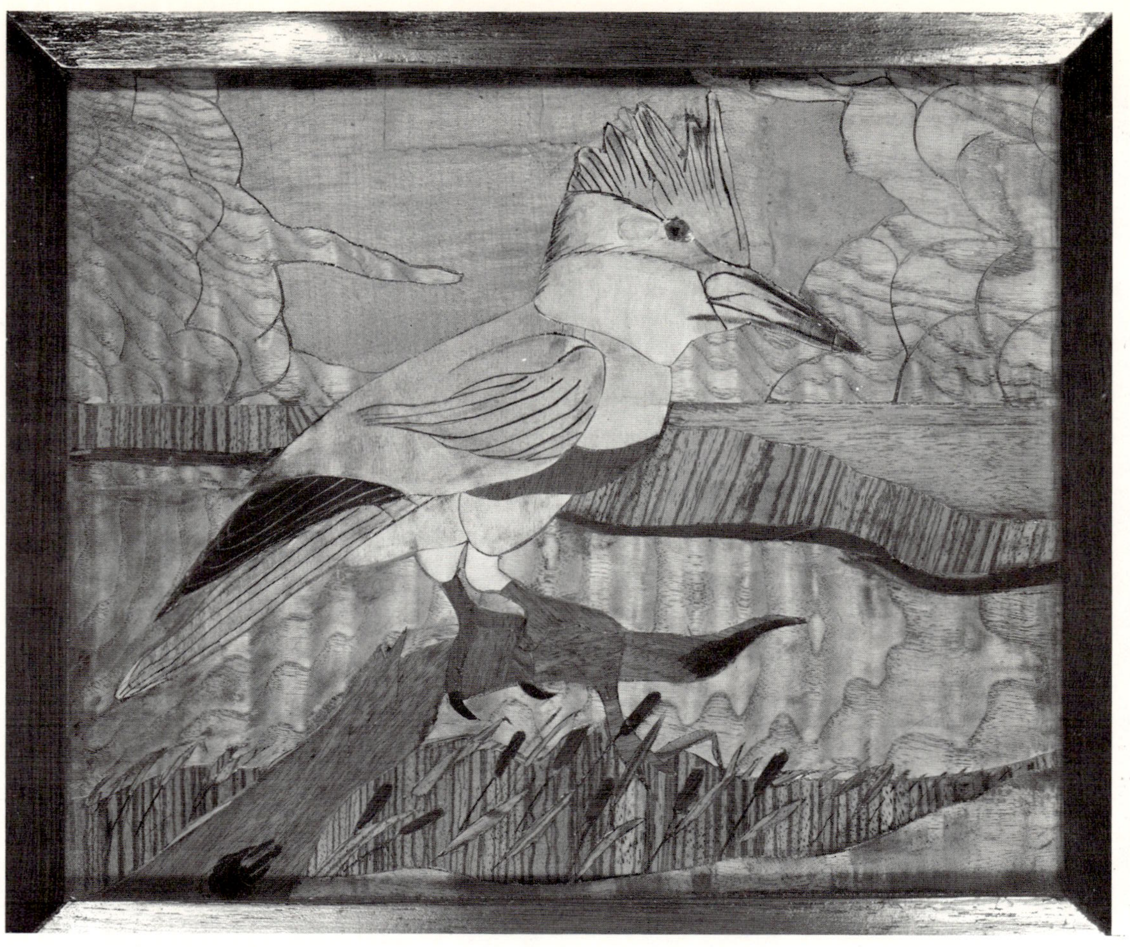

Figure 50. Marquetry. Kingfisher

Clouds—Tamo (Japan) peanut figure
Sky—Zebrawood (Africa)
Meadow—Light walnut (U.S.)
Shoreline—Ebony (Africa)
Reeds—Lacewood (Australia)
Cattails—Rosewood (East Indies)
Kingfisher—Holly (U.S.)
Legs, feet and breastband—Mahogany (Africa)
Dead limb—Dark walnut (U.S.)

follow. You are cautioned again about controlling the space between the inlays. Cut the claws from ebony with a sharp knife and inlay them after the entire picture has been bonded.

The whole picture may be cut out before assembling any of the parts. This method might require more willpower but it could result in greater efficiency. Coat a portion of the backboard with veneer glue and allow it to set for twenty minutes. In the meantime, coat the parts of the picture concerned with glue and allow to set for the specified time. Begin with the sky and work downward and to the right and left, as before. When the glued portion of the backboard has been filled, glue another section and another set of inlays. Continue the process until the picture has been completed. Be sure all parts are matched perfectly. Allow the picture to set overnight.

Next morning survey your work and make any necessary corrections. Enhance your reeds and cattail section by making separate inlays to point up the design. Rosewood makes excellent cattails.

To surface your picture use an old-fashioned cabinet scraper. They are now difficult to find in hardware stores because power sanders have replaced them. Grind all four edges straight and at right angles with the sides. Whet the edges on a sharp oilstone until the corners are sharp and free of wire edges. Next, burnish the edges to turn them over in a hook. A burnisher is also difficult to procure but a nail punch can be used to stroke the edges and, to lift the hook, the point of the nail punch can be ground to a fingernail point beveled on both sides. Stroke the edges firmly the entire length at an angle of about 60°. If this operation is done effectively the turned-over edge will be as sharp as a razor. Sometimes the hook is turned over too far and must be lifted from the blade. Do this with the point of the burnisher or the improvised nail punch. In the absence of a cabinet scraper, freshly cut pieces of glass may be used, but glass is not nearly as effective as a sharp scraper. The regular scrapers on the market do not cut clean. They may, however, be used with caution.

Hold the cabinet scraper firmly at an angle suitable to the cutting angle of the hook. Use the thumbs for pushing the scraper forward. If it does not cut a clean shaving, it has not been sharpened correctly. Scrape obliquely across the kerfs and with the grain. When surfaced, the picture may be sanded with very fine "sandpaper." Your sanding block should have a felt surface between it and the paper. I use Production Paper, an aluminum oxide coated sheet, 120 grit followed by 220. Regular sandpaper is unsatisfactory. Sand whenever possible with the grain. After your surfacing operation, rub the picture with a soft cloth soaked in turpentine. Your picture should stand out beautifully. There may be places you can improve. Do not hesitate to do so, but remember your laminations are now paper-thin and will not tolerate much more reducing.

If there are any parts to be dyed, now is the time for this operation. Merely tint the wood, allowing the beautiful grain to show through.

Repair the iris of the eye. Mahogany with an ebony pupil will be just right. This operation will test your carving skills. A sharpened 1/4″ pipe will cut the mahogany keenly when turned in a power drill. Bond the iris and allow to set overnight. When the glue has set thoroughly, drill a hole for the pupil. Carve the pupil and insert it. White glue instead of veneer glue may be used for the eye as it will set up harder. If there have been spaces left in the corners of the eye, fill them with holly.

Next, fill the saw kerfs with a filler. Black will be satisfactory in many places, but matching the wood is desirable in other parts. Before applying the clear varnish or lacquer, seal the surface with a good wood sealer (*see* Chapter 13). If there is a chance of the filler's bleeding into the unfinished veneers, apply the sealer and one coat of finish before using them. Rub down each coat of finish with fine steel wool after it has set several days. Three coats of varnish should be sufficient to complete the job.

The framing operation is next. Make the frame parts and veneer with the kind of wood you wish to use. Do this before cutting the miters (not the outside edges, however; these edges are veneered after the frame has been glued to the backboard and both parts planed in a true surface). Join the frame parts carefully, using small finishing nails. Coat both the frame and backboard with veneer glue and allow the parts to set. Be sure the frame is in the exact location before contact. Use the paper trick to assist you in this operation. After the frame has been bonded, plane the edges of the backboard and the outside edges of the frame to coincide. The frame should extend over your picture about 1/4″ all around. Next, veneer the outside edges completing the job, except for the varnishing operation.

When your picture has been completed it should bear a close resemblance to Figure 50. I made this piece of marquetry by following my own directions given in this lesson. If you have made a wise selection of veneers and done your work carefully, your picture should be a thing of beauty: a unique piece of art—a conversation piece. With the imagination of Mehitabel's son you may observe your Kingfisher fishing all year round. Stretching this mental power a bit farther you can hear the sound of her voice, like the rattle of a fishing reel, as she swoops over the still waters like a boy on a scooter. Barring an accident, she will rest on the dead limb of the tree overhanging the creek as long as you shall live.

NOTE: A marquetry craftsman has several tricks up his sleeve to correct his mistakes. If you have never tried a piece of marquetry before, you might be wise in trying a simple pattern first. Try the Mallard duck on a plain background. This project will help you become familiar with the process. Of course, when you become skilled in the art you will discard the pile technique and build up your picture piece by piece. The inlays, however, will still be cut by overlapping the wood and cutting the adjoining parts in one operation. This technique will insure a perfect fit. But your main guide will be the master drawing and there will be no surplus parts.

Chapter 12

CHECKING, SHRINKING, AND BLEMISHES

John Rood, who has been referred to in several instances in this book, states that the question most frequently asked of him is: "How do you keep it (wood) from cracking?" "I don't," he frankly replies and goes on to minimize the matter. This is small consolation to the beginner who has enough shortcomings of his own without borrowing more from his carving medium. Recently a young man from suburban Washington, D.C., called me over long distance telephone to ask the same question. He had carved a barn owl out of redwood and it was seriously checking. Like Rood, I replied, "I don't," but I did give the caller some simple directions concerning his problem that may have helped him.

Checking is a natural weakness in all woods in varying degrees. Physically, it is caused by the unequalization of the drying procedure. While the core section remains comparatively green, the outside layers dry out and shrink. Then something has to give. So the outer layers of the log crack to increase their diameters over the unyielding core. The ends of the log, having been more directly exposed to the air, crack along the radial axis, penetrating according to the dryness of the surrounding air. Some carvers paint the ends of their logs to discourage rapid drying, and recently the author has noticed kiln-dried lumber being shipped with the ends painted an orange red. All materials expand and contract under temperature variations, the degree depending upon the kind of substance involved. One form of thermostat makes use of this principle in metals. Two strips of metal having great variance in their expansion and contracting ratios are bonded together. The expansion of the one is resisted by the other. Again, something has to give, and in this instance the metal with the greatest ratio of expansion increases its comparative length by bending. This displacement either closes the gap or opens the points of contact, thus closing or breaking the electric circuit, depending upon the design of the instrument. So the phenomenon, while unfortunate in wood, has many mechanical advantages.

Wood is very sensitive to moisture, so the humidity of the air has as great if not a greater effect upon the drying process as temperature. A log will not check if the core dries at the same rate as the outer layers. A drying procedure that will encourage this condition is difficult to attain. So, the carver must accept checks and the more serious cracks. Fortunately there are ways to alleviate this weakness in wood. Cracking and splitting can be repaired in seasoned logs, but green wood must be chemically treated (PEG—1000). Both techniques will be discussed later. In any event, the carver must learn to be the master of his medium or live with its weakness.

Therefore, more important than the kind of wood is the state of its dryness. An unseasoned log or block is difficult to control. It is a heap of trouble from the beginning to the very end. The outline may shrink, warp, or check out of control, destroying the preconceived design. Some of these faults may create a condition beyond repair; then the work becomes one

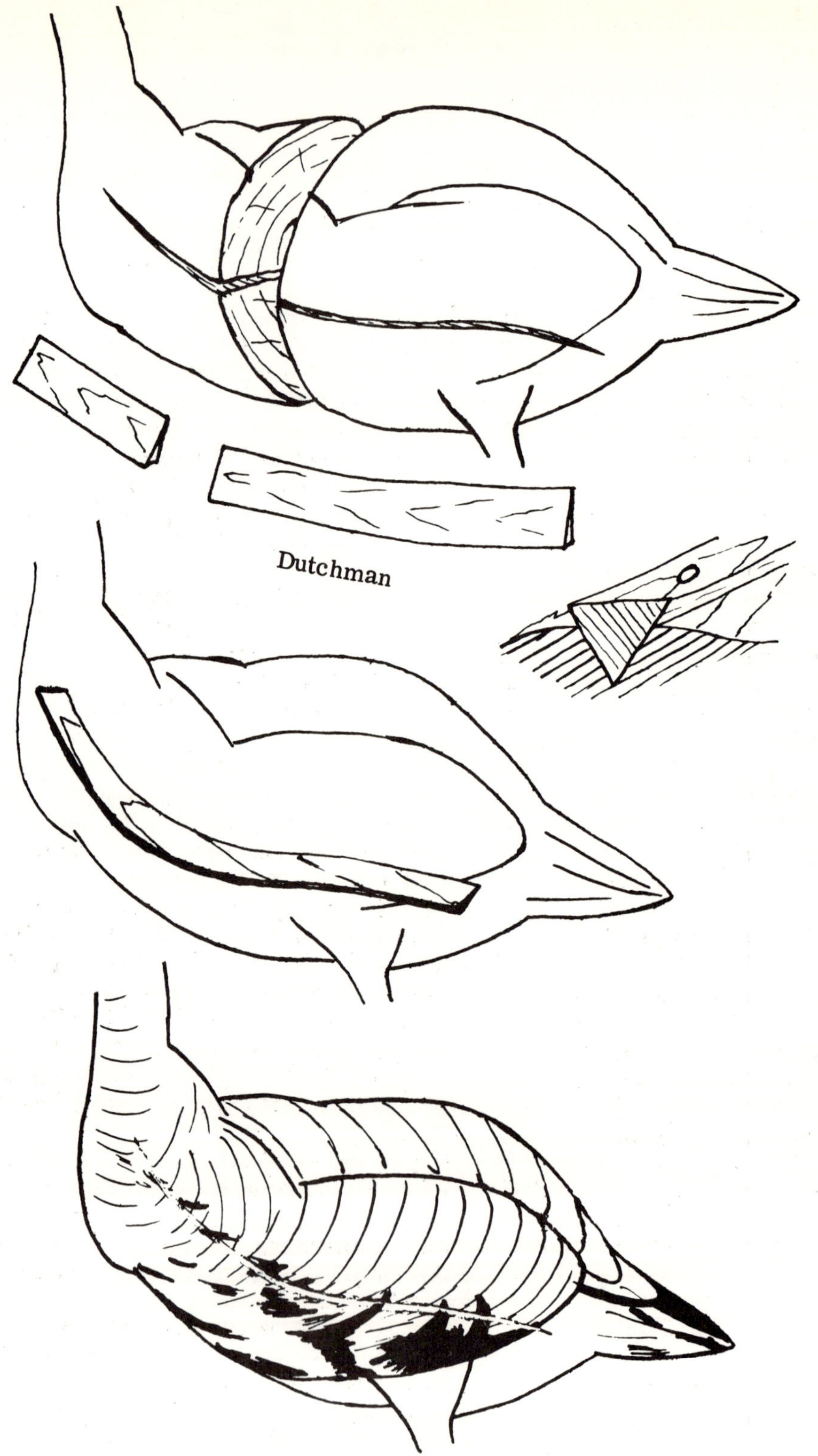

Figure 51. Correcting defects with a "Dutchman."

of love only and is lost. The wood to be carved should be either kiln-dried or dried naturally by the air over a long period of time. If the log is large it should be stored in a dry place for several years before using. This method does not work so great a handicap as might be expected. Most professional carvers have a stockpile of logs or timbers that are in a continuous state of rotation; that is, when one log is used, another takes its place on the unseasoned end of the pile. Several logs will insure plenty of time between storage and carving. I, myself, have enough logs to keep me busy for the rest of my life, but I will, from time to time, add to my stockpile. I have just completed a carving from a red cedar log that had been in storage for over ten years. As the bird began to emerge from the log, check marks appeared; not serious ones but enough to cause some concern. Some even required remedial treatment. Fortunately, after the check marks have been repaired and the finish is applied, dry wood will "stay put" and cause no further trouble.

Correcting Check Marks. There are several ways of correcting check marks. Hairline shakes should be ignored; the chances are that they will disappear before the finish is applied. But the larger cracks must be repaired before the final finishing operations. If the crack interferes with contour, it should be repaired at once for when carving, the eye is guided by surface contour and without it a serious error might result. Also blemishes should be cut out and new wood substituted. Avoid using any of the plastic fillers for cracks or other defects in birds, or any other carving, which is to be given a natural finish. A skillfully inserted "Dutchman" is preferable.

On polychromed carvings, plastic wood, famowood, a polyester filler or shellac sticks may be used to fill small cracks and minor defects. Famowood is good as it comes in several colors and will take a finish. "Pay Day," a filler manufactured by Martin Senour Paints, may be used for rather large cracks. It is the polyester filler used by automobile body mechanics to even out depressions which were formerly filled with lead. There are other trade names for the same material. It adheres to both clean metal and wood. It is strong and may be carved like the wood in, or over, which it is molded. It comes in paste form with a separate liquid catalyst. Only enough of the material is mixed at one time to do the job. (*See* Chapter 14 for other uses of "Pay Day.") Shellac sticks may be ignored entirely for all practical purposes for they are awkward to use and require heat to melt or soften them. They are mentioned because they come in various shades and might be more suitable on finished birds than other fillers.

In either the polychromed or naturally finished carvings, large cracks and blemishes should be filled with wood. In the naturally finished carvings the grain and color of the Dutchman must closely match direction and shade respectively, or the repair job will show. A poorly performed effort is sometimes more noticeable than the crack. Inserting Dutchmen requires as much or more skill, than the carving operations.

Repairing Deep Cracks. To properly repair a deep crack there are a few important steps. First, clear the crack of all loose fibers and sharp irregularities. The recess should be slightly negative wedge-shaped to conform with the inserted wood (Figure 51). If the crack is not too sharply curved the Dutchman may be bent to follow it while being "driven home." The cross-sectional form of the inserted wood should be wedge-shaped as shown in the illustration. The penetrating angle should be small, as a larger one will not allow the Dutchman to hold of itself. If the crack is so large that a greater angle is necessary, the recess should be cut to conform with the angle of the wedge-shaped wood to be inserted (Figure 51). In this instance, the Dutchman will not hold of itself but must be nailed in place. Use fine wire nails with heads. Holes for the nails may have to be drilled to keep the inserted material from splitting. When glued in place the nails should be driven down tightly, making a close-fitting seam. The surplus material of the small-angled wedge-shaped material may be dressed down to the surface immediately after being driven in place. In the latter case, the wide-angled insertion must wait until the glue sets. The inserted material should be well above the surface of the carving, so the wood next to the nailheads may be removed sufficiently to use a claw hammer or a pair of pliers to remove the nails. Then the surplus wood may be dressed down to the carving surface. The direction of the grain should be watched closely while removing the surplus wood in both instances, or the Dutchman may split below the surface. Always cut downhill with the grain when removing chips; that is, cut the material so it will not split into the surface.

Do not shave the inserts below the carving contour. In large inserts be careful that the contour of the surface is preserved.

In some instances the crack affects contour by being large and located in a critical place in the carving. When this is the case, the crack should be repaired before continuing with the carving operations. Also, serious defects may develop which were not anticipated by the carver. A decayed spot or a hole in the log must be removed at once. All of the unsound wood should be removed at least 1″ below the finished surface. The shape of the cavity is important for the Dutchman is difficult to carve to fit irregular places. The preferred method is to carve the Dutchman first, slightly wedge-shaped and large enough to adequately cover the cavity. Be sure to match the grain and color. When the plug is completed, place it over the cavity and carefully scribe around it with a sharp lead pencil. Cut out the cavity, religiously following the scribed outline. The sides of the cavity should not be slanted one way or the other—cut straight down. The plug should have sufficient angle to tighten itself. Of course, the grain and color of this insert should match the surface it is to replace. After several trial efforts, the Dutchman should fit "to a hair." Coat the contacting surfaces with glue and drive into place. The edges running perpendicular to the grain may be given considerable pressure without danger, but the edges running parallel to the grain should not fit too snugly or the surface of the carving will split. In other words, do not let the wedge action of the insert split your carving. Before tightening, the plug should drop into the cavity 3/4″ if it is a large one; another 1/4″ should make a tight seam. When the Dutchman has been installed, the carving should rest until the glue sets thoroughly. Then shave it down to the proper contour.

How to Handle Knots. A knot sometimes appears in an unfortunate spot on the surface, marring the total effect. It should be removed, either by the process described in the preceding paragraphs, or by the following method. If the knot is not over an inch wide, it may be bored out with an auger from 1/2″ to 1″ deep. Usually much less depth will be sufficient. The plug to fit the hole must be turned on a lathe or carved, with the grain perpendicular to the radial axis. The end grain showing will be as unsuitable as the knot, but with the grain matching, the repair job will go unnoticed. The plug should be slightly tapered. It should drop into the hole at least 3/8″

or more before tightening, depending upon the size. Be sure the grain is running in the right direction or the repair job will be conspicuous. After the plug has been glued and driven in, it may be shaved down immediately. Determine the direction of the grain by splitting off the top part of the plug. Do not attempt to cut the plug off flush with the surface the first time. It is apt to go below the surface and ruin your job. When you learn the direction of the grain, you can then cut the plug off carefully by running your chisel uphill until it is shaved down to the surface.

In some instances the knot may be helpful in accentuating a particular spot in the carving. Recently I observed a nude carving with the knot serving to point up the navel cavity. But such usage is rare. Usually a knot is an eyesore and should be removed. Sometimes a peculiarity of the grain or the color of the sapwood may mar a carving. In either case, the faulty part should be removed and repaired. In polychromed finishes these precautions are not necessary, the only requirement being a smooth surface, but in natural finished carvings, grain and color are important aspects of the total effect. Generally, color and grain will cause no trouble but rather will enhance the work.

Hiding Seams. There are times when the most skillfully performed repair work leaves conspicuous seams. A poor selection of wood will often cause an unsightly seam. The simplest way to correct this condition is by camouflaging the grain and color. Mix a daub of paint on a palette or some other smooth surface, the exact shade of the grain of the wood and another daub matching the color of the soft wood. When the colors have been mixed, cleverly brush the seam and surrounding surface with them to conform with the color of the surface wood. This operation is not as difficult as it may seem. This camouflaging art is unnoticeable and sometimes the effect is amazing. Again, this technique is not necessary for the polychromed birds, but tight seams are just as important, for poorly joined inserts show through the finished surface, marring the feathering effects. So, do not get the idea that the natural finished birds are more difficult to make than the painted ones. In natural finished work the emphasis is on woodworking skills; in polychromed birds the emphasis is still on tight seams, but the more difficult operations are the finish and the elaborate details of feather markings. The difficulty of the first is offset by a different difficulty of the second, for painting in the feathers realistically is the most meticulous job of all. Competition in this latter technique is keen among bird-carvers, each craftsman striving to outdo the others by trying to breathe life into his subject.

Treating Green Wood Chemically. The age-old problem concerned with cracking and shrinking of wood improperly seasoned has now been solved—at least partially. Craftsmen in several important industries are now using green wood for turning out their products and with satisfactory results. In fact, green wood works better with the new process than partially dried stock, as will be discussed later.

There was bound to be discovered a method of treating green wood to stabilize it, so that it could be used immediately. The scarcity of timber on the one hand, and the tempo of industry on the other, demanded a method for treating unseasoned lumber. For the discussion of this method, the author is indebted to the U.S. Forest Products Laboratory. The research is maintained in cooperation with the University of Wisconsin at Madison. While the wood is apparently stabilized effectively by the new method, the change is not chemical but a physical transformation of the wood fibers. As explained previously, the checking and cracking of wood is caused by the uneven drying of the outer layers of the wood and the core. The chemical treatment simply equalizes these stresses by substituting polyethylene glycol for the moisture evaporated, in the outer fibers of the wood. There may be a softening of the fibers and some flexibility also imparted to the wood, but this latter deduction is not brought out by written accounts of the experiments conducted by the Forest Research Laboratory. In this substitution of chemicals for moisture the green wood becomes stabilized, and apparently does not noticeably check afterward.

Research of the Forest Products Laboratory indicates that the use of polyethylene glycol for reducing checking and splitting in green wood is very effective. Several articles by the authorities of this branch of the Agriculture Service have frequently appeared in *Forest Products Journal.*

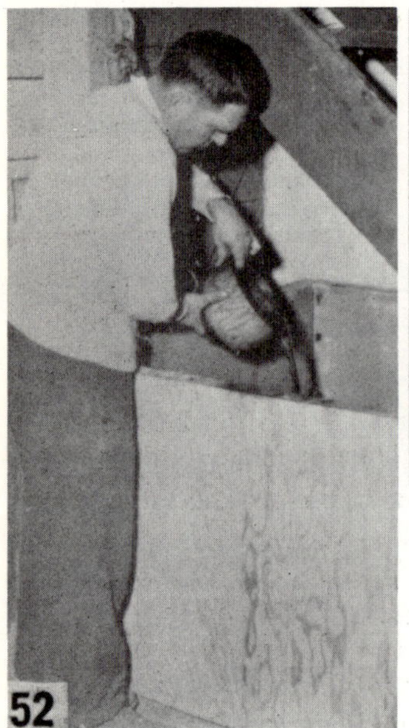

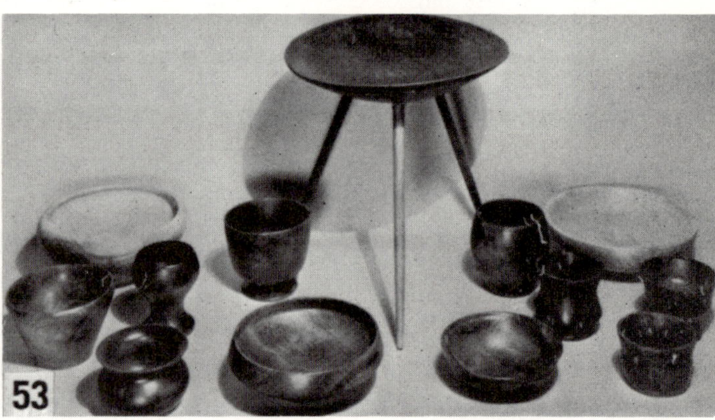

Figure 52 (left). Removing green-wood bowl from polyethylene glycol solution following treatment. Home workshop treating vat shown is made of exterior grade plywood lined with fiberglas of the type used to cover wooden boats.
Figure 53 (above). PEG-treated bowls that have been turned to final dimensions, sanded, finished, and polished.
Forest Products Journal, U.S. Dept. of Agriculture.

These articles discussed the use of polyethylene glycol (PEG—1000) for various objects made of green wood and methods of application. This chemical may be purchased from any of the major chemical companies and manufacturers. Mine came from Forshaw Chemicals, Charlotte, North Carolina. While my experiments have not been as extensive as desired, my findings tend to agree with those of the Forest Products Laboratory. Therefore, the important aspects of using the stabilizing chemical will be briefly discussed.

The Service emphasizes that the best results are obtained with green wood. Kiln or air-dried woods are not so effectively stabilized. In fact, poorly dried woods should be thoroughly soaked in water before treating with PEG—1000.

First, a vat must be made large enough to immerse the largest log, block or carving (Figure 52). Either a stainless steel container or one made of plywood and lined with fiberglas (the type used for covering wooden boats) is ideal. The professional carvers who have a large volume of work should have a liquid temperature-controlled device since the treatment is hastened in heated solutions (30–50% solutions are recommended). Quoting from *Circular 64—011*, the following mixing solutions are discussed.

> The two commonly used solutions are 30 and 50 percent PEG by weight. Exactly 4.46 pounds of polyethylene glycol (a standard commercially available package) dissolved in 5 quarts of water will make 7 quarts of 30 percent solution having a specific gravity of 1.05 at 60°F. Or 10 pounds of polyethylene glycol dissolved in equal weight of water (about 4.8 quarts) will make 7.4 quarts of 50 percent solution having a specific gravity of 1.039 at 60°F. A precision hydrometer that is accurate for the desired range of specific gravities is needed to maintain proper concentration of the solution during treatment.

This rather technical paragraph should not scare away a carver who is interested in chemically stabilizing his woods. The formula can be simplified without the use of laboratory instruments, but without the laboratory accuracy of information. If the block that is improperly seasoned shows evidence of serious cracking before it is carved, it may be treated in a 50% solution for about two weeks before the carving begins. The block should be thoroughly soaked before the treatment begins. After the carving is completed it should be treated again for best results, as the "glycoled" wood has been cut away leaving new untreated fibers. If there is some way of maintaining a temperature of about 140°F., the time necessary will be shortened. The following information is supplied for guidance. In this instance, the solution was 30% and penetration was found in the outer ⅛″ of the carving.

Time Soaked Days	Temperature °F.	Glycol %
4	140	10.1
8	130	6.7
14	130	8.6
14	65	6.4
21	65	11.8

According to the table the experiments tend to show that the time soaked is about as important as the temperature. Apparently, a low concentration of PEG is sufficient to stabilize the wood.

The foregoing studies were made with green wood that already had been carved and finished in humid foreign countries. A number of the carvings were treated with polyethylene glycol after being immersed in water for as long as two weeks to restore the "turgid green condition essential for satisfactory diffusion of the large molecules of the chemical into the fine structure of the wood." After the water-soaked carvings were treated from 3 to 7 days in a 50% solution and dried in a 73°F. room, the carvings were stabilized and protected from further checking.

From these findings I conclude that a carving giving evidence of undue checking may be immersed in water for about two weeks and then treated with PEG—1000 for another week in warm water (depending upon the size of the carving) to prevent further checking problems. Here is an interesting field of study. If green wood can be used as effectively as seasoned stock, both the original cost and much of the carving difficulties can be eliminated. The effectiveness of this technique must be learned through trial and error methods by the carver himself, a field of experimentation not yet entered into by myself to any great extent.

A number of craft industries are already using PEG for treating their green stock. These concerns, according to their managements, have found their manufactured articles as good as those made from seasoned woods. Such articles as gunstocks, lathe turnings, small carvings, even archery bows, are now made from green wood by many manufacturers (Figure 53). Only recently has the polyethylene glycol treatment been applied to wood carvings by some sculptors. Homer Lawrence first introduced the treatment to me. The practice is yet very limited, but the scarcity of properly seasoned logs will eventually force most craftsmen to use green woods that will require chemical treatment.

Both the experienced carver and the neophyte should experiment with this new technique. Green wood is always available. Aside from being conveniently accessible, the initial cost of the wood is greatly reduced, sometimes to the mere trouble or expense of hauling it away.

Those who use the polyethylene glycol treatment for their carvings should know that *only a polyurethane resin finish will* work satisfactorily over the waxy surface of the treated wood. Other kinds of finishes will not adhere firmly—will not even dry properly. They may blister and peel off entirely, caution the authorities. Once the decision has been made to use the PEG—1000 treatment, the findings of the researchers should be followed carefully in the finishing techniques. This conformity should work no serious handicaps as polyurethane resins provide an excellent finish and are readily purchasable from most paint suppliers. If other finishes are preferred (as is the case of the polychromed birds) they may be applied after the "glycoled" wood has been sealed off with the polyurethane resin finish. One coat of the material should be sufficient. This sealing off of the treated wood may be thought of as a sealer coat which is usually applied to the raw wood in the customary method of wood finishing. The waxy fibers of PEG—1000-treated wood must have an initial finish more sympathetic to their surface. The finishing of polyethylene-treated carvings is thoroughly discussed in the following chapter on finishing.

Chapter 13

FINISHING THE CARVINGS

The development of wood finishes and color techniques has been a slow process until comparatively recent times. Prehistoric man used natural minerals and vegetable residuals to paint pictures on his cave walls more than 15,000 years ago. He painted his idols and domestic utensils and tools with a crude finish, usually polychromed, but sometimes with a natural sheen by the use of vegetable or animal waxes. Much-used tools were given a beautiful sheen by the friction and oil of the user's own hands. Therefore, the idea of finishes is by no means new. But these primitive attempts were little improved for thousands of years, not until some ingenious individual discovered that pigment ground into the whites of eggs made a good painting medium. This discovery happened sometime during the eclipse of the dark ages. This tempera technique was used by artists of this backward period and was so satisfactory that it continued to be used after better mediums were discovered—even up to the present time. An impregnation of wet plaster with pigment was also used. This wet fresco treatment of walls is also in use today. But both tempera and fresco techniques are now used with a dexterity and skill by modern artists little dreamed of by the original developers of these media.

According to authoritative sources, Jan and Hubert van Eyke introduced the process of oil painting in the early 1400's and paved the way for the various schools of painters of the Renaissance. Modern society is indebted to those master artists for their famous works which are now preserved in art museums throughout the civilized world. Their valuable contributions might not have been possible without the van Eykes' oil medium, which almost entirely superseded the tempera and fresco techniques. In fact, oil paint became the satisfying and preferred medium of artistic expression for the next five hundred years. It still is popular with most creative artists and will continue to be in the foreseeable future. But many modern artists are now turning to acrylics that may become as popular for future generations of creative individuals as the oil media was for those following the Renaissance.

Finally, the art of dissolving natural resins produced from the sap of various trees and the residuals of certain fossils and insects was discovered. Then followed a new concept of wood finishing; a new era of resin finishes, the shellacs, lacquers and varnishes.

During World Wars I and II, the demand for oil and other fats became so pressing that the development of substitutes to take their place became imperative for both the arts and industry. Under the pressure of this need emulsified synthetic resins were developed that are now generally known as acrylics, or plastics. This fortunate breakthrough not only solved the perplexing problem of a durable and beautiful finish for automobiles, but for all finishes in general. The long-sought-after glass that would bend without breaking had been discovered. Plexiglas could not only bend without shattering, but under pressure and heat, it could be molded in a multitude of unusual and interesting forms, including hoods for airplanes. The synthetic resins revolutionized several industries. Due to their versatile uses they could be molded into all sorts of objects hitherto made of wood or steel. They could be formed as thin as paper and make a better wrapper. Old animal wools and vegetable cotton and flax could not compete with the new fibers made of synthetic resins, but of most concern to us was the impact the development had upon the paint industry. Most of the large chemical concerns now specialize in the manufacture of synthetic resins. To give credit where credit is due, the Dupont Company and Rohm and Haas have been the pioneers and foremost in the development of this modern miracle of science.

All major paint companies now have their own brand of plastic paint. "Hyplar" is the trade name of the Grumbacher product and is probably the best known of the acrylics used by artists.* The old medium of oil has nearly been eliminated for outside finishes, and creative artists are turning to the acrylics in greater numbers for their media. Plastics have many advantages over oil paints. For example, the main failing of the latter medium was its inherent weakness in drying. The paint not only took longer to dry, but oxidation of the linseed oil and pigment underwent a chemical change leaving a thin film which became quite brittle with age and cracked, or peeled off entirely. The acrylics dry by a process of evaporation of the solvent which, in most cases, is water. A durable film results that is nearly impervious to weather conditions. The acrylics are very flexible and simple to use. Their quick-drying feature saves much time as the painting may be a continuous process. Synthetic resins have had a spectacular beginning and the end is not yet in sight.

Loosely speaking, there are mainly two types of finishes: the natural and the polychrome. In the first instance no attempt is made to give the object color emphasis, the finish consisting merely of several coats of clear varnish or lacquer, including a sealer for the first coat. The "modernist" would even eliminate the varnish or lacquer treatment, being content with a wax paste or liquid finish. Enid Bell uses transparent shoe polish. In the second instance, the pertinent colors are painted on the object for various color effects. For the carvings of this book every effort will be made to duplicate the colors of the bird concerned and to apply the finish to give a realistic "skin" effect.

Most artists prefer a natural finish; the raw wood without a sealer is preferred by some. These latter artists are apparently not concerned with check marks or serious cracks. Even a good sealer discourages checking and makes the carving virtually dustproof. But the collector, and there are thousands of them, desires his birds to be finished in the faithful image of the model. This technique is quite difficult and demands not only a patient disposition but artistic skills to achieve best results.

The first requisite in either finish is a clean, dry surface, free from wax, oil or grease. No kind of finish will adhere to an unsuitable base. Each coat of finish is rubbed down with fine steel wool (natural finish especially) leaving a residue of steel waste in all small openings. This waste must be brushed off or blown out with a bellows, or an air-pressure hose. Cleanliness really is next to godliness in wood finishing and if "divine" results are to be achieved, this rule must be religiously observed above all others. In fact,

* Use of acrylics was seriously considered in painting the polychromed birds of this text. In fact, the novice may use them in preference to the oil paints recommended. The polyurethane resin finishes *must* be used on carvings given the PEG—1000 treatment.

if there are any trade secrets in wood finishing, cleanliness is one of them.

After the surface has been carved and prepared for the finishing operations, the first step, in either the natural or polychrome finish, is a coat of primer or sealer. Sealers are designed and manufactured for this specific purpose and most of them do a fine job. A sealer closes the pores of the wood and provides an ideal base for either varnish or paint. A good sealer tends to prevent further checking by removing, to some extent, the reasons for this natural phenomenon. It keeps the moisture out and tends to allow a more uniform temperature distribution throughout the whole block. Sherwin-Williams manufactures a good product called "Beauty-Lok." It is the sealer used on my carvings illustrated in this book and used as projects. Other good sealers are "Firzite," manufactured by the U.S. Plywood Corporation, and "Tung Seal." There are others and, in the absence of any of them, thinly cut shellac will work satisfactorily.

In every instance the sealer should be rubbed down with steel wool (00-000) after it has set overnight. This operation will smooth out the finish and remove slight blemishes and any sheen that may have developed. Every coat of finish should be lightly rubbed down with fine steel wool to give "teeth" to the surface for holding the next coat.

Some woods, like white pine, are rather lifeless when given a plain natural finish. To enliven the subject a coloring process is usually performed consisting of a penetrating oil, spirit, or water stain. This technique brings out the fine grain in contrast, making the wood more sophisticated than before. Many cheap woods are given a walnut, mahogany, or some other finish to imitate expensive woods. When some woods are stained (birch, for instance), they are as good as the real McCoys. When stains are used, the sealer coat is not needed because the stain seals the pores as it dyes the wood. In fact, a sealer preceding an oil stain removes most of its effectiveness since the pores already are closed and cannot "drink up" the penetrating stain.

Natural Finish. As has been emphasized, the surface must be clean of all foreign materials or blemishes. Even a sandpaper scratch will show up like a sore thumb through the transparent finish. Lacquer sprayed on or varnish brushed on must be even and lean; otherwise, it may pile up in ripples or form "fisheyes." Many thin coats are preferable to one flowing application. Each coat is allowed to dry thoroughly so that it will not pull when rubbed down lightly with fine steel wool. Several days may be required for the finish to harden. The last coat may be rubbed down with powdered pumice stone using linseed oil as a lubricant. Steel wool may be wet with linseed oil while rubbing down the final coat. Rottenstone is preferred by some wood finishers to use in rubbing down the last coat. Experience will prove to be the best teacher in polishing your birds. The pair of Mallards (Figure 54) are finished in this manner; also the Bald Eagle (Frontispiece). As cautioned previously, apply the finish in thin coats. Flowing applications will not only require more time setting up, but there will be danger of blemishes resulting.

Finishing the Polyethylene Glycol Treated Carvings. I have had no experience in finishing wood carvings that have received the PEG—1000 treatment. In the absence of authorative studies of my own, I am indebted to the U.S. Department of Agriculture, Forest Service Laboratory maintained at Madison, Wisconsin, for the leaflet on finishing polyethylene glycol treated carvings, reproduced in this chapter.

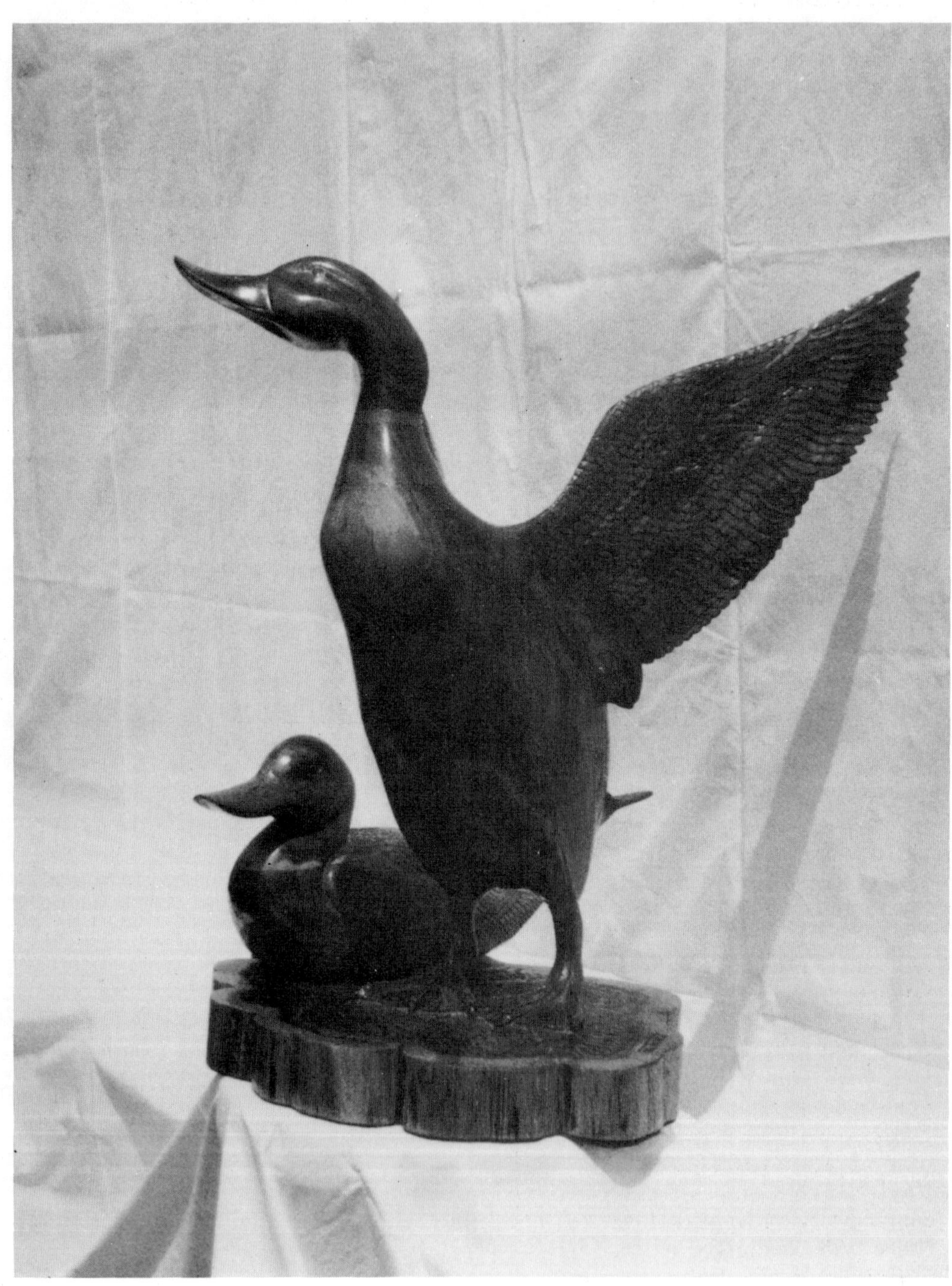

Figure 54. Pair of Mallards.

WOOD FINISHING LEAFLET - 24

APPLYING A POLYURETHANE RESIN FINISH TO WOOD STABILIZED WITH A POLYETHYLENE GLYCOL TREATMENT

Forest Products Laboratory,* Forest Service U. S. Department of Agriculture

The only finish known that will dry properly on the waxy surface of wood that has been treated with polyethylene glycol to give it stability is polyurethane resin (single component) finish. The polyethylene glycol treatment has a considerable effect on the manner of surface preparation and finishing procedure; it must be done carefully and correctly. The following steps are recommended for a successful finish job.

1. Initial Sanding
Sand initially with very coarse sandpaper, stroking with the grain. Fine or medium papers will clog quickly and thus cannot be used for this first sanding.

2. Bleaching of Dark Areas
Due to the nature of the polyethylene glycol treating process, there may be an accumulation of about 1/16-inch thickness of dark material near the surface of the wood. These materials are concentrations of pigments, minerals, and extractives, and may be removed by brushing on a solution of 4 heaping tablespoons of oxalic acid crystals in a cup of hot water. Extreme care should be used in handling oxalic acid, as it is a poison. After about an hour of drying, remove and neutralize the excess acid by sponging with a cloth dampened with a dilute solution of household ammonia. Allow 24 hours of drying time before proceeding with the finish sanding.

3. Finish Sanding
Using wet-or-dry sandpaper (4/0) and hot water for lubricant, sand out all rough spots and scratches. Allow the wood to dry thoroughly before proceeding with step 4.

4. Application of Sealing Coat
Stir polyurethane resin finish thoroughly and then pour into clean container, mixing in an equal volume of turpentine or mineral spirits. Apply to wood. Allow 24 hours for drying; then sand lightly with 6/0 paper.

5. Application of Toner-Filler
When toner-fillers are to be used, shake thoroughly and apply liberally with a clean brush, stroking with the grain. After 1/2 hour of drying or when the solvent has evaporated, work the filler into the pores by rubbing across the grain with a soft cloth or the palm of your hand. Allow to dry at least 1 day in a warm, well-ventilated room. When thoroughly dry, sand lightly with 6/0 paper.

6. Final Finish Coats
Apply the first finish coat of polyurethane resin full strength or diluted only slightly. Allow to dry, sand lightly with 6/0 paper, and then rub with 3/0 steel wool, being extremely careful not to cut through the finish. Then apply the final coat or coats. Four or five finish coats will result in a really professional-looking job. Sand lightly between each coat with 6/0 paper and follow this with light rubbing with 3/0 steel wool. After final coat has dried thoroughly, polish with fine pumice and an oil lubricant. Further protection may be achieved by applying furniture polish, wax, oil, or whatever you desire.

Additional Comments

1. The stabilizing chemical, polyethylene glycol (p. g.), will quickly absorb water vapor from the air during hot, humid weather. The resulting film of moisture that forms on the wood surface can prevent the sealer, filler, or finish coats from setting firmly or adhering properly. For this reason, p. g. treated wood should not be finished during hot and humid weather unless done in an air-conditioned room. If finish drying difficulties are encountered, dry the wood before continuing the finishing process.

2. Polyurethane resin finish will normally set within an hour or so in a warm, dry atmosphere. If desired, the drying time can be reduced by adding a little (a few drops) additional hardener (6 percent cobalt naphthenate) to the finish just prior to application. If added earlier, your supply of finish will solidify in the container.

3. Checkering or like processes should be completed prior to application of finish coats due to the hardness of the polyurethane resin finish.

*Maintained at Madison, Wis. , in cooperation with the University of Wisconsin.

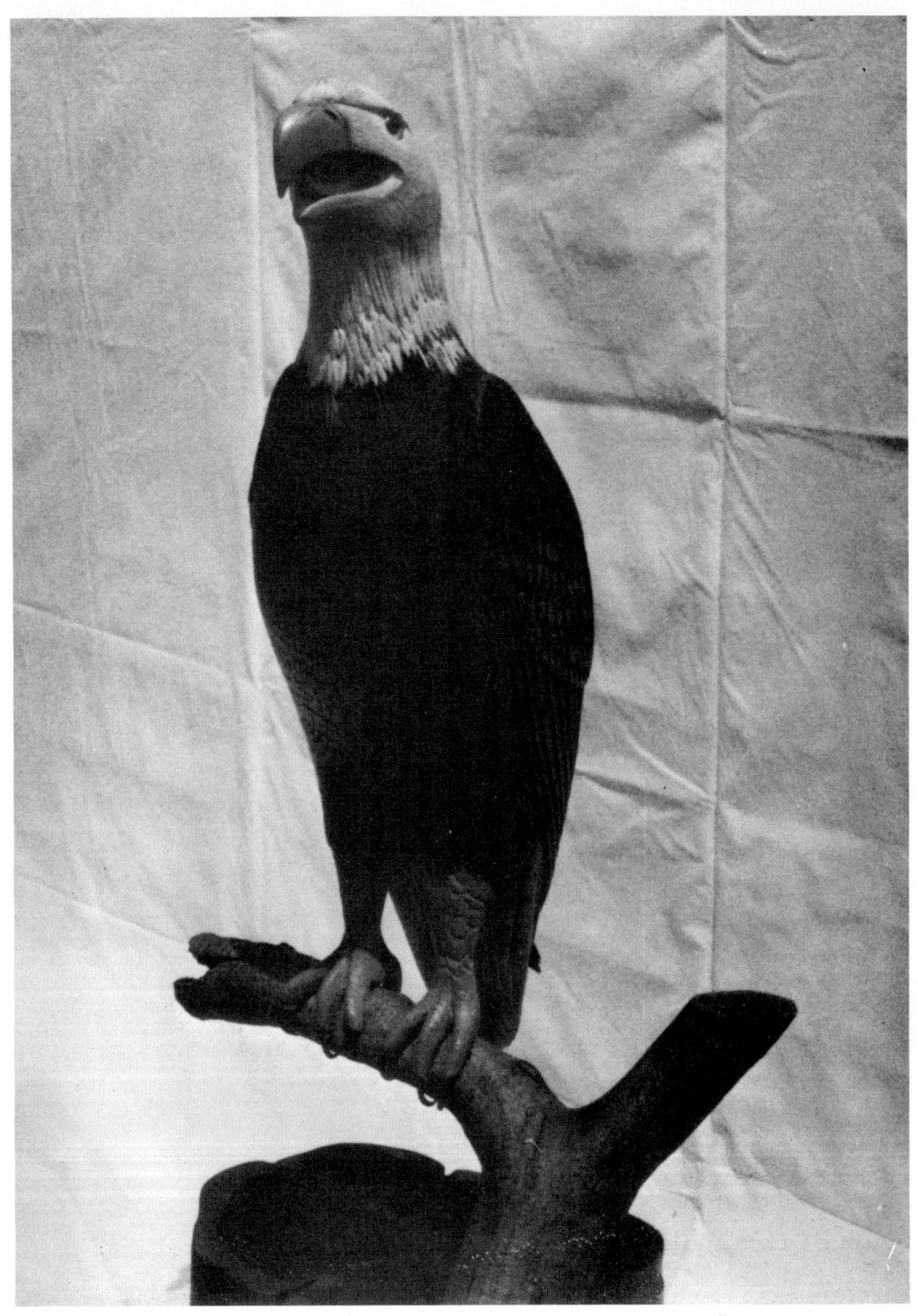

Figure 55. Bald Eagle, erect on bough.

The Forest Products Laboratory has made extensive studies in treating green woods with polyethylene glycol, and finishing the carvings with polyurethane resin varnish. Carvings from tropical countries are often made of poorly seasoned wood. They have been brought to this country and soaked in water to make them sensitive to the chemical treatment and then finished with polyurethane resin with amazing results.

A technique often used is a combination of the natural and polychrome finish. The birds for costume jewelry in Chapter 4 were finished in this fashion. The carving is either stained or painted to represent the identifying markings of the particular bird (usually the head or some unique feather color), and the remainder is left natural. The whole is then given the usual transparent finish treatment. A Bald Eagle, not previously mentioned (Figure 55), was finished in this manner. A walnut penetrating stain was used for the whole bird (carved in white pine) except the white head and tail, and the yellow bill and feet. Titanium white powder was mixed in penetrating oil and brushed on the head and tail parts. The surplus was later rubbed off. Enough of the white pigment penetrated to give the "bald" effect. White is the most difficult pigment to penetrate into wood pores. The author has found no satisfactory way to penetrate white like the other colors, or to bleach the wood to give a similar effect. "Blanchit" is a product on the market whose manufacturers claim will bleach wood. It comes in two units, one used after the other. It cannot be sent through the mails, so many carvers will find the product difficult to obtain. After the pigmenting process, clear varnish was used for the remaining finish.

When using oil or any of the other penetrating stains the most important operation is rubbing off the surplus material to expose the beautiful grain in all of its glory. This rubbing procedure is highly important for it either makes or breaks the job. Clean rags make a suitable rubbing material. After the stain is applied evenly over the entire surface with a flowing consistency, reaching every crevice, it is allowed to set up until it becomes dull in luster. Experience will indicate the best time to start the rubbing operation. If started too soon, the stain will be too lean; if allowed to set too long, it will not only be difficult to remove but the appearance will be affected. There may be some instances when the stain should be "starved," but again experience is the best guide. When oil stain is skillfully removed, at the proper time, the effect is impressive. Make every effort to achieve an even, clean texture; that is, do not allow the finish to dry in spots, indicating poor workmanship. Some areas will naturally absorb more stain than others because of their more porous composition, but in this instance the effect is desirable, enhancing the appearance and emphasizing the characteristics of the particular kind of wood.

Several years ago I built a number of bookshelves for the library of the local Women's Club. After they were installed, I gave specific directions for finishing them. The room trim was dark so black walnut oil stain was recommended for the shelves. Several days later I inspected the finishing job. When I saw the shelves I felt sick to my stomach. My excellent job of craftsmanship had been irreparably ruined. A walnut oil penetrating stain had been used as suggested, but the directions for using the finish had been figuratively thrown to the four winds of heaven. It had been applied like paint and never rubbed off; so the beautiful grain of yellow pine boards was buried beneath a grimy opaque cover of dried oil stain. Indeed, the shelves looked as though they had been daubed with mud. They were an offense to the eyes and altogether ugly and objectionable. Not only had the instructions of the builder been ignored, but the directions of the manufacturer as well. This unfortunate experience is mentioned to give emphasis to the rubbing procedure. Any rational individual should have known something was wrong after the oil stain began to appear dull and muddy, but the operators brushed merrily on until every shelf was ruined.

After the wood has been rubbed down to expose the grain design, the object is allowed to set until the stain has dried throughly. Then it may be lacquered or varnished until the desired results are achieved.

In porous, open-grain woods, such as oak, another technique of treating the raw wood is used. A paste, called wood filler, is brushed thoroughly into the open grain. When it has set up to a dull luster it, too, is rubbed off, this time across the grain to avoid pulling the filler out of the pores. All solid particles of the filler should be removed from the surface leaving it smooth and clean. After drying overnight, the object is finished with lacquer, varnish or wax. As in the case of the oil stain, the wood filler serves two purposes: (1) to fill the grain and close the pores, and (2) to dye the wood the desired color and to emphasize the grain structure. Incidentally, limed oak is treated with lime so that the grain shows up white. Other colors, of course, may be introduced in this manner. The rubbing process is probably more important in this type of finish than in the oil stain technique for when the wood filler sets up, it hardens like stone. In fact, most fillers are made of silicon compounds.

Polychrome Finish. "If you can write your name, you can paint," states a brochure on painting. This is an oversimplification of the matter, especially in the case of painting the skin effects of ornamental birds. It is much more difficult than painting pictures because there is less freedom of technique. So far as this text is concerned, the steps of painting birds in their natural colors are as follows: (1) sealer coat; (2) painting in the feather patches in their true colors; and (3) painting in the feather effects. The second coat of oil paint may be a quick-drying paint like "Craftint" (Defoe) a Japan type of showcard colors. It dries with a flat finish and for this reason is used by some carvers for the final coat, as well.* But there are others who use tube colors entirely for all of their painting procedures. Mrs. Black says she uses oil paint the consistency of water for her feathering coat, a technique I intend to use when painting my next bird.

As previously stated, most collectors insist that the birds they purchase be colored as realistically as possible. Only a few artists really object to polychroming the birds; the technique is just not their "cup of tea." But, because of the peculiarity of the birdcarving cult, the collector, and the times, ornamental birds, as well as decoys, must be painted exactly like their models. In fact, polychromed carvings are almost universally preferred over the natural finished birds.

* At least two carvers to my knowledge use oil paint straight from the tube when painting their birds. Both say that the oil paint used for the first coat, not only provides an opaque surface, but penetrates the raw wood and provides a better base for the second coat. The last coat is usually applied *alla prima* (wet in wet). Both are masters of their craft. Both paint the second coat the color of the markings of the particular bird. Their method must have merit for their birds look natural enough to fly. Lem Ward cuts his colors with turpentine and kerosene in equal proportions to achieve the desired flat effect.

In polychromed birds the color markings are just as important as the carving itself. Painting them like the birds concerned permits slight color variation without serious unfavorable effects, simply because different individuals see differently and none see them as they really are. For example, one portrait artist sees the skin of his model a shade of pink, while another, equally skilled, sees brown or some other color. With the present art concepts going hog-wild, the variance is amazing, from light pastel shades to bright green. But the skilled bird-carver is allowed no such latitude in his painting. Otherwise, his clients will seek other sources of supply. Every effort must be made to paint the birds authentically in every respect. In fact, one of America's best bird-carvers makes no attempt to paint his own birds. He employs a formally trained artist to do this work for him. His creations are, therefore, superb, always finding a ready market. Some other carvers use other techniques that are popular because of the unique character of their art. Two of these methods will be discussed later. Others stylize their carvings, more or less, making no attempt to paint in the feathers realistically. In any event, irrespective of the technique, the carver who thoroughly learns his craft must be a sculptor and painter rolled into one personality.

The novice who reads these lines is not expected to be so masterful with his carving tools or brush as the individuals referred to in this book. The author is merely trying to encourage him to "hook his wagon to a star," as the old adage goes, and "keep your seat and there you are." The artists whose works are represented in the picture gallery of carvings have labored long and diligently to achieve their distinctive places in their craft. But the beginner may be surprised at his own efforts if he seriously applies himself to his task and follows the directions of this book faithfully.

Three steps have been advised in painting the birds in this book. A fourth step should really be included for most carvers touch up their work after they have laid it aside to dry after the feathers have been painted. There is always a spot that may be improved.

The application of the sealer coat has already been discussed. For both types of finish, the first step is the same, except for wood that has received the PEG—1000 treatment. Instead of the regular sealer, a polyurethane finish is used to seal off the waxy surface of the chemically treated wood. Two coats of this finish may be necessary before brushing on the color patches.

The second step is marking off the color patches and painting them the same color of the feathers to be painted on later. Study a picture of the bird or, even better, a living model. Carefully lay out the color patches with a lead pencil.

Next, mix the colors. Squeeze from the tube enough paint of each color to complete the second coat. If the bird is small, a regular artist's palette or a piece of clean glass may be used on which to mix the colors. I use a palette made of many sheets of paper that may be discarded as used. Mix the colors to closely resemble those of the real bird concerned, using turpentine as your thinner. A good opaque coat should be brushed on, but not piled up in a flowing manner. A few drops of paint dryer may be used to cause the colors to set up faster. While the colors used for this particular coat will not be used for the final finish, you should try to match the colors of the model for practice, if for no other reason. Be careful where the colors meet; do not pile up a ridge. Paint the colors adjacent to each other and then straddle the border with a dry brush and smooth the paint uniformly. The colors should be the same as those used in the final coat to serve as a guide and to reinforce the final coat. The feathers will be brushed in thinly in some spots, but because of the undercoat no harm will be done. A careful application of the second coat will simplify the feathering technique. Some carvers use their feathering paint as thin as water, so an undercoat of the same color is highly important.

There may be some instances where a different technique is desirable. There are times when the undercoat is allowed to show through for fringe effects, or vice versa.

If the painting is not continuous, the mixed colors may be sealed off with "Saran Wrap" to keep them from setting up. Press the edges down firmly to prevent the air from reaching the paint. This precaution will keep the colors moist for several days.

If your bird is large, small containers for your colors are desirable. The Ward Brothers use clamshells, others use paper cups (the small ones used by restaurants to serve a dab of jelly). Tops of pressurized cans are a little large but useful, and soft drink cans cut down to size are ideal.

When the first paint coat has dried thoroughly, rub down lightly with fine steel wool to teeth up the surface slightly. Do not rub through your paint. Be sure the surface is free of steel shavings and dirt before applying the next coat. Most carvers do not use steel wool or sandpaper to teeth their finishes, but apply coat on coat without any apparent ill effects.

At this juncture, the carver will discover that some device for holding his carving while it is being painted is desirable—if not necessary. The wet paint cannot be touched with the fingers and the bird must be held so that its surface may be painted conveniently. I use sticks or rods in the leg holes. These are fitted in a heavy block which may be turned in any direction. The block may contain a number of holes bored at various angles to hold the carving in various positions. For small birds, Wendell Gilley clamps the legs in a pin vise, and the metal handle (wooden handle removed) is clamped in an engraver's block. This device should give the carver some idea even though he may not want to invest enough money to buy such equipment. A clever carver will work out for himself a suitable holding device for his birds while they are being painted. The hand may be steadied by an improvised rest of some sort, a box, a mahlstick, or any contraption that will allow controlled movement of the brush. A cramped movement will show in your painting.

To obtain excellent results, the painting in of the feathers is a difficult procedure. Fortunately, mediocre jobs have pleasing effects, too, or many carvers would be unable to sell their work.

Mix the paint as before and this time be sure of the color. Study your picture, your live or stuffed model. Thin the colors with turpentine to cut the high gloss; a flat finish is desirable. Start at the tail end and paint toward the head for the soft feathers. They should be brushed on in short strokes trying to show where the stroke ends over the last row of feathers. A smoothly painted job does not look natural. Stroke the feathers on your bird. A slight color difference is effective where the feathers end and high places on the bird should be lighter than the lower parts. Incidentally, if your colors are so thin that they run, add a few drops of dryer. Remember the shingle effect of your feathering job. Paint both sides simultaneously so that you get corresponding effects; that is, you paint a little on one side and then switch to the other. Soft feathers are generally found on the breast and belly, neck and head. After they are painted, the wings may be started.

Where the colors coincide, an *alla prima* technique will be necessary. The brush must be kept clean for this work. Have several old clean rags available to wipe the paint off of your brushes. Sometimes brushing with a dry brush down an outline will blend the colors properly. The colors should have set up an hour or so for this operation. At other times, actually allowing the colors to come together will work best. Experiment with your techniques until you have found the most suitable methods for you. Two or three brushes should be sufficient. The brush should be as wide as the feathers being painted since each stroke should represent a feather.

Often the lower edge of a feather is fringed with a different color, simplifying this operation. The Canada goose, for example, has most of its large feathers fringed with brown. There are traces of this color on the soft feathers too, but here the predominant colors are grey and white on the breast and belly. These fringe markings are almost as characteristic of the bird as the white cheeks. There are many other birds with fringed feathers and they make excellent carving models.

The primary and secondary feathers are the largest, and the wing bars are next in order. There are usually ten primary feathers. These are easier to paint, but not a gentle breeze of an operation. If large enough they should be painted in two parts, the shafts and the barbs. The shafts are the backbone of the feathers and the barbs are those parts fastened to it. The barbs are a miracle of construction design. Long before man appeared on earth, birds had incorporated the zipper principle. In the bird's rugged task of flying, the barbs often split or are torn apart. When the bird preens itself, these torn parts are "zipped" together in exactly the same way as a metal zipper works. Thousands of microscopic barbicels ending in interlocking hooklets are forced together by the bird's beak and by this natural phenomena are made whole again, and as strong as they were before. These feathers require different brush strokes, running in the direction of the shaft on the one hand and the barbs on the other. In large feathers this painting technique is important, making the difference between a realistic feather and a stylized one.

Wing bars should be pronounced. I carve them with light incisions, but many professionals depend upon their painting skills to bring them out in a realistic manner. Many birds, like the Kingfisher, have wing bars tipped in white or some other color. Also different colors appear that may or may not be visible while the wings are closed, but are quite evident when the bird flies (Mockingbird). In any event, if the softer feathers are successfully painted, the larger ones should be an easier task. Finally, attention is called to the arrangement of feathers. Remember that only a part of a feather shows. The other part is under the adjacent one. Do not paint a "leaky" spot in the bird's coat. A novice can spot a feather out of place.

After the bird has been painted there still remains some touch-up work to perform. A "dry" brush can sometimes work wonders. There may appear spots that can be improved and while the paint is still wet or tacky, the correction should be made. Remember to keep your brush clean or you will rub in colors you do not desire. Rub off your brush with each stroke. Experience and patience will temper your work as you proceed.

Some well-known carvers stylize their painting procedures, brushing in the color markings, but make no attempt to paint the feathers realistically

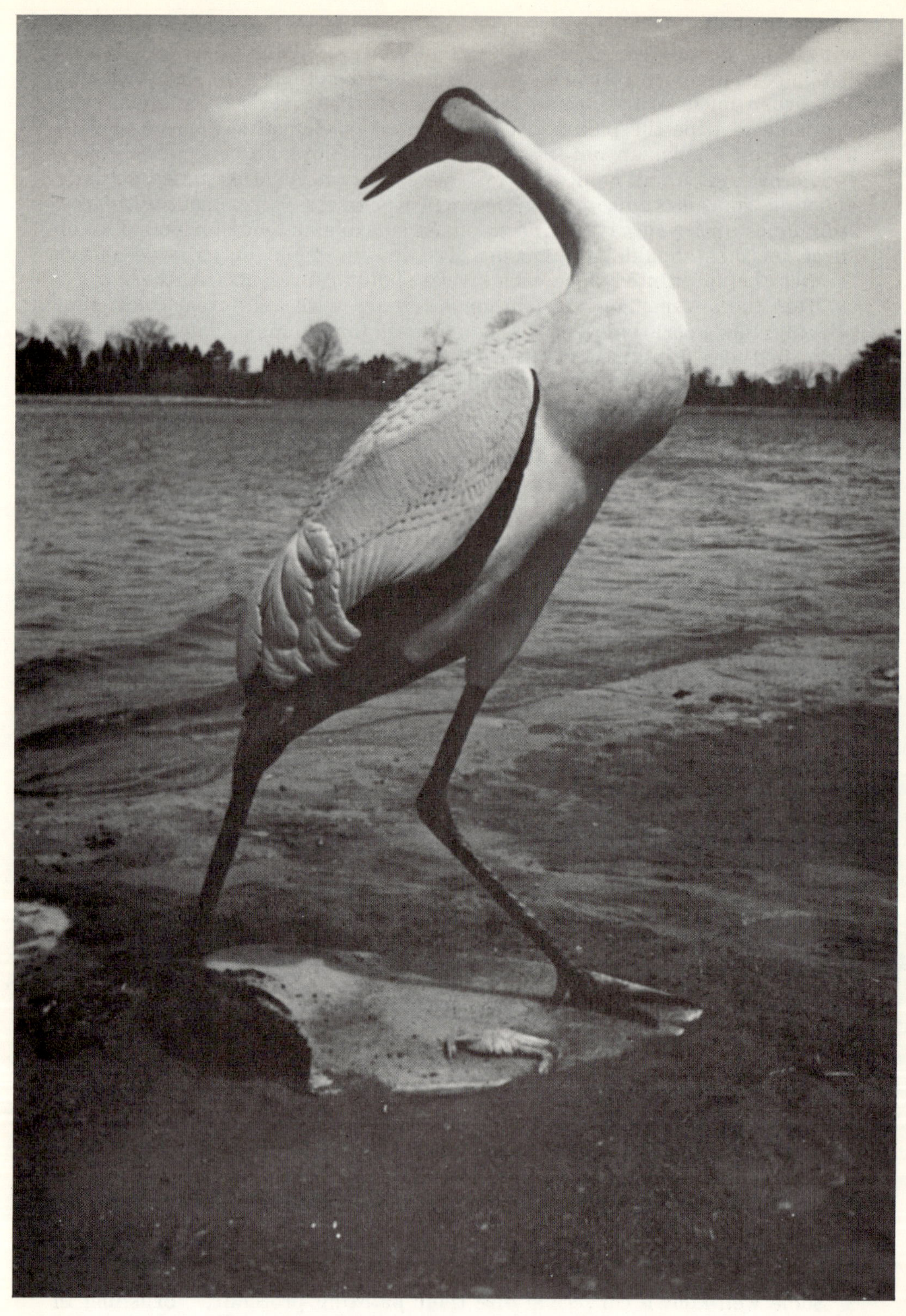

Figure 56. Whooping Crane. Crab also carved.

(Figure 76). They are concerned with the whole effect as if viewed from a distance. Yet, so far as painting is concerned, I feel that brushing in the feathers to look real separates the men from the boys. Many skilled carvers have learned to do this difficult task with the skill and perfection of a professional artist.

The painter of carvings should remember that the surface of birds is not a consistent shade of color. Like all objects, feathers reflect light, forming lighter and darker areas. There is always enough difference to give effective contour. For example, the head of a Mallard is not a consistent green, but darker in the eye cavity and under the cheeks. The highlight of the cheeks is where the most light is reflected. The effect is achieved by some painters by brushing in *alla prima* the darker and lighter shades over a base color. Remember the painting principle: dark shades recede and light shades advance. This fact is very well known to painters and the principle can be used to good advantage by bird-carvers. Some birds, like the grackles, have a radiancy of color which changes with their position from the sun. The bird-carver must catch some phase of this brilliant color in his carving. A clever use of varnish will sometimes emphasize a highlight.

Besides the use of the painting technique in finishing carvings, there are other effective and popular methods. Two of them will be discussed briefly. Mr. John A. Hilleary of Baltimore, Maryland, carves his birds in high relief and finishes them with an electric needle. His interest is to show birds in flight and to carve the wings as they look at some particular instant. To achieve his effects, he uses a pyrograph to convey the idea of motion, and the true markings of the different species. He carves pets, animals, and other wildlife but his main interest is in ducks and geese.

The birds are first cleverly carved, forming the deeper incisions with the chisel before the pyrographic process begins. He controls the shade both by pressure on the needle and the time of exposure. The sepia color merely takes the place of paint and Mr. Hilleary believes it is more effective. Figure 64 pictures a sample of his exquisite work.

Another technique using charred wood contrasts for effects is the work of H. J. Waite of Westchester, Pennsylvania. He carves miniatures mainly and actually burns in his shades with an oxyacetylene blowtorch. The softer fibers are burned first, leaving shading effects on the carving depending on the density of the various parts of the wood and the intensity of the flames played upon them. The hard grain usually stands out in contrast with pleasing effects. A cutting torch is used for the flame and Mr. Waite uses it with the skill and perfection of a true artist. The carvings are later given a transparent finish. His work is popular with the public, attracting not only collectors, but individuals in search of a suitable mantel or niche decoration. Unfortunately, Mr. Waite did not supply the author with a photograph.

The novice should realize that there is no one way of finishing birds. There are as many ways as there are bird-carvers. This chapter has been written as a guide for beginners who are starting from scratch. No doubt ideas have been expressed and discussed which experienced carvers will "salt down" in their thinking. But the point to remember is that all serious beginners, after some experience in painting their carvings, will learn other ways of using their finishing tools and materials. They will even "stumble" upon some in an awkward moment. These different methods will become uniquely their own style, differentiating their work from all of the others. A bird-carving friend of mine, speaking of this progression toward individuality, said: "I noted at the recent Babylon show, 14 Canada geese all lined up for the judging. Each was a fine representation of its species but none resembled the other."

Read a good book on wood finishing. A study of the manufacture of paint, especially the acrylics, will help you to appreciate the nature of preserving and decorating wood surfaces. You will learn new tricks you never dreamed of before. Next to experience, reading related information concerned with your work is the most important training you can receive. The more you learn of such material, whether it is directly concerned with your painting or carving or not, the more your nervous system will respond to your work and be attuned to the rhythm of the composite whole. The more you learn about matters related to your work, the more skill will flow through your fingers. The carver does not carve by enthusiasm and energy entirely. There are the spiritual, the inspirational, concomitant forces that really transcend the spirit of the forms. Such integration of subject matter and experience has been stressed in this book. Too much emphasis cannot be given to this aspect of learning.

Chapter 14

ODDS AND ENDS

In this chapter an effort will be made to tie up the loose ends of the carving techniques already covered, and to discuss some important aspects of the work that have not been mentioned in earlier chapters. The material was not included at the time for fear of distracting the reader's attention from the subject matter to less serious detail. While the ideas were pertinent, they tended to clutter, somewhat, the how-to-do-it instructions. For example, the last chapter on wood finishing was concerned solely with finishing the carvings, not with how to care for the materials involved. Yet, after their initial use, caring for brushes, and the finish itself, is rather important considering their cost and efficiency.

Brushes are not very rugged tools. They are easily made worthless with improper care. Protect them and they will serve you faithfully until the bristles wear down to their ferrules. Neglect them and they have only a one-time use. During the period while finishing is in progress there is little point in cleaning them every day. They will keep soft if left submerged in a can of solvent or cleaner unharmful to their bristles. Of course, the bristles should not touch the bottom of the container. I use kerosene as a solvent and cleaner. Even water will work satisfactorily for an overnight interval. Before continuing the finishing process after a day's intermission, the bristles should be washed in turpentine and restored to their former working condition. The foregoing concerns varnishes and oil paints only. Brushes used in shellac or any of the lacquers must have a different cleaner and solvent according to their respective media. If the brushes have been used in the water solvent acrylics, they should be washed in plain water after use.

There are several ways of holding brushes in solvent so that the bristles will hang free. A very effective method is to cut a piece of gasket rubber (about 1/8″ thick) a little larger in diameter than the can to be used. Holes to fit the handles of the brushes are punched in the rubber so that the handles will be friction-tight. The brushes may be suspended from the rubber gasket which also serves as a lid for the can. A simpler way is to tie a string around the brush handle and run the loop over a straight piece of wire resting on the rim of the container holding the solvent. A common clothespin (spring type), clamped around the brush handle and balanced over the rim of the can, serves the purpose. There are devices on the market to hold brushes in a can of solvent but none of them are any more effective than the examples just discussed. An artist friend of mine uses the pan in which painters roll their felt applicators for plastic paint. She places her brushes side by side on the inclined plane with the bristles extended over the well designed to hold the paint. She fills the well with kerosene and her brushes are ready the next day for instant use. In any device the important feature is to keep the bristles submerged but at the same time hanging free from the bottom of the can. Again, these instructions do not apply to brushes used in plastic paints.

When the brushes are not to be used for an indefinite period they should be thoroughly washed with a cleaning solution until not a trace of the pigment remains.Then they should be washed with yellow soap and water. Brushes should be allowed to remain on their sides or handle ends in a jar. Bristles warped out of position are worthless for meticulous work.

Caring for the finish after it is used is important too. Carvers use very little of it at one time. There is a limit to the small amount which may be purchased, so it should be preserved in its container to serve at some other time after its first use has been satisfied. Keep the air from all paint media. In the case of oil paint, air causes the pigment and linseed oil to oxidize and harden. In the case of acrylics, the solvent will evaporate and the pigment will become unworkable. With proper care, finishes may be kept for a year or more. With a friction-top can, the groove may be filled with the finish before pressing down the lid. A tight seal is formed to preserve the finish for a long time. Linseed oil poured over paint will form a tough film and seal the pigment for an indefinite period.

Mounts and Bases. Driftwood is preferred by most bird-carvers as a base. Fortunately, it is not difficult to find. In rural sections, especially, the material may be found near streams, tributaries and seashores. I recently pulled ashore the bole of a large tree with my tractor. The tree fell a long time ago upstream and drifted down in front of our waterfront where it became stranded in the mud. Over the years it has been an impediment to small craft visiting our creek. Observing it at low water, I noticed that many unique formations had developed on the trunk and near the roots. The sap had long since rotted away but the heartwood was as sound as the day the tree fell. Pulling it ashore was quite a task but well worth the effort. In addition to supplying many mounts for birds, the bole will make a life-size carving of a human figure, for it was about two feet in diameter. Even in the fields suitable weathered tree forms may be found. Old farms still have chestnut fence posts that have been in the ground for more than a half-century. They have unique forms caused by the softer wood rotting away and leaving the harder, more durable grain. Old cedar stumps of trees, fallen many years ago, are also a good source of "driftwood." The sap has long since decayed, leaving beautiful gnarled reddish-brown roots. These stumps are usually so loose that they may be kicked out of the ground or pulled free with the hands. When sandblasted they present many interesting shapes, very suitable for bird mounts. The more rustic the perch, the more it is in keeping with wildlife.

What has been said of rustic mounts does not entirely rule out the use of formal bases. In fact, there are occasions when the cleverly constructed base is more suitable than driftwood. The Kingfisher base (Figure 29) is Plexiglas set in a trim of mahogany. The perch, however, is a weathered piece of black locust found on our waterfront. The base seems just right, and the whole carving makes a very interesting centerpiece for the table or mantel.

An excellent base for ducks, geese and other aquatic birds may be made of plywood covered with sand. The construction is as follows: First, shape the base of a piece of 3/4″ plywood (life-size birds) to the desired design. Trim the under edge with a 3/4″ border glued fast to the base so that it becomes a part of it, raising the bottom off the floor. The edges may then be beveled or rounded down to about 1/4″ to the floor (a feathered edge will break off). A gentle sweep will look natural. When the base has been formed, give it a flowing coat of spar varnish, but not enough to run and form "curtains." When the surface becomes tacky, sprinkle fine sand over it quite liberally for the surplus will dust away. To give the sand a more "beachy" effect, shell fragments may be added—even a shell or two. If one foot is higher than the other on the carved bird, the raw base may be given a mound; in fact, any number of effects may be carved in the base before it is coated with sand. A beautiful conch shell may be artistically placed upon the base to create a point of interest. The loose sand should be blown off, leaving an even-sanded surface. The Whooping Crane (Figure 56) and Heron (Figure 57) are screwed to such a base.

Steel rods used to reinforce the legs of the mounted birds should extend through the base and be tightened with a washer and nut on the under side. Of course, the rods should be threaded to receive the nuts.

Generally, the mounts and bases should be in keeping with the nature and habitat of the birds concerned. For example, you would not mount a web-footed bird that wades or dives on a limb. You could do this, however, with a tree duck. Both ducks and geese are more natural when mounted on flat bases. The sand-covered types are very effective. Birds native to rocky terrain or coastline are appropriately mounted on rocklike bases carved of wood or molded from plaster of Paris. Cormorants are usually mounted on rocklike formations. Charles Graveney's Cormorant group is so mounted and it has become a museum piece (Figure 65). Remember that bases and perches are important for eye effects. They make the difference between the commonplace and the unique carving.

Legs and Toes. Metal rods are usually used to reinforce the legs of large birds; wires may be used for smaller ones. In long, slender legs like those of herons, cranes and yellow legs, steel reinforcement is almost a necessity. Short, squatty legs may be strengthened with a dowel pin, but a threaded rod is necessary to fasten them to a base. For small birds the wire may be bent with the hands, but the rods for larger birds must be formed in a vise. If made of copper or brass, the carver may solder the toes to the legs, but if made of steel they must be brazed for satisfactory results. Figure 58A shows the legs and toes held in position while being brazed. Of course, the same technique may be used in the soldering operation. Notice that the claws are designed on the same principle as the nails of the human fingers, that is, the claws come out of the top of the birds' toes, leaving them blunt. The leg rods should always extend below the bulge of the foot where the toes meet the legs. In some instances the ends should be threaded as already indicated. This extension penetrates the limb mount (Figures 58B and C) and when the toes are bent in position the legs are fastened securely. When used in ducks or other birds standing on a flat surface, the extension rod need not be threaded but friction-tight so the carving may be removed while dusting or polishing. Birds having steel legs without covering of any kind may be further improved by hammering to the proper leg shape and scoring with a sharp cold chisel. A file will be useful, too.

If wood is desired for the legs, but reinforced with steel cores, the operation may be performed in one of two ways. First, the leg pieces should be cut extra wide and a hole to fit the rods bored from end to end. The legs may then be carved around the hole. The pieces are slipped over the rods, coming together with a miter joint at the knee. The lower section must be slipped in place before the toes are brazed or soldered. The second method consists of forming the legs in halves and gouging a half-hole to fit the

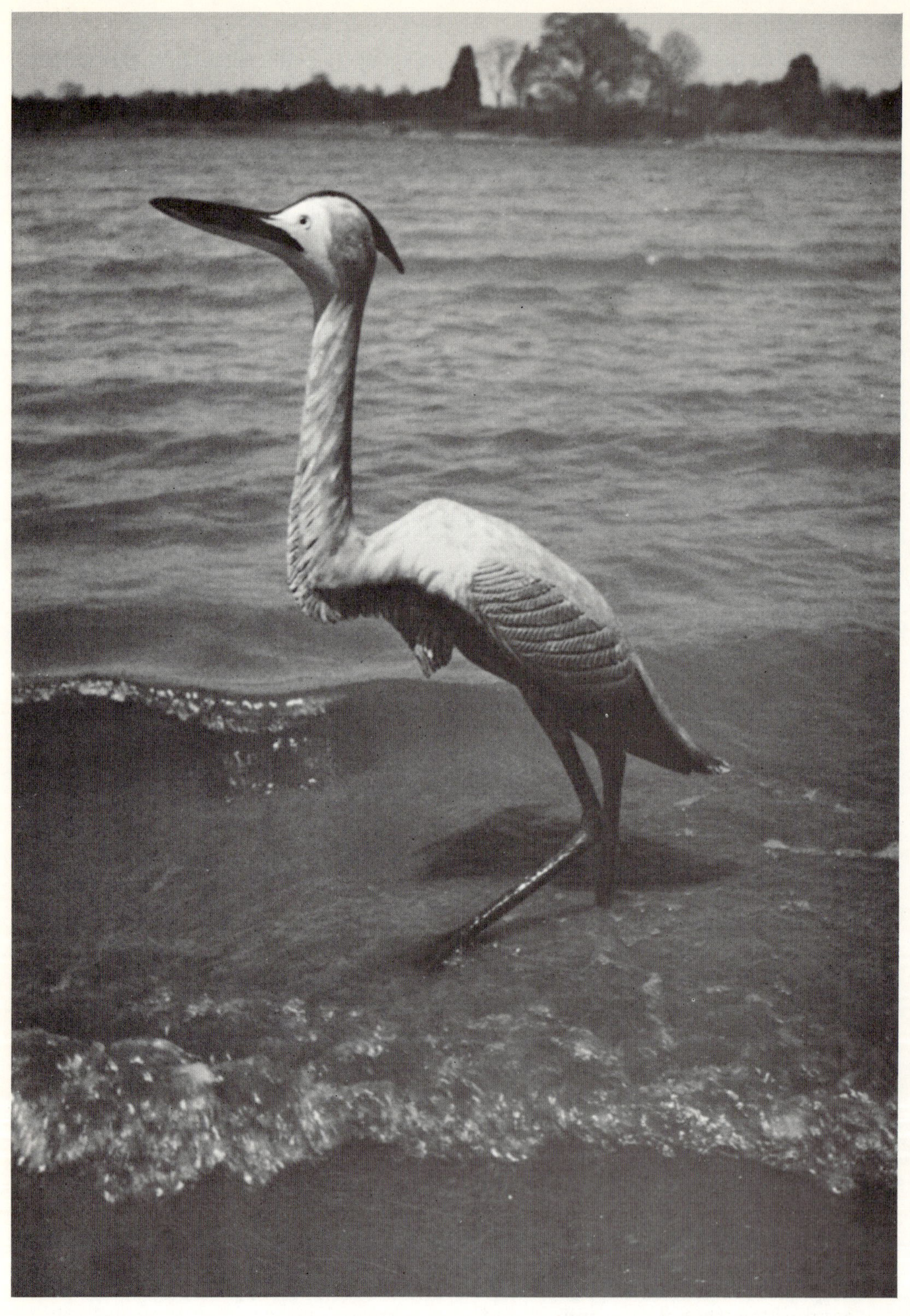

Figure 57. Heron (Great Blue).

rods. The wood may be cut to proper size before the holes are formed. The halves fit together at the knee with a miter joint as in the first case. When the holes have been formed, the halves may be glued together around the rod. The toes are incased in the same fashion, and when the whole leg unit has been fabricated, it may be carved to proper contour and scales carved on it (Figure 58D). The Whooping Crane's legs were carved in this manner (Figure 56).

Another way of covering the legs and toes is with a polyester filler, the kind body and fender mechanics use to smooth out dents in automobile bodies. Martin Senour Paints' body filler No. 6379 is what I use, but there are several comparable fillers sold under different trade names. Number

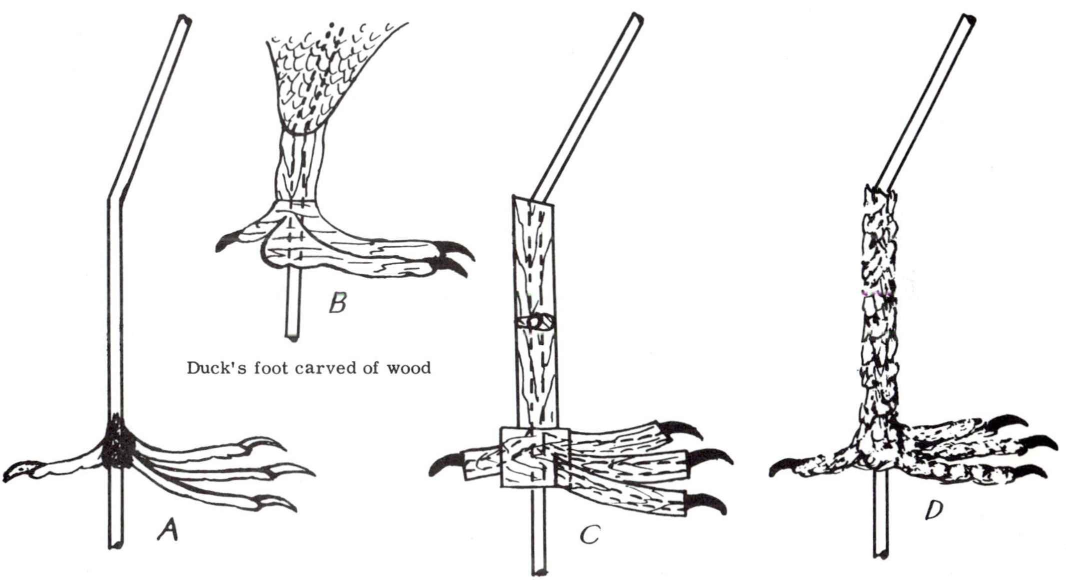

Figure 58. Leg construction. A. Brazed steel leg and toes. B. Foot carved from the original block. C. Steel reinforcing legs and toes of wood. D. Brazed steel legs covered with polyester filler.

6379 is called "Pay Day." It is catalyzed with a yellow cream hardener and when it has set it can be filed, sanded and feather-edged to a satinlike finish. Follow the directions on the can carefully. Mix only enough filler to do the job for it sets up quickly and cannot be used again. To cover the legs (steel reinforcements), spread enough of the filler on a ribbon of wax paper wide enough to go around the rods and leave space for the filler. Place the rod in the middle of the ribbon and turn the edges over until they meet. Press the edges together. The job does not have to be perfect as some patchwork around the feet will be necessary. The toes are covered in a similar fashion. The steel must be clean, down to the bright metal. The mill scale, rust, and any foreign material will prevent the filler from sticking. Cold rolled steel must be clean of all oil before being used. Use plenty of filler at the bulge of the feet where the toes are joined so that the feet may be carved without evidence of where they were attached. When sanded or carved to the proper contour, the scales may be cut in.

This latter method might be used for naturally finished birds but is not recommended for birds with legs heavy enough to be carved from wood. Whenever possible, wood should be used for legs to keep the subject in sculptural form.

As already suggested, some carvers make a coarse texture around their birds' legs with thread. This is a satisfactory method, but not the best technique; legs of wood (reinforced with steel) or steel covered with polyester fillers are better.

Whenever possible, I make the legs (even the feet) of wood and reinforce the wood if necessary. The grain should run with the length of the legs, and the feet should be made separately with the grain running with the toes (Figure 58). In many instances the legs may be carved with the body. However, if the grain runs crosswise, the legs should have a dowel rod inserted into their centers before the carving takes place, that is, after the rough cuts have been made. It is much easier to carve the feet before they are glued to the legs. After the web is carved, it may be varnished and when tacky, sprinkled with fine sand. This will give a realistic touch to the polychromed birds.

Wings. Often a bird is carved with open wings. They represent a problem to the carver in two respects. First, the wings must be attached to the body separately in some effective manner; in the second place, the irregular contour of the wings usually presents a difficulty with reference to the grain. Wings carved of one piece of wood are likely to be fragile if given beautiful curves. The primaries are usually shown open and if the grain is not right, they will break off easily. An effective way to fabricate wings is to bend the contours of laminated stock using the same wood as the body. In full-sized birds the laminations should be ¼″ thick carefully surfaced to make a tightly glued joint. Figure 59 shows a type of form for bending the wings to any desired shape. The laminations should bend in the form easily, but if they do not, soak the boards in hot water to soften their fibers and clamp them in the form until they have dried out. Then the surfaces may be coated with glue and returned to the form. Place a block of wood on both the top and under surface and clamp them together with a C-clamp. After the glue sets the laminations will remain in their formed positions as strong as if they had grown that way. In full-scale large birds, the thickness should be at least an inch to provide plenty of material for carving. The tenon should be cut ½″ thick and extend the whole wing breadth. The shoulders of the tenon should be formed to suit the mortise sunk into the body of the bird. The tenon should be inserted about 2″ deep, following the contour of the bird's body.

The mortise recess may be cut with a ½″ auger, in a series of holes, in tandem, at the same angle with the axis of the bird. The surface at the mortise should be flat and left uncarved with sufficient material remaining to form the fillets with the wings. The angle of the auger may be controlled by constructing a frame fastened to the back of the bird with guide boards to determine the pitch. As the angle of the mortise determines the pitch of the wings, this operation is important. A little time spent in constructing a gadget to guide the auger will be well used. The wings of the drake Mallard (Figure 54) were formed in this manner.

When carving wings, study wing construction; the design, shape, wing bars, direction, form, and other aspects of this vital member of a bird.

Remember that the advancing edge is thick, giving the necessary lift factor required in flight; that the wing tapers toward the primary feathers lengthwise and toward the secondaries crosswise. The trailing edge is one feather thin. There is a decided concave depression just under the advancing edge of the wing to keep the air from spilling out. Carve the feathers carefully, using a good picture for your guide in the absence of skins or a stuffed or live model. The wings should be carved before they are attached to the body. Make several trial fittings, however, until the wings slip into their mortises without much effort. Be sure the pitch is right. If it is not, correct it. Even at this stage, a mistake is better corrected than allowed to remain to mar the appearance of the finished bird. Poise your bird as if it is ready to take off.

If the wings do not have a pronounced camber, they need not be laminated; otherwise, these directions hold.

Eyes. There are several ways of making eyes. In most cases commercial glass eyes are preferable for the beginner. But there are times when they are neither available nor even desirable. For example, a truly sculptured bird should have no such trappings. Whether commercial eyes are used or not, the eye chart prepared by J. W. Elwood Supply Co., will be of invaluable help in selecting the size and color of the eyes when making them yourself. A skilled sculptor would carve the eyes directly on the head of the bird, but this method is not advised for the novice. An easier and surer way is to make the eyes of wood, separately. A wood-turning lathe is convenient for this, but in the absence of such equipment, a dowel pin of the proper size will suffice. Drill a hole the size of the pupil in the end of the dowel pin and insert a cylindrical piece of ebony or a piece of soft wood saturated with India ink. The end grain should be used, of course. Round off the dowel pin with the inserted pupil to a near hemisphere and dip in clear varnish. Shake off the surplus and hang on a hook to dry. For full-size large birds the dowel should be cut off 3/8″ to 1/2″ long, providing plenty of length for gluing the eye in place. Color may be added to the iris of polychromed birds after the dowel pin has been prepared, but before the pupil has been inserted. When dry, the pupil may be tapped in place and the eye varnished. The bottom edge of the eyes should be slightly chamfered to facilitate the inserting operation. If the eyes fit tightly, varnish may be used instead of glue.

If a wood-turning lathe is available, the eyes may be given a French polish.

The holes for the eyes must be located in the head of the bird accurately and at corresponding positions. Determine the spot for the first hole by sight; that is, where you think the eye should be placed. Locate the hole on the other side of the head by triangulation. From a desirable point on the crown of the head above the eye, strike an arc corresponding to the distance of the located hole. Measure off the distance from the end of the bill to the center of the located hole with dividers and cut the arc on the other side of the head. The intersection of the arc should be the correct location for the other eye—but check to be sure. Your geometry may be inaccurate. Stand off from your bird and check by sight. Installing the eyes after the finish has been applied prevents mutilation of this important feature of the bird.

The next technique is quite simple after the gadget has been constructed. A piece of pipe, the inside diameter of which is the same as that of the iris, is countersunk until the edge is very sharp. This edge is further

BIRD EYE CHART

Bird	Size	Color
Bittern—American	11	Yellow
Bittern—Least	8	Yellow
Blackbird—Red Wing	5	Brown
Rusty	5	Brown
Brewers	6	Yellow
Blue Bird	4	Brown
Blue Jay	7	Hazel
Bobolink	5	Brown
Bob White Quail	8	Hazel
Buzzard	12	Brown
Canary	2	Brown
Cardinal	5	Brown
Cat Bird	5	Brown
Chapparel Cock (Road Runner)	10	Yellow
Chicken—Domestic	10	Hazel
Coot	9	Red
Cormorant	12	Green
Crow	11	Brown
Cuckoo	7	Brown
Dove—Turtle	7	Brown
Mourning	7	Brown
Duck—Black	10	Black
Buffle Head	10	Brown
Bald Pate	10	Yellow
Blue Bill	10	Brown
Canvas Back	10	Red
Gadwall	11	Brown
Golden Eye	11	Yellow
Harlequin	10	Brown
Mallard	11	Brown
Merganser American	11	Red
Merganser Hooded	9	Yellow
Merganser Red Breast	11	Yellow
Old Squaw	10	Brown
Pintail	9	Brown
Red Head	10	Yellow
Scoter	10	Yellow
Shoveller	10	Yellow
Spoon Bill	10	Yellow
Ruddy	11	Hazel
Scaup Lesser	11	Yellow
Shell Drake	10	Red
Teal—Bluewing	9	Brown
Teal—Cinnamon	9	Yellow
Teal Greenwing	9	Hazel
Widgeon	10	Yellow
Wood Duck	11	Red
Whitewing Scoter	10	Straw
Eagle—Bald Young	16	Brown
Bald Adult	17	Yellow
Golden	17	Brown
Falcon	11	Brown
Flicker	8	Brown
Goose	12	Brown
Grackle	5	Straw
Grebe—Am. Eared	8	Red
Horned	9	Red
Pied Billed	8	Red
Grouse—Ruffed	10	Hazel
Gull—Bonaparte	9	Brown
Franklin	10	Brown
Herring	12	Yellow
Glaucus	14	Straw
Laughing	10	Red
Ring Bill	10	Yellow
Hawk—Chicken	14	Hazel
Cooper	12	Straw
Fish (Osprey)	14	Yellow
Gos-Hawk	14	Hazel
Hen	14	Hazel
Marsh	12	Yellow
Pigeon	8	Brown
Red Tail	14	Brown
Rough Leg	14	Hazel
Red Shoulder	14	Hazel
Sharpshinned	10	Yellow
Sparrow	9	Brown
Swainsons	14	Hazel
Shoveler	10	Yellow
Kingfisher—Belted	10	Brown
Killdeer	7	Black
Loon	14	Red
Magpie	8	Brown
Mocking Bird	5	Brown
Mudhen	10	Red
Nighthawk	8	Black
Osprey	14	Yellow
Owl—Arctic	19	Straw
Barn	14 or 15	Brown
Barred	18	Special
Burrowing	10	Yellow
Great Horned	20	Yellow
Long Eared	14	Yellow
Pigmy	12	Yellow
Richardson	13	Straw
Screech	14	Straw
Sawwhet	12	Yellow
Snowy	19	Straw
Short Eared	13	Yellow
Partridge	10	Hazel
Pelican	17	Straw
Pheasant	10 or 11	Special
Pigeon	7 or 8	Orange
Plover	6	Brown
Prairie Chicken	10	Hazel
Quail	7 or 8	Hazel
Rails—Clapper	10	Hazel
Carolina	7	Red
Little Black	5	Brown
King	9	Brown
Virginia	9	Hazel
Yellow	6	Brown
Road Runner	10	Yellow
Sparrow	8	Brown
Starling	5	Brown
Sandpiper	6 or 7	Brown
Snipe	6 or 7	Brown
Swallow	4	Brown
Tern	6	Brown
Teal (See Ducks)		
Turkey—Wild	12 or 13	Brown
Woodpecker	7	Brown

Courtesy J. W. Elwood Supply Co.

All eyes have black pupils. Color refers to iris. 1–16 sizes and millimeter measurements are identical. Size 17 = 18mm.; 18 = 19mm.; 19 = 20mm.; and 20 = 22mm.

sharpened with a small round rifler file, or a small Carborundum cone. (A small power carving set is ideal to sharpen this pipe.) The pipe is next fitted with a tight wooden plug driven directly below the bevel of the pipe just formed (Figure 59). Shape the convex surface of the pipe inside with soft plastic wood. Shape with the finger or a small stick prepared for this purpose. After the plastic hardens, coat the surface with varnish. When it becomes tacky, sprinkle coarse Carborundum dust on it (or fine sand) to form the abrasive surface. Let set for a week at least so that the varnish will be sufficiently hard to hold the grits. This gadget will form a beautiful eye and may be applied directly on the bird. Be sure to locate the eyes accurately for once the eyes are formed, their positions are difficult to change. The gadget is held in a hand drill or brace while forming the eye. Do not generate too much friction or the varnish will soften. The pupils may be inked in with India ink or drilled for a black wood insert. In a bird like the eagle, the upper eyelid slightly folds over the eye. The surface of the fold should be prepared carefully and an inlay of wood glued in place to be carved after the glue has set. The eyelids may require further treatment in the case of a few birds, but generally the circular shape conforming to the iris is satisfactory. This pipe gadget is mainly for large birds; smaller carvings require only the pipe sharpened without further modification. Be careful not to cut the circular shape too deep.

A slight variation of the above technique can be effected by the use of a flat auger with the lips sharpened in the convex shape of the iris. In this method the center hole is already drilled (or located), requiring only a follow-up with a drill of proper size for pupil insertion. Of course, the size of the flat auger determines the size of the eyes. This method is unsatisfactory for eyes under ¼″ diameter For smaller eyes, a sharp countersunk nail punch will work very well.

The skilled carver may want to form the eyes without gadgets, but a beginner will find such aids are rewarding and improve his work to a remarkable degree.

Most professional bird-carvers use commercial eyes for their painted models. The eye chart shows the size and color of the eyes of most ducks and birds. This chart is invaluable to beginners. Even experienced carvers refer to it to determine the size of the eyes of their birds if commercial eyes are *not* used. The sizes from one to sixteen (smaller sizes not indicated) and millimeter measurements are the same; that is, a size 11 eye measures 11 millimeters in diameter. All other sizes have been changed to millimeters in a note below the eye chart.

The chart sizes should be converted into fractions of an inch to determine the size of hole to be bored. Taxidermists' catalogs provide a good source of information for the bird-carver and all of them advertise glass eyes for sale.

Commercial eyes are usually supplied with pairs of fine wire twisted together. Some carvers cut the wire off flush with the eye, but a better method is to leave about ¾″ of it and turn up the last ¼″ to form a barb (Figure 59). First drill a small hole at the correct eye location to receive the barbed wire. Next, counterbore with an auger the same size as the glass eye. Fill the small hole with glue and fill the larger one with plastic wood. When the eye is inserted to its proper depth, the surplus plastic is forced out and the barb is securely submerged in the glue of the small hole. The excess plastic wood is rubbed off without marring the paint (or varnish) of the finished bird. When the plastic and glue have set, the eyes are securely fastened in place.

In natural finished birds the iris may be turned with a sharp plug cutter from a piece of burly grained wood to highlight this vital feature of the bird. The pupils are always black. Inlays or inserts of various woods are often effective. For example, the Bald Eagle (Frontispiece) is marked with the sapwood of cedar for the white tail and head. Holly could have been used with still a better effect here; the bill and feet could have been carved

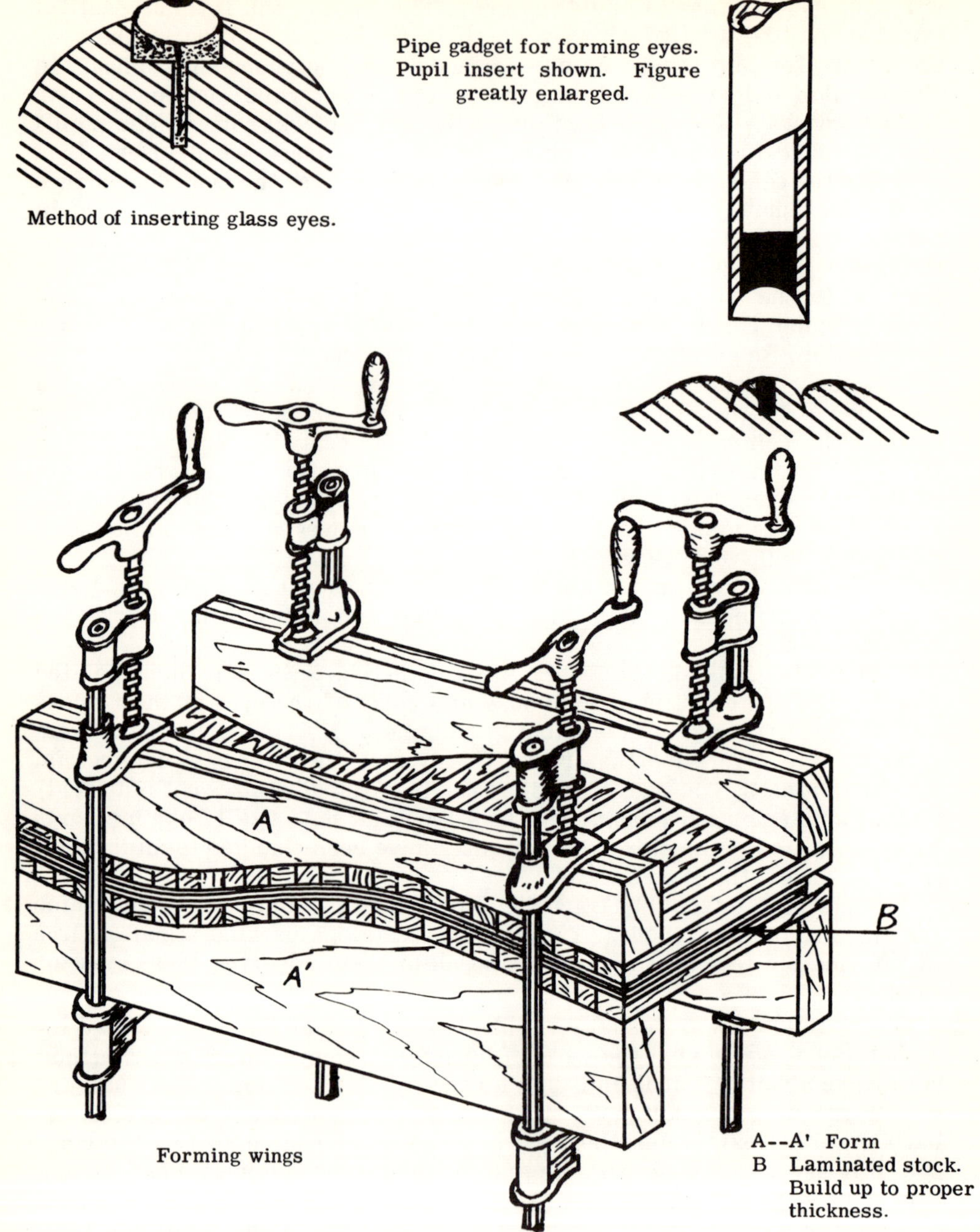

Figure 59. Gadgets for construction of wings and eyes.

of Osage orange to further carry out the color scheme, but neither of these two woods was available at the time the bird was carved. Where the head joins the body, the seam is completely hidden by droopy feather inlays in red cedar wood.

A truly natural finish demands that only natural wood be used, without stains or other finish colorations. This is the general feeling of sculptors who even avoid the use of inlays. John Rood's bird (Figure 66) is made of solid mahogany. It is cleverly designed in a near abstract technique. Charles Chase's Goliath Heron (Figure 67), carved from a black walnut log, is more realistic. Both works are fine examples of the sculptor's art. But the public is quite sympathetic toward color and I indulge my weakness in this respect by using colored wood inlays rather than paint.

Most bird carvings will require some modification of the block or log to achieve proper strength. This is especially true of woods that splinter easily, like cedar and ebony. The necks, heads, tail feathers, and like members should be designed, wherever possible, with the grain running their length, even if the operation means carving separate parts. Decoy duck makers always carve the heads of their birds separately. In this way the bills can be carved with the grain running in the right direction. Also, there is freedom in arranging the angle of the head without much carving difficulty. Decoy ducks, whether made for working purposes or for ornamentation, must pass a floatation test in all judged shows. Bill Birk takes advantage of the angle of the head to balance his decoys after they have been carved.

In long-necked birds the neck is usually carved separately requiring, in turn, that the bill be inserted as in the case of the Kingfisher. Many parts may be laminated as the wings, a technique already described. Contact gluing techniques now allow the laminations to be built up on small parts without a press, the parts becoming bonded together on contact. Dowel pins may be used effectively in many parts to reinforce cross-grained material. The key factor in carving wood is to take advantage of the grain; it must always be skillfully controlled.

In natural finished birds the seams must be made accurately or the work will be less effective. A carver's work should not give the impression that his fingers are all thumbs. In polychromed birds a little plastic can cover a multitude of joinery sins, but when the raw wood shows, the evidence of craftsmanship is highly important. Always use razor-sharp tools. An effective way to join the neck of a bird to the body is to form the joint as accurately as possible and then glue in position. After the glue sets, draw a line across the joint to serve as an index mark. Then with a fine crosscut saw, saw down the seam carefully. When separated, the two parts should fit back together perfectly as the saw kerf has removed all previous inaccuracies. Coat the two surfaces with glue and place back in position, with the index marks forming a straight line. The hole for the dowel pin (if used) should be bored after the head has been fastened in place. It may be bored either from the crown of the head or from the breast. In either case, in natural finished birds a plug having the corresponding grain and color of the particular surface should cover the dowel. No evidence of reinforcing should be seen.

Polyester fillers have been mentioned from time to time in this book. The fillers are synthetic resin products and when mixed with their catalysts harden quickly into a very desirable fine-textured surface for carving or painting. Its uses cannot be overemphasized for wood-carvers who paint their models. In many respects it is better than the regular fillers. It has taken the place of lead in automobile body and fender work because of its flexibility, texture, and strength. Follow the directions on the can for applying this new development to fill holes and defects in wood and for large and small curved fillets. It is comparatively inexpensive considering the results achieved. Some well-known brands are: "Bondo," "White Plastic," and "Pay Day."

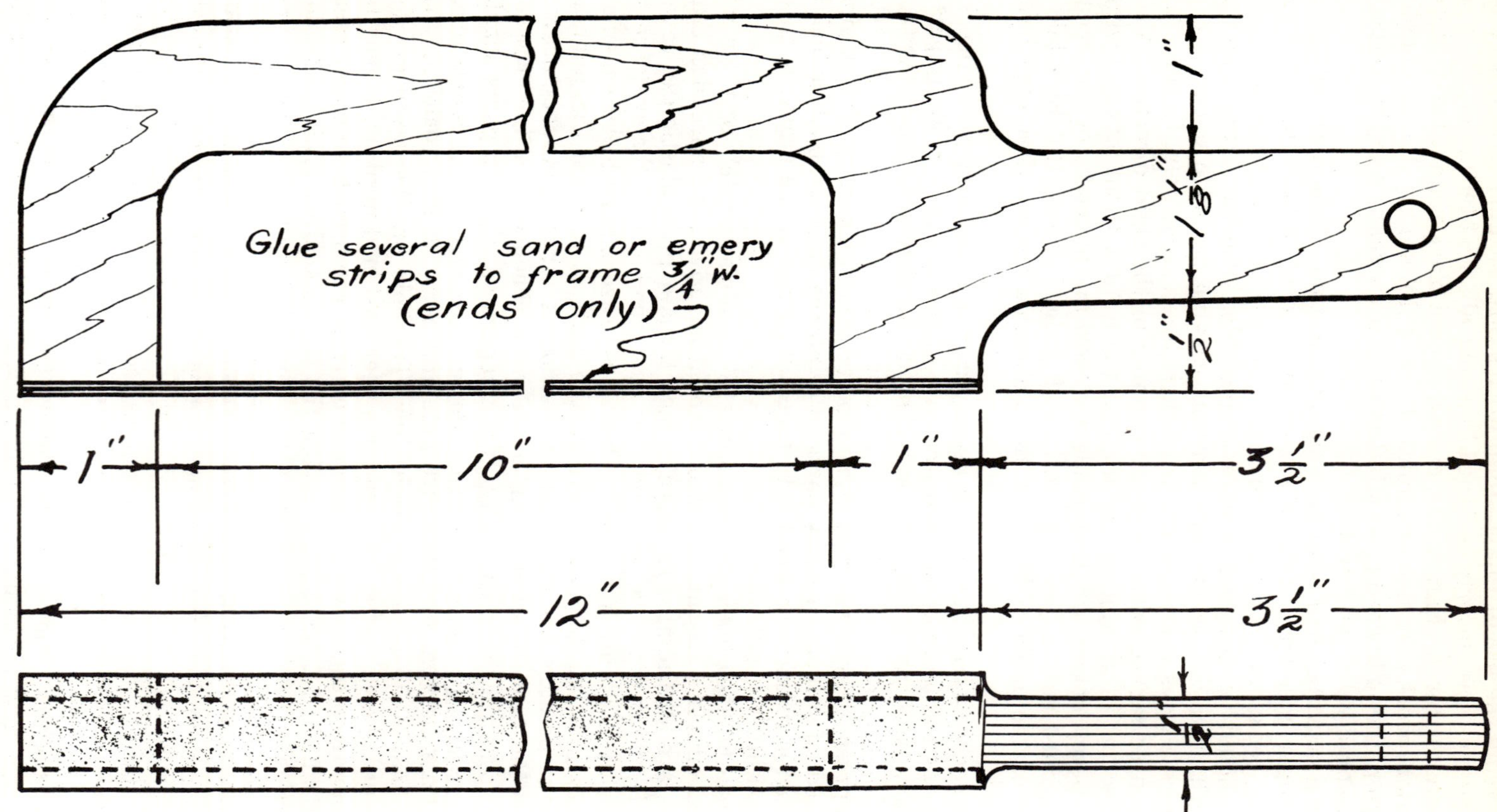

Figure 60. A handy hand sander.

A convenient hand sander may be made of ½″ plywood designed as shown in Figure 60. Emery cloth may be torn in strips (about ¾″ wide) and glued on each other at the ends of the frame. When the top strip becomes worn and useless it may be torn off to expose a new strip. Abrasives come in cloth strips in rolls which may be used instead of emery cloth. There are contour sanding wheels on the market that do a good job but they are dusty and should have a vacuum system connected with them. Under no circumstances should they be used where painting operations are performed.

The foregoing shortcuts and improvisations are invaluable to the beginning carver. At the very start he learns effective ways of performing his work which has taken me a lifetime to stumble upon in my woodworking experiences. There are many others, of course, developed by other carvers and the novice himself will find convenient methods of performing his work which may be uniquely his own. The thought expressed in the preceding chapter concerning the individuality of the finishing process among bird-carvers applies to these shortcuts, improvisations, and differences in carving techniques. If the reader of this book is seriously inclined, sooner or later he will become a skilled craftsman with a method of doing his work a little differently from all others in his field. There is a tendency to streamline one's efforts to make the job less tedious and difficult. This natural tendency has resulted in laborsaving devices in use today throughout our domestic and industrial life. In the field of the arts this phenomenon is no less present; so the novice will, as he progresses, develop a system of carving strictly his own. Only after a well-organized procedure has jelled in a symplified system can he feel that his efforts are original and done according to the techniques he has worked out for himself. Then in the congregation of the skilled men and women of his craft he can say with confidence: "Now I do it this way"—the earmark of a carver who knows his work and is not afraid to compare his methods with those of the experts. His persistent efforts have paid off; his incompetency is behind him. He never lost hope; he kept the faith! But of all his successful urges, none was greater than his dogged will to persevere.

Chapter 15

IDEAS: FROM EVERY BURNING BUSH!

Another question that I am frequently asked concerns the source of ideas. Personally, I feel that the search for ideas presents no great problem. The question is indicative of an inquiring mind, however, and a person who is interested in carving but has little experience in the art on a high performance level. Certainly, the skilled carver will never be idle because the well of his imagination has run dry. Of course, there will be times when he claims he has "run out of soap." But the truth of the matter is, more likely, he has run out of incentive, a driving force to spur him on to his next job. He just did not have the will; he did not want to work! The lack of ideas is a plausible excuse but the reason is not entirely valid. Oh, for the time and energy to carve all of the ideas stored in the mental bin awaiting fruition!

Most of the better known carvers are years behind in their work, a backlog which the collector does not appreciate. Steve Ward tells the story of a little old woman (not from Pasadena) who ordered a decorative decoy from him and seemed quite disappointed when she was informed that she should not expect delivery for a year, at least. Several weeks later she wrote Steve and wanted to know how her carving was progressing. She was politely informed that it would be several months before work on the decoy could be started. She waited a few more weeks and wrote again to inquire about her carving. Finally, Steve's artistic temperament rose to the surface and he canceled her order.

Experienced carvers have ideas stored away, an abundance of them, awaiting the time to be expressed in wood. Less popular bird-carvers, or amateurs, may not be so fortunate, but they should not have to probe their minds to distraction to discover new ideas. In fact, this method is poorest of all possible techniques. Ideas cannot be forced; they are usually spontaneous, bursting upon the conscience sometimes with the brillance of a Roman candle. The incident setting off the fuse may be a magazine article, a picture, a TV show, or any of a thousand other everyday experiences. The real reason for the doldrums, therefore, is not a lack of ideas but an absence of the compelling force to move the carver to pick up his tools and chip out the ones he already has.

Because of the difference in the way individuals think—the manner in which their minds have been inhibited—there are, no doubt, some potential carvers who do thirst after ideas. They have not yet learned to discern the grain of wheat in the chaff of their observations. This inspirational attitude is perhaps acquired, or comes naturally to some individuals, but in any case must become a well-developed characteristic of the carver's personality. It is in the nature of acquiring this disposition that the following discussion is presented.

One is reminded of the poet who called upon his typewriter to write him a verse because he lacked inspiration. To paraphase his thought:

Carve me a figure, my old jackknife;
I lack for inspiration.

Such blind hope and wishful thinking will accomplish little, but the fact that the would-be carver is "browsing" is a point in his favor. For it is from the retort of the mind that outside stimuli are distilled into intelligent ideas. The beginner must learn to stimulate his reflexes and his mind will take over the closure aspects of the remaining pattern. This means that the mind, if given a chance, will create ideas out of basic stimulations of perception. This attitude can be acquired but, like the physical nature of

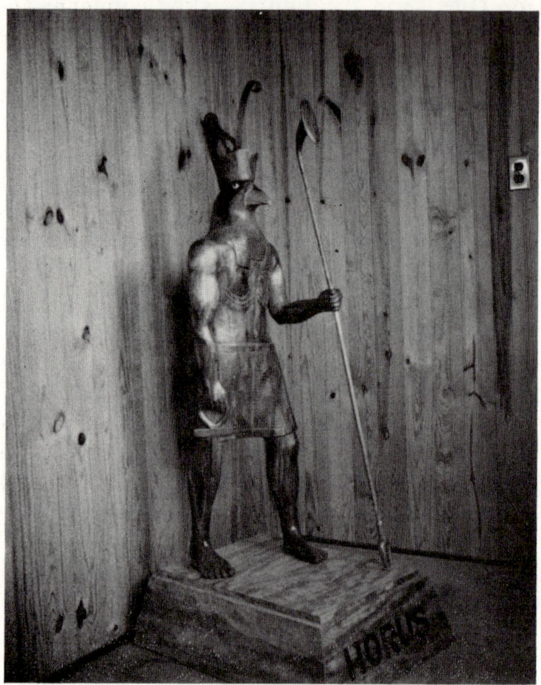

Figure 61. Falcon-headed god, *Horus*.

the body, it must be exercised. The neophyte must learn to see the tree instead of the woods; to learn to isolate from common, everyday experiences the motif related to his art. Ideas permeate his environment and when he has learned to make the right synthesis he will see an idea in every burning bush. The Muse is the close coordination of the observing and inspirational faculties of the mind.

How I chance upon my ideas is quite simple. While writing the first chapter of this book, the Egyptian god, Horus, strangely affected me. The falcon-headed king of the Upper and Lower Kingdoms seemed to cry out: "Carve me!" The double crown on his head, the *ankh*, the symbol of enduring life, in his right hand, and the staff of well-being in his left, were all of inspiring dimensions. While writing these lines the idea has been further etched in my conscience. I will certainly carve the Falcon-headed god, Horus, the son of the Egyptian trinity. (Note: *See* Figure 61.)

The sculpture is after a stylized limestone relief painting of Ptolemy I rendering sacrifice to the god Horus. It was found in a chapel of Ptolemy I at Tuna el-Gebel (Hermopolis), Middle Egypt.

The double crown indicates that Horus was ruler of both upper and lower Egypt. The tenpin shape of the crown represents upper Egypt and the frying-pan shape represents the Lower Kingdom. The feather was usually worn on the Lower Kingdom crown. The cross (ankh) was the symbol of life. The scepter (a modified hieroglyphic sign) was the symbol of well-being. It also indicated (topped with a shepherd's crook) the attribute of gods and king—symbol of the power to rule.

The very first idea of a bird carving came to me because of a challenge. This assault upon the egotistical nature of an individual is often all that is necessary to move him to action; to set his imagination on fire in a creative effort. James Fenimore Cooper was goaded by a friend to write one of his best novels. His friend was discussing Scottish literature and made claims concerning Sir Walter Scott's *The Pirate,* to which Cooper took exception. The claim made by his friend, a polished gentleman, qualified by both taste and extensive reading to speak authoritatively, was that the nautical experiences in *The Pirate* were real and indicated a profound knowledge of the sea. Cooper, a newly-commissioned midshipman in the U.S. Navy, was so provoked by his friend's naive remarks that he boastfully declared he could write a better sea yarn himself. His friend smiled condescendingly and suggested that he try. He did! The result was *The Pilot.*

A similar experience happened to me several years ago. I visited a wildlife carving show where I knew I would find my boyhood friends, Steve and Lem Ward. Since the days we were schoolmates in the Creek community, the Ward brothers had become distinguished throughout the country as professional bird-carvers. They had learned, without formal training, to carve the birds and ducks of their native marshes so realistically that they were unable to supply the demand for their work. While observing the outstanding craftsmanship of some of the best wildfowl carvers in America, I chanced to say boastfully, in the pseudo-voice of the Creek community:

"You know, Steve, I can carve just as good as these fellows."

Steve turned sharply toward me to better understand my remark. Perceiving that I was talking in the vernacular of the old home village, he smiled and answered accordingly:

"Yep, I bet you can!" Then changing the tone of his voice to more serious intent, he continued, "Bill, I dare you to try."

This was the challenge. Up to this moment the thought of applying my woodworking skills to the carving art had never entered my mind. Impulsively, I replied: "OK, Steve, I will—you bet I will."

My mind then became a beehive of stirring thoughts. I actually felt that I could carve birds with a fair degree of skill. Then suddenly the seed of an idea took root and flowered. I clearly saw a pair of Mallards, the drake with outstretched wings, and his mate resting quietly beside him on the sands. I could hardly wait to get home to begin carving the image so plainly seen in my imagination. In about a month I had carved the pair of Mallards from a cedar log which, fortunately, had been stored away under the woodshed for some years before. The ducks were given a natural finish (Figure 54) and immediately won the favor and praise of all who observed them. The work proved to be so popular that I was offered $500.00 for them by a young lady of a prominent family. As the carving had sentimental value beyond price, the offer was respectfully denied. These ducks have been an ever-present source of inspiration over the years and they could have been sold many times. They have won blue ribbons in art shows all over the Eastern Shore.

While the elation resulting from the pair of Mallards was still being enjoyed, I chanced to see the *National Geographic Society's* publication: *Water, Prey and Game Birds of North America.* I read the subject dealing with Whooping Cranes with burning interest. I recalled seeing a flock of these large birds feeding in the neck of a small waterway in lower Maryland when I was still a small boy. I was searching for crabs, wading in a shallow gut, when they came into view as I turned a bend in the shoreline. The Cranes turned their heads toward me nervously, but did not fly away. Appreciating their fears, I observed them for a few moments and retraced my steps toward the creek. After reading of their dire plight to survive, I decided to carve one of these marvelous birds, life-size (Figure 56). The soft crab, upon which the cranes feed, was carved as an afterthought, but it has excited as much interest as the bird itself. A trip to Rock Hall, Maryland, was necessary to obtain the model. It is so life-like that one observer wanted to know how it was preserved, believing it to be a real crab.

After the Crane, I turned to statuettes, each inspired by a significant incident. A visit to the seashore resulted in the *Sun Bather,* a bikini-clad beauty sitting on a blanket spread on the sand. A TV review of an ice-skating frolic gave the author the idea for the *Ice Skaters,* two shapely girls performing a difficult feat on the ice (Plexiglas). A chance examination of a Sunday supplement of a large metropolitan newspaper provided the idea for the next carving—an advertisement showing a half-nude woman standing on floor scales weighing herself. She had a towel wrapped around her hips and her expression was one of utter disgust. This subject has been carved twice with equally unsatisfying results. The idea is good, however, so it has been stored away in the mental hopper awaiting an opportune time to be tried again.

The heron has always stirred my imagination. It is a stately bird, possessing a graceful though lumbering gait—a motion all its own. While flying, the heads of geese and swan stretch out from their bodies as do the heads of Flamingos and Cranes. But the head of the heron is curved back on its shoulders like the Pelican. The heron is not a sociable bird outside of its own species and then only when it roosts and breeds. It even feeds alone. It keeps far away from the curious eyes of human observers and can be studied only with the aid of binoculars. These interesting birds are clever in the art of camouflaging themselves. Recently, while visiting Rock Hall, I observed a heron flying toward a black spar buoy driven in the harbor. When it perched, it straightened itself in line with the pile pointing its long neck and bill straight up toward heaven. The black buoy and the bird appeared to be one object. Bitterns are often shown in such a pose in the reeds, but this camouflaging technique of the heron was strange indeed. After witnessing this protective feat my respect for the bird increased. I knew I must carve one of these amazing birds (Figure 57). Before my enthusiasm abated I had carved two life-size models. I have not yet carved the heron with its body in line with the perch.

The Pintail duck is a beautiful bird. The characteristic markings of the drake make it a favorite among bird-carvers. The two outstanding markings are the pin tail from which it gets its name and the white neck stripes which nearly meet back of the eyes. The Plexiglas fever was still running hot when I conceived the idea to carve a drake feeding, with his feet showing through the shallow "water". The duck was partially completed while demonstrating the art of carving at the Chestertown Tea Party celebration. I had never seen a carving of a duck feeding, so I selected this pose instead of the more common positions. When finished it inspired little interest. The carving was fairly good, but the base "ran away" with the subject. With some modifications the bird will again be carved some day; still another idea stored away for future fruition. The next time some thought will be given to the use of a plate-glass mirror for the base.

One of the customs of my sect is to present to the hostess an appropriate gift expressive of the guests' appreciation when invited to dinner. In searching for a suitable "offering" the custom can become quite frustrating. The problem was solved last summer when an artist friend of the family became excited over a small cardinal bird, carved to test out a thought of design. The perch was screwed fast to a piece of 3/8″ Plexiglas and did present a nice effect. As she gushed over the carving I knew I had solved the problem of a dinner gift for her. I have made several such carvings of various songbirds with very satisfying results. Always the hostess is enthused and overwhelming in her praise and appreciation. Here is an example of an insignificant carving causing a chain reaction of several such efforts. The idea presents an insistent urge once the custom is begun. There is no question for need of inspiration or interest; the carving *must* be done. The task is similar to a commission and, what is just as important, it must be completed within certain time limits.

While writing these few lines ideas have been popping up all over the place: a tree, for example, full of small native birds. An old cedar stump with a complex root system, sand blasted, and turned upside down would be just right for the tree. Imagine a pair of Baltimore Orioles perched upon the topmost branch, the male hovering with open wings while his mate sits restfully beside him! Also, in the picture see a woodpecker pecking at a lower branch or the trunk; a nuthatch inspecting the underside of a limb, with cardinals, cedar waxwings, and other species appropriately located all over the tree! Perhaps a Blue Jay should be included, squawking raucously just for the hell of it. Figure 62 shows some of my garden birds.

One of my very early carvings is shown in Figure 55. The erect eagle, perched upon a limb was carved without any soul-raising experience. A picture published in the *National Geographic Magazine* caught my fancy, and I realized that I had never carved an eagle. The Bald Eagle has become the emblem of this country as it was of so many other nations in the past. Its likeness has topped the standards of many armies. The Romans used the symbol in many ways. Its likeness has been incorporated in totem poles all over America. With such thoughts in mind I set to work and carved a life-size model. Again, nothing succeeds like success! The carving won instant praise and attracted considerable attention, even though there were certain features which were not authentic. When I was invited to give carving demonstrations at the American Bird Carving Exhibition, sponsored by the local chapter of the *Maryland Ornithological Society,* I decided to carve another eagle, this time from a solid log. Most of the work had already been done before the show began, leaving only enough carving to keep me busy during the hours of demonstration. Both eagles were on my bench when a representative of the *Washington Post* arrived to cover the

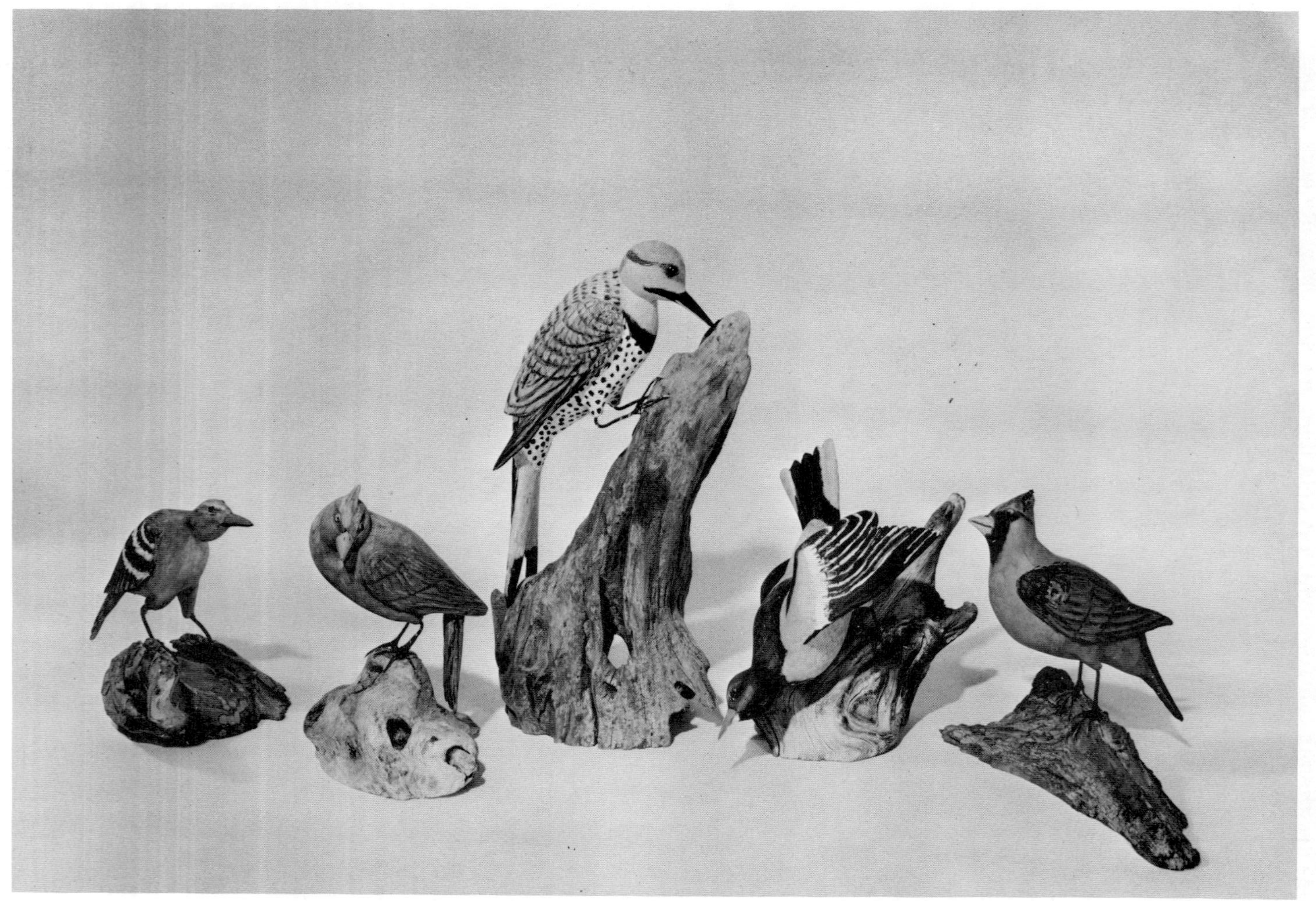

Figure 62. *Garden Birds.* Carved by the author.

exhibition. The birds were photographed in color and were published the following Sunday. The picture and the article created considerable interest among the *Post's* readers, many of whom wrote or called me asking for further information concerning my work.

Mrs. Gladys Black, mentioned earlier, was inspired to do her *Mallards Dropping In* from a Federal Duck Hunting Stamp (Figure 63). She says the work is the most photographed and publicized of her carvings. It was first shown to the public on television last year (NBC; June, 1967). The source of her inspiration created nearly as much interest as the carving itself. Jay N. (Ding) Darling, the famous syndicated cartoonist of the *New York Tribune* designed the stamp. As it was the first issued, and being designed by such an outstanding conservationist, the stamp has now become a collector's item. Mrs. Black spent about 1200 hours in research and carving the beautiful work. "A live pair of Mallards in the backyard and another pair in the freezer served as models," says Mrs. Black. As I remember the carving, it was done in perspective rather than the full three dimensions. The background was painted in—a pond of water fringed with rushes. The work will probably end up in a wildlife museum.

There are few better examples of getting ideas from a picture than the one just noted. Pictures are an important source of inspiration. Even ideas conceived in other ways usually have to be supplemented with picture information.

The reader has already learned how I conceived the ideas for the first two chapters of lessons in this book. Any number of examples could be cited concerning how subject ideas were conceived in the writing of this text. The geese that I carved to test out the written directions of the second lesson were fastened to a piece of dark cloth tacked on the wall of my studio. They were positioned similarly to those of the newspaper photograph and then were photographed. A visitor at this time noticed the skein of geese on the wall and began to ask questions. She was shown the original photograph (Figure 15) and the polaroid picture that I had taken and enlarged (Figure 22). She then approached the carvings and stroked the relief forms. She was amazed at the similarity of all three interpretations.

Many professionals conceive ideas merely by chancing upon a unique shape or object. This might be called the primitive approach, for predawn man saw spirits in all kinds of forms in trees, rocks, and other natural objects. He also used natural shapes for tools and weapons, even food containers. A curly grained burl carved by weather and time could well have been the first vegetable and meat bowl. Even today, natural shapes, trees, boulders, even little pebbles on the bench, have moved sculptors to further develop their shapes into the likenesses they first saw in them. Ossip Zadkin saw in a tree a crucifix. The spreading limbs became the arms of Jesus and the bole His body. This technique is unusual, however, although it is said that Michelangelo saw King David in a piece of discarded marble before he ever sank his chisel into its surface. Certain shapes do inspire sculptors and carvers, and collectors interested in such natural forms roam beaches and fields in search of them.

Generally, sculptors and carvers of wood desire their media to be clear, without any preconceived shapes. The modern trend is for compact work, the figure held totally within the block or log, without "flying buttresses" or parts easily broken off. There are seldom any pierced openings in the more astute forms, despite the feeling of at least one authority who says that an

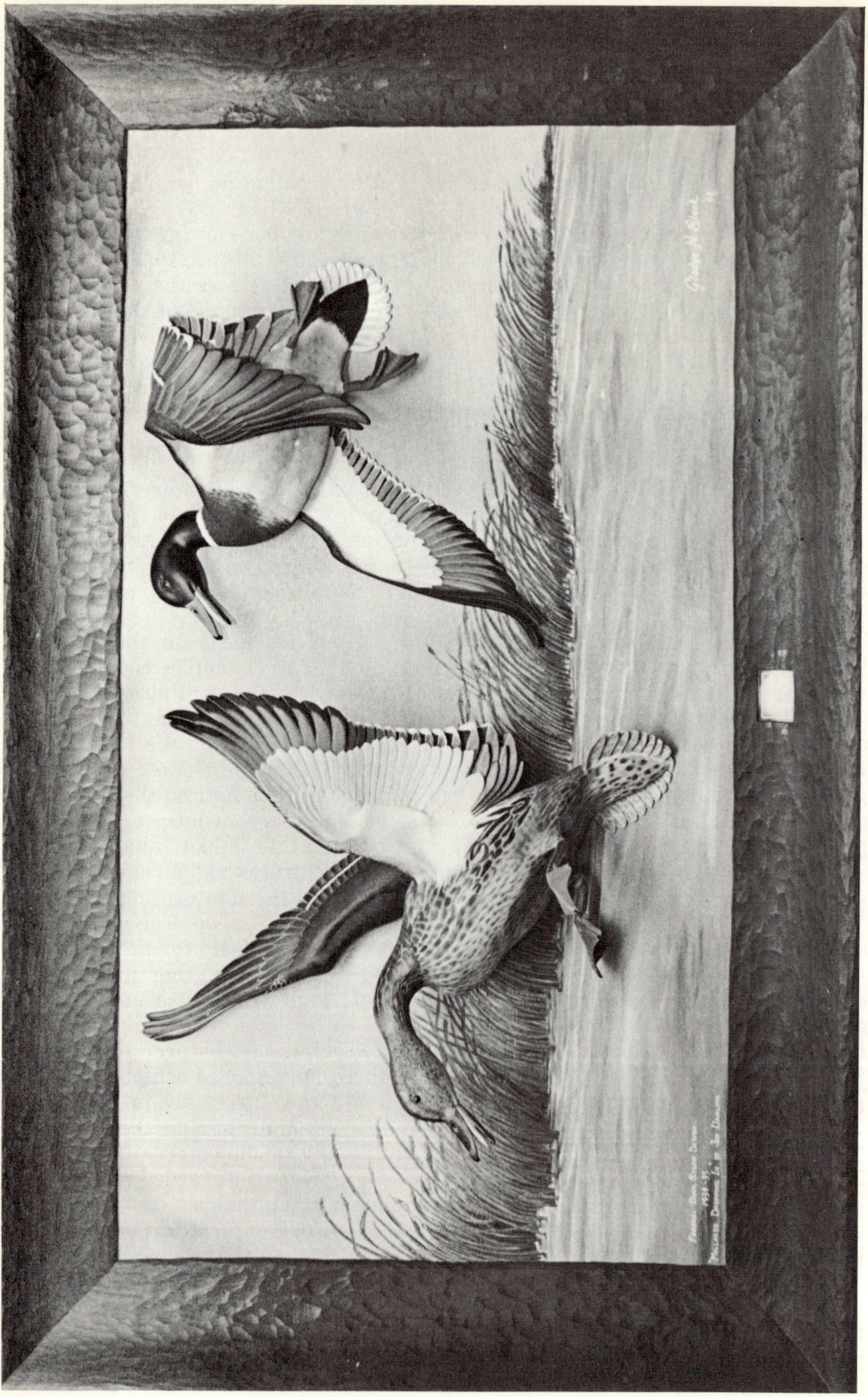

Figure 63. *Pair of Mallards Droppin' In*, by Mrs. Gladys N. Black.

opening in a sculpture brings the opposite side into a more meaningful relation with the whole. The *Laocoon* group is not now considered good sculptural design, irrespective of the fact that it is the most famous for portraying pathos in suffering mankind. Ordinarily, wood carvings should be compact, without projections, but in bird carving some exceptions should be made to the rule. All bird-carvers carve outstretched wings, head and feet standing clear of the block. So, in this text little emphasis will be given to "flying" parts except in a more literal sense, or where the design tends to be weakened, or indicates poor taste. Most bird-carvers do not follow the methods of John Rood who has rigid ideas concerning certain aspects of his work. His superb bird (Figure 66) is a masterpiece of "technique moderne." His more realistic work is rugged but provokes much feeling and, in most instances, is a sensitive portrayal of the idea intended. His techniques should be studied by everyone who seriously dreams of a future in the carving arts.

Now, back to the subject again, after this appropriate digression. Look for the human interest aspect in your work. Inject some humor, for even birds get themselves into some comical situations. Visit game reserves, ornithological museums—any place where birds can be found. Just as important is to study books about carving and sculpture, and books about wildlife. Get yourself in tune with the whole of the creative effort. Begin to collect a good library of texts, pictures, and how-to-do books. Start a natural museum of your own. Your background of materials and information cannot be too elaborate. Once the idea is conceived such helps will be invaluable.

Finally, if all of the foregoing discussion does not lead you to a more sensitive awareness of your environment—seeing ideas where others see only the bush—still more study is necessary to achieve this power of observation. In the meantime, if you persist, there will develop a pattern of concept in your mental powers and ideas will eventually come without studied effort. When you have arrived at this point in your training, you will be able to appreciate good craftsmanship, be more sensitive to your surroundings, and appreciate art in all of its varied forms. You will not have to worry about ideas; you will have more than you can ever bring to fruition. Remember always, in passing, that ideas, like Conwell's diamonds, may be found in your own backyard.

Chapter 16

WOOD: THE WOOD-CARVER'S MEDIUM

There is nothing more familiar to man than wood. He cannot remember when he first used it to warm his bones on frosty nights and to cook his food. In his long struggle upward in the evolutionary night, wood has always been his most important aid. Pottery, generally considered to be his first creative effort, was conditioned with sticks as tools to mold the clay after it was displaced from creek banks with crude wooden or stone scoops.

Wood was the material of the first weapons, tools, and food containers, preceding stone which he somehow learned to chip for arrowheads and tools later. In primitive countries wood is still the material used for carving articles of domestic utility and weapons for defense. In modern times wood enriches our homes which are often made entirely of this material. Wood is familiar to all peoples everywhere. To the carver in both primitive and progressive countries it is his most flexible and important medium.

White cedar and basswood are most frequently used by wildfowl carvers of the Eastern Shore of Maryland. This locality is mentioned because there are probably more bird-carvers here than in any other geographical area of equal size in America. White pine, too, is extensively used. Old telephone poles of chestnut or white cedar were used until the supply was exhausted. Chestnut logs may still be used in a few instances for many older farms still have fence posts of this material available after they have been in the ground for more than fifty years.

White Cedar. White cedar is a light wood of even texture, easy to carve, and will not waterlog. So, when the carving is to be used for a working decoy, the wood is ideal. It is difficult to obtain on the Eastern Shore, however, since it is not native to this area. Sometimes a number of duck-carvers will pool their interests and hire a trucker to haul a load of the logs from southern New Jersey or some southern state to which it is native. The logs are usually green, so they must be laid aside to air-dry, or treated chemically to prevent the carving from checking. (So far as I know, chemically treated logs are not used by the 'Shore craftsman.) White cedar is almost imperishable. At one time large quantities of it were excavated from the saturated peaty soil, or drawn up from swamp water, to be used for timber in boatbuilding, shingles, fence posts, and for other purposes where weather-resistant wood was important. The wood is easy to carve, as stated previously, and the texture is regular and even. It is a close-grained wood, light and otherwise suitable for carving decoy ducks and ornamental birds.

White Pine. White pine is now very scarce. Usually the purchaser is supplied with ponderosa or sugar pine, both excellent substitutes. The grain is close in all three species, usually straight, and without patches of matty fibers. It, too, is light in weight and a light brown in color—almost blond in some instances. It is soft and carves easily. It has a waxy surface when cut with a sharp tool, slippery to the touch. It may be purchased from most local suppliers and may be obtained in heavy boards up to twelve inches wide and three inches thick. Boles of the tree are always green and must be obtained in the locality where the tree is native. As this wood is one of the more important media for carving decoy ducks and birds, the carver should always be on the lookout for old houses being demolished. If they are old enough, heavy beams and sills of white pine may be found and purchased at a reasonable price.

Basswood. This is one of the light-colored woods—nearly white (white basswood). In fact, it is called white wood in some sections of our country. All of the basswoods are of the linden family. The linden basswoods range from New Brunswick west to the Lake Superior region, south to Virginia, and along the mountains to Georgia. Downy and white basswoods are found along the eastern coast from New York to Texas. All species are ideal woods for school shops and there are dealers specializing in supplying this wood to educational institutions. The wood has a fine grain and texture. The grain is not prominent, even less than in white pine. It is not usually carried in stock by the local supplier, but may be obtained through him from the larger lumber establishments located in major cities. The trees are abundant along the St. Lawrence River where native carvers use it to turn out bowls, lamps, carvings, and other attractive articles for the tourist trade. Some of them season their own wood by boiling it several hours in water. One of my prize carvings was done by a young man named Timmons who cut down the tree on a lot behind his shop and dried his wood in this manner. The carving of two bucking stags has remained stabilized over the years and is just as free of checks as it was the day it was carved, more than twenty years ago.

Red Cedar. I use this wood more than any other kind, simply because I have an unlimited supply on my farm. In the woodshed are many logs of various kinds of trees waiting for the chisel, but most of them are red cedar cut after the trees had mysteriously died. The wood is not recommended by carving authorities because of its tendency to split easily and its contrary grain. Matted fibers in patches are present throughout the tree, making it quite difficult to carve. Red cedar is the wood from which lead pencils are made; because of its aromatic fragrance (believed to repel moths), it is used in the manufacture of chests and for lining clothes closets. So, to this extent the wood is familiar to most individuals. It, too, is imperishable and is used by local farmers for fence posts. The grain is complex in spots, but so far as I am concerned, its chief fault is the abundance of knots and numerous places of decayed sapwood and old growth sections. These have been healed over by the growing tree and are invisible to the carver when he starts his project. The wood is not difficult to repair, however, and with patience and skill all of the blemishes may be cut out and repaired with sound wood. The yellow-white sapwood is more difficult to carve than the brownish red heartwood. When first exposed to the air red cedar is a lustrous, slippery red, as beautiful as any exotic wood. But the color soon oxidizes to the duller shade. The larger logs usually contain little sapwood which is a light yellow to white; flashes of it appear throughout the whole log, sometimes resulting in unique effects—and sometimes a pain in the neck, appearing in critical areas with undesirable results. In such cases I cut out the sapwood and insert a matching Dutchman of heartwood. Red cedar cuts easily, but the direction of the grain must be watched closely during the carving operation. It can change abruptly and cause the tool to enter the finished surface. Because of experience and familiarity with the wood, I prefer it to other local woods despite its many faults. The pair of Mallards (Figure 54) were carved from red cedar. Note how the breast merges into the sapwood.

Black Walnut. For carvings which are to be finished in clear varnish or wax no finer wood exists than American black walnut. It is the favorite of all native woods, especially for serious works of sculptural art. It should never be used for polychromed birds for obvious reasons; it is much too valuable and beautiful to be covered with paint. The grain is usually straight in the bole, but very complex in the crotches and where the roots form. These irregular grained parts are the most valuable of the tree for veneer purposes. Stumps that have been weathered for years have been excavated and sawed into beautiful veneers. The curly, burly grain is indeed spectacular, comparing favorably with the most valuable exotic woods imported from foreign countries. The American black walnut is chocolate brown in color (heartwood, sap yellowish), but I have worked with it in shades approaching purple. It is now difficult to come by in logs because of the great demand for them by veneer-producing companies. I have a standing order with several loggers for walnut logs if they happen to find them.

Mahogany. This popular wood varies according to the country from which it is imported. The wood from the West Indies is usually preferred, but for carving purposes, any or all of the species are good. The softer varieties come from South American countries and southern Mexico. Philippine mahogany is a trade name for various trees that are not true species of the tree, but are, nonetheless, good carving media. Mahogany varies in color from light tan to dark reddish brown. Although it is a tropical evergreen tree which technically would classify it with the soft woods, it is considered hard wood, and is, as compared with the needle-leaf trees. But it cuts easily and is an ideal wood for the wood-carver. Like black walnut, the wood is difficult to obtain in logs as it is in great demand for making fine veneers. Also, the wood is usually sawed into lumber and not sold in logs except to a few dealers in sculptural supplies. The Cuban variety is now scarce, not because of Castro, but because the supply of these valuable trees has almost been exhausted. All of the mahoganies take on a high polish and are mainly used for the manufacture of furniture.

The wood is not used extensively on the Eastern Shore although its price is comparable to white pine. For laminated blocks it should have a wider use.

Cherry. This wood is found in most parts of the country, both the wild and cultivated species. Wild cherry is just as suitable for carving as the fruit variety. The wild cherry grows rapidly, sometimes attaining a diameter of 2–4 feet, but this is unusual. It is often free of limbs for many feet along the lower part of the trunk. The color is light brown to red; the sapwood is yellow. The grain is fine and straight and the wood takes on a fine polish; in fact, it must be finished to bring out the grain effectively. Its checking and warping characteristics are favorable for carving, and it is in much demand for costly interior trim. Sculptors use this wood for some of their most serious work. Cherry is an excellent medium for natural finished birds.

All fruit trees are good carving woods; some (the apple, for instance) possess a beautiful grain complex, being widely used for tool handles (planes, hand drills, etc.). The wood-carver should always be on the lookout for orchards being torn out and make arrangements for procuring the boles. As most of these trees are of relatively small length and breadth, they may be given the PEG-1000 treatment to stabilize them and carved while green. (*See* Chapter 12 on Checking, Shrinking, and Blemishes.)

All native woods may be used successfully for carving if they are properly dried. Some are preferred more than others, but all of them have some advantages. Sour and black gum, tupelo, and pepperidge may be found in low wetlands along the Atlantic coast and as far west as Arkansas. They are excellent carving woods when seasoned properly. The grain is sometimes very complex in the gums, now and then twisting spirally around the bole. The oaks are used where rugged texture and effect are desired. The grain might be too conspicuous for birds because the carving should be given a natural finish. To carve such hard woods for polychromed birds is unwise. Charles Graveney's Cormorant group (Figure 65) appears to have been carved of oak; so in the hands of a skilled sculptor open-grained woods may be used to create certain effects. Elm, maple, and locust are other woods which the carver should consider. They all should be seasoned thoroughly before using or given the chemical treatment. I am anxious to carve a large figure of black locust. I have used it for some bird mounts and it seems so smooth and even-grained when planed with a sharp tool.

Redwood has not been mentioned. It is not very plentiful in the East in large boards or timbers. Some large growth wood carves well, but it, like red cedar, is prone to split easily. When finished, its color is much like mahogany and the layman can hardly tell the difference. There are two main species: the big trees, *Sequoia,* and the heavier redwood, used for siding for houses and for other surfaces where weather resisting woods are necessary. Some of the Sequoia are thousands of years old—were fair-sized trees when Christ was born. They are now protected from the lumberman's axe, but other redwoods are being used for lumber in vast quantities. At the present rate of consumption they, too, will become scarce. Although a continent apart, both species are close relatives of the bald cypress.

Cypress. There are three well-known cypresses, the yellow, Lawson, and bald cypress. The latter is an eastern tree growing in the southern swamps as far north as Sussex County, Delaware. It is often entirely surrounded by water. The roots are well buttressed for this reason and they usually send up conical forms, called "knees," which are very light in weight and good carving media. The wood of the tree is denser than white pine. It is easily worked, however, and the old growth timber is in demand for interior decorations, panels, trim, and doors.

Yellow cypress, sometimes called Alaska cedar, closely resembles white cedar. It ranges in the Northwest from the coast to an elevation of 7,000 feet. It is slow in growth, a tree 275 years old measuring only 20 inches in girth. The wood is quite yellow, a bright sulphur color, has fine, straight grain and is easily worked.

In contrast to yellow cypress is the magnificent Lawson cypress attaining a height of 180 feet and 4½ feet in diameter, the largest tree of the genus. It is located in the fog belt of the West Coast and, unlike bald cypress, ranges to an elevation of 5,000 feet. It is widely cultivated, both in this country and abroad. The wood is yellow and has good carving texture. All of the cypresses are highly weather resistant.

Readers who are convenient to ocean beaches or the shores of large rivers may collect driftwood in considerable quantities. Occasionally an old shipwreck will yield some large timbers of teak. As mentioned previously, the carver should be on the lookout for carving woods. When dried out, old waterlogged boles are excellent media.

Many wood-carvers prefer to use the exotic woods for several reasons, but these media should not be used by the beginner. They are too expensive for his inexperienced efforts and, in some instances, are sold by the pound rather than by the board or linear foot. They should never be used for polychromed birds, except in the case of inlaid colored veneers, which is quite different than the painting technique. The exotic wood should be given a natural finish, perhaps only a sealer to stabilize the carving and make it dustproof. Some sculptors use "Minwax" for this purpose. In any event, exotic woods are used mainly for their grain effects and any treatment to emphasize this dominant characteristic is satisfactory. For the benefit of wood-carvers who desire to carve some of the foreign woods (this is the ultimate goal of all carvers), the more popular and better known species will be discussed briefly.

Coco Bolo. This wood is the choice of many sculptors. It is heavy, dense, but with an even grain texture. It ranges in color from yellow to red to purple. It takes on a very high polish.

Lignum Vitae. This is the hardest and heaviest of all woods used by the carver. It, too, possesses a very fine grain, so fine that it is barely perceptible. It works crisply and is jet black in some grain formations and golden brown to green in others. Its texture is tough; mallets are made of this wood. It is so dense that it sinks in water.

Ebony. This is the king of carving woods. Its regal rights are due largely to its jet black color. It is not suitable for some types of carvings, but in other types where an exotic effect is desired, it cannot be surpassed. Ebony has a fine grain structure. It works crisply, but can be carved easily with razor-sharp tools. It takes a very high polish and is superb for certain sculptural work. A raven, for example, or any black bird is effective if carved in ebony. It is very expensive. I recently purchased a square foot of ¾″ gaboon ebony; it cost me $7.50. Even the beginner should have pieces of ebony in his shop for pupils of birds' eyes and other spots requiring similar emphasis.

Rosewood. This is probably nature's most beautiful wood. It is excellent for making costume jewelry, as shown in Figure 11. In bird carving it should be used for highly decorative effects and by experienced carvers. John Rood's bird (Figure 66) could well have been carved in rosewood instead of mahogany. Some of his other miniatures, too, could have been carved from this wood with good effects. Rosewood is deep red with an almost black grain integrating its structure. It carves well and takes on an excellent polish like the other exotic species. Its greatest use is in the manufacture of musical instruments. It is presently listed by some suppliers at $.60 per pound in logs.

Teakwood. No list of carving woods would be complete without the famous teak of southeastern Asia. Kipling's description of elephants hauling teak logs from the swamps of Burma, India, and Thailand is readily called to mind:

> Elephants a-piling teak
> In the sludgy, squdgy creek,

In former days it was the perfect wood for shipbuilding. It weathered well, was durable, and its oily texture tended to discourage tiny sea organisms that are prone to foul ships' hulls when they remain in water for long periods of time. Recently a friend visiting the family told of the old naval ships which President Theodore Roosevelt sent around the world during the early days of Japan's confrontation with this nation. Their steel hulls were lined on the inside with heavy teak timbers throughout their entire length *below* the waterline. If a steel projectile pierced the steel hull no great danger to the ship would result because the fragmented wood timbers could be stuffed with rags, cotton waste, or other material from the inside. When the vessels were scrapped there was a great demand for the teak timbers by carvers and furniture makers. It does not necessarily require a finish since the natural oil in the wood results in a lovely surface when polished. The wood is scarce and difficult to obtain, but for carving purposes it is available for craftsmen who do not mind the expense. All carvers dream of owning a teak log and carving a masterpiece.

Teak is light to dark brown with characteristic dark streaks. It carves well and easily, but is somewhat gritty, quickly dulling the carving tools. It is excellent wood for costume jewelry, for abstracts, and other decorative effects. Any carving of teak, if skillfully executed, possesses an appeal all its own.

Bird carving in recent years has taken a turn toward the more sculptural technique. As indicated earlier, sculptors do not lean noticeably toward painted works that are so popular with the public. Some of our best carvers are using woods that have a unique and beautiful grain structure for their media, depending on the grain formation to enhance their work. The art is akin to the use of highly figurative grain of burls, crotches, and other parts of trees in veneers to make sophisticated furniture. Even pictures without the use of pigments are skillfully made, using veneers alone to emphasize the various color effects. Some suppliers of expensive veneers offer kits with already cut and matched veneers to simulate the masterpieces of the painting artists, leaving only the work of gluing the "jigsaw" parts to a background of plywood. After the surface has been finely finished, the pictures are quite decorative and sometimes spectacular in their effect.

For decorative purposes the stylized and abstract forms of birds are ideal subjects for expensive woods, either native or exotic. One of the better known English carvers, Charles Graveney, makes use of the grain to enhance his subjects. His *Cormorant* group has already been cited as an example of expert craftsmanship (Figure 65). His other subjects are beautiful naturally finished figures varying from seals and fish, to abstract figures. His *Ruth and Naomi* is a beautiful work of abstract art done in English walnut. Hardly less interesting is his *Cricketer* in willow. I know of two other craftsmen who carve beautiful birds, emphasizing the natural finished form rather than the realistic polychromed effect. One carver specializes in Peruvian mahogany and the other uses American black walnut. The *Goliath Heron* by Charles Chase (Figure 67) is a superb example of a carving bringing out the grain effects of the medium which, in turn, enhances the subject.

Actually, any kind of wood may be used to carve beautiful models. The skill and imagination of the carver are much more important than the kind of wood used; remember, however, John Rood's dictum that the choice should be in keeping with the subject. Rood's sculpture, *Johnny Appleseed,* is carved in applewood; his *Smasher* from tough oak. The skilled fingers guided by an active, artistically fertile mind can make a common piece of yellow pine come alive. Lack of wood, like the lack of ideas, is no excuse for the ambitious carver whose fingers itch to grasp his carving tools. Ah! Here is the rub! But the creative impulse and the fortitude to bring forth the imaginative image from a wooden block is the "Open Sesame."

Now the lessons are over! You are on your own course, my patient carver, without a pilot. A *bon voyage* to you in your exciting adventure on the high seas of carving. When you finally reach your port may the birds you have carved, scattered all over the land or lining the shelves of your shop, be convincing evidence of your arrival. Even so, may the chips of the master continue to fall profusely to the floor, sharp and crisp. When the imprisoned bird has escaped the bonds of his shapeless block and stands poised majestically on his perch before you, may he speak to you in unheard words of praise and adoration; may his message stir your soul in grateful appreciation of your will to excel and your determination to carve and carve until the perfect day.

Chapter 17

PICTURE GALLERY OF CARVINGS BY THE LEADING WILDFOWL CARVERS OF AMERICA

This chapter has been designed to illustrate to the readers the art of the best bird-carvers in this country. There may be others just as gifted but they are not known to me, nor do they exhibit their work in bird-carving shows, several of which have national significance. Some of the carvers represented are not only experts but they are "tops" in any group of skilled carvers of wildlife. They are always invited to exhibit their work at the nationally famous shows and collectors from all parts of the country attend the exhibits to observe their work.

An effort has been made to illustrate the various techniques in both the natural and polychromed finished birds. To illustrate the technique of leaving raw tool marks showing in a rustic manner, the picture of Charles Graveney's *Cormorants* was borrowed from the Tate Gallery in London, England. To show the possibility of abstracts, John Rood's bird was included, although his model is not strictly an abstract. In addition to carving in the round, high relief work is illustrated by several excellent examples (Black's painted *Mallards Dropping In;* Hilleary's electric-needle-treated *Lesser Scaup Ducks;* and Hanks' natural finished birds). Also, there are sculptured forms, birds carved from the solid log—somewhat different than birds and waterfowl carved from blocks of wood used in regular decoy duck designs. Charles Chase's *Goliath Heron* is an excellent example in this category. Also, my *Drake Mallard* (not the superimposed duck) and *Bald Eagle* satisfy the conditions of true sculpture. With such varied methods, the beginner has a wide choice in deciding the kind of birds he will carve—not including a technique of his own.

Study the pictures carefully and critically. Get acquainted with the work of these master carvers. You will hear and learn more about them as you progress in your carving activities.

John A. Hilleary

Mr. Hilleary was mentioned in Chapter 13. The photograph shows two Lesser Scaup ducks in flight. They are superimposed on a neutral background of plywood.

Mr. Hilleary is one of the few carvers who use an electric needle to finish their birds. They are carved in high relief, nearly in the round.

His work is an excellent example of skillful carving and outstanding originality in the carving art.

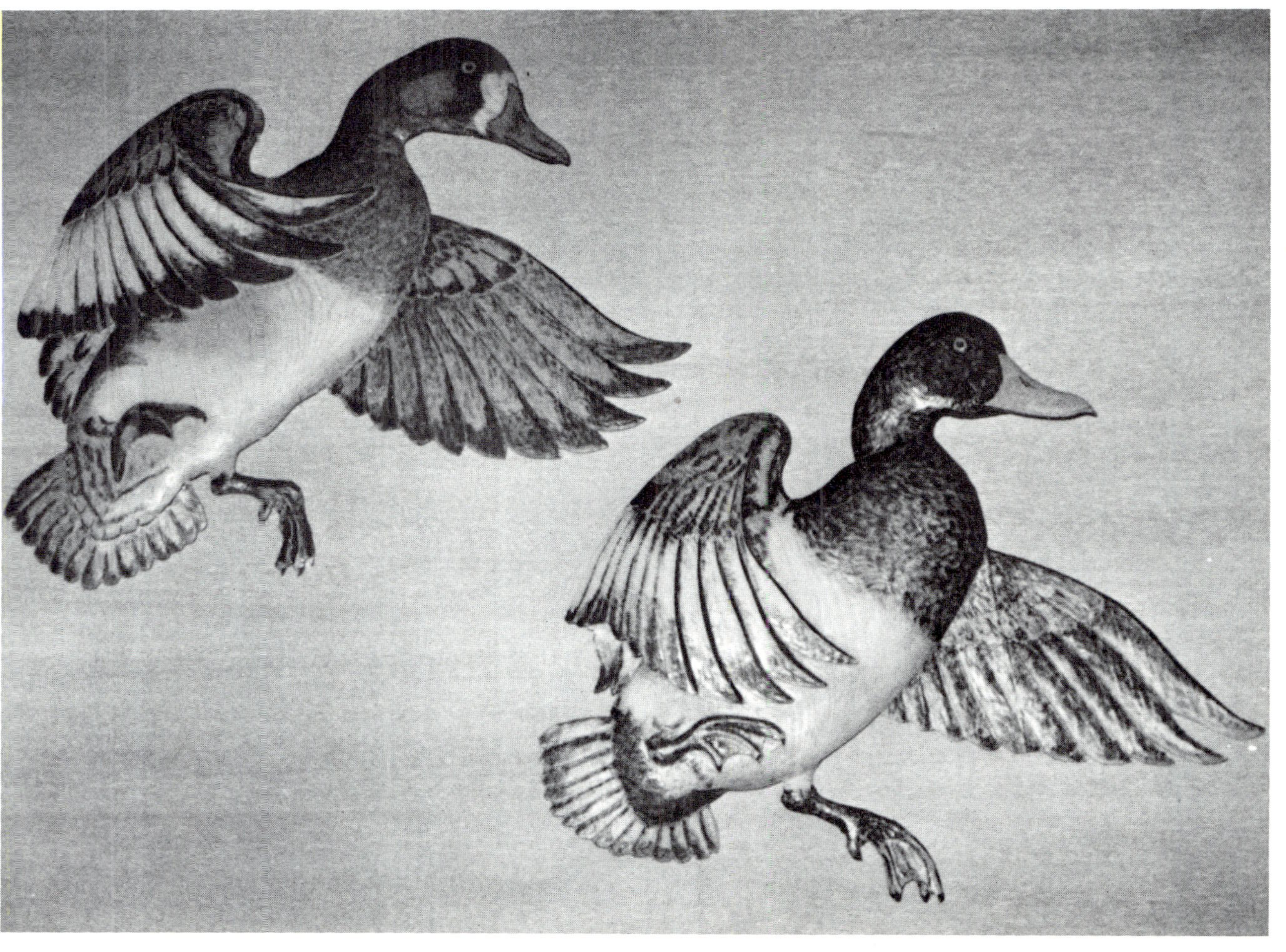

Figure 64. *Lesser Scaup Ducks*, by John Hilleary.

Charles Graveney

The Cormorant group shown in the photograph reposes in the Tate Gallery at London, England. It was reproduced to illustrate the chiseled texture of a skilled artist. Carved from what appears to be an oak block, the birds are expressive and all "Cormorant." The beauty of the haughty poise of the larger one complements the stoic expression of its companion.

A smooth or polychrome finish would not have been nearly so effective. This technique requires considerable skill, belying the impression received by the layman. When the beginner can make each chisel stroke count for so much form he can appreciate "removing all chips which are not Cormorant."

"There is always a fascination in being able to make something, whether it serves a utilitarian purpose or fills an emotional or esthetic need, and wood in its variety, being clean and readily obtainable, has always been a universal material to satisfy these demands," says this skilled English carver.

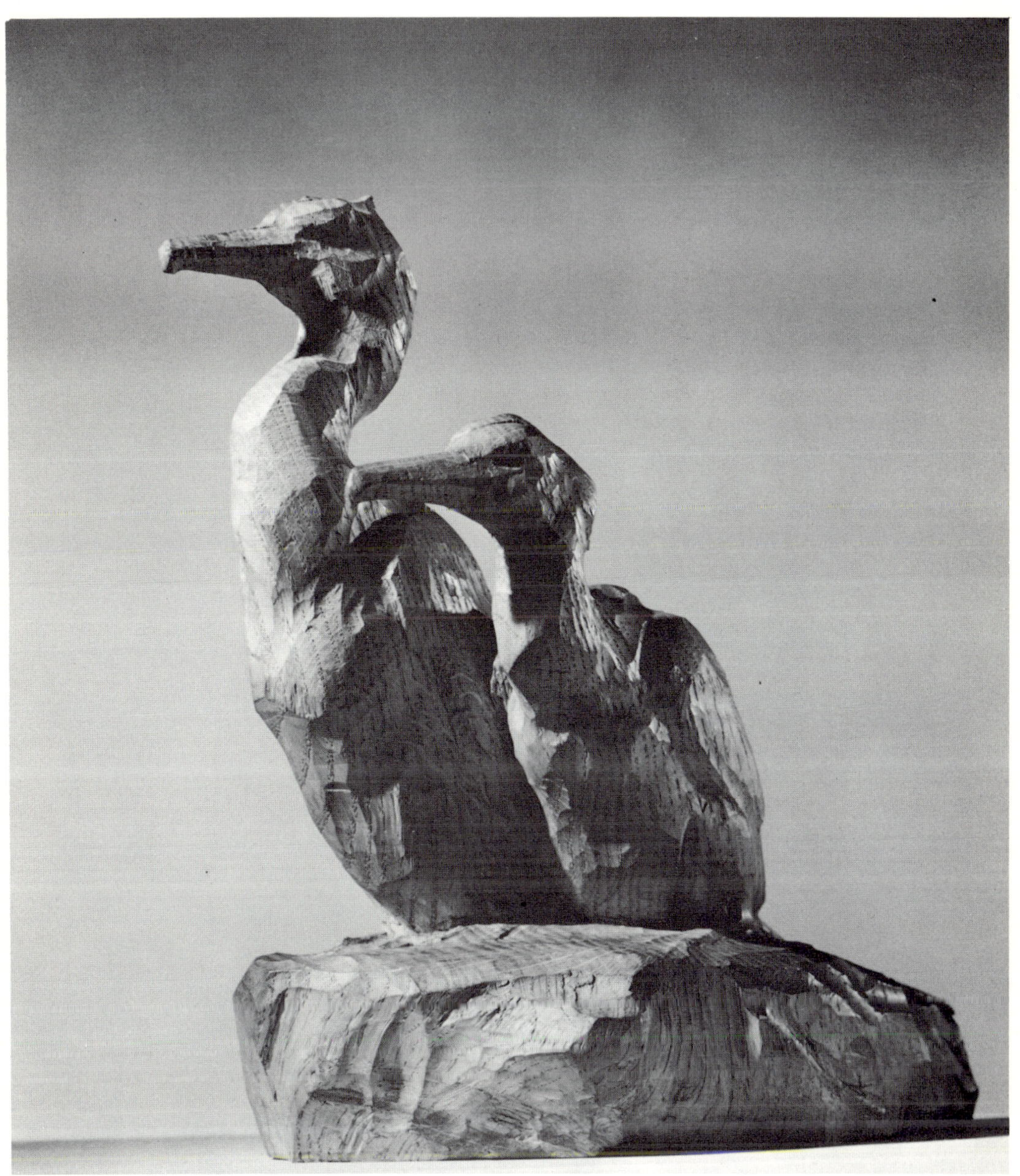

Figure 65. *Cormorants,* by Charles W. Graveney. Tate Gallery, London.

John Rood

The bird shown in the photograph (opposite) represents one of John Rood's early carvings. It is a near abstraction, formed almost entirely with a wood rasp. To a layman this bird may seem a simple idea to imagine and to carve. To carve, yes, with some degree of skill, but to conceive as a creative product of the mind, no. I have been trying to think of an abstract bird since I started this book. I am no nearer to a satisfying idea than when I started.

John Rood is referred to several times in this work. He is an excellent craftsman. "He is a moving force in the art world—a human, sincere artist with a strong sense of direction and a feeling for the American scene. Critics and gallery-goers have been struck by his impressions of American life at its grass roots as expressed in his sculpture."

Beginners in wood carving will be wise to study the techniques of this skillful artist.

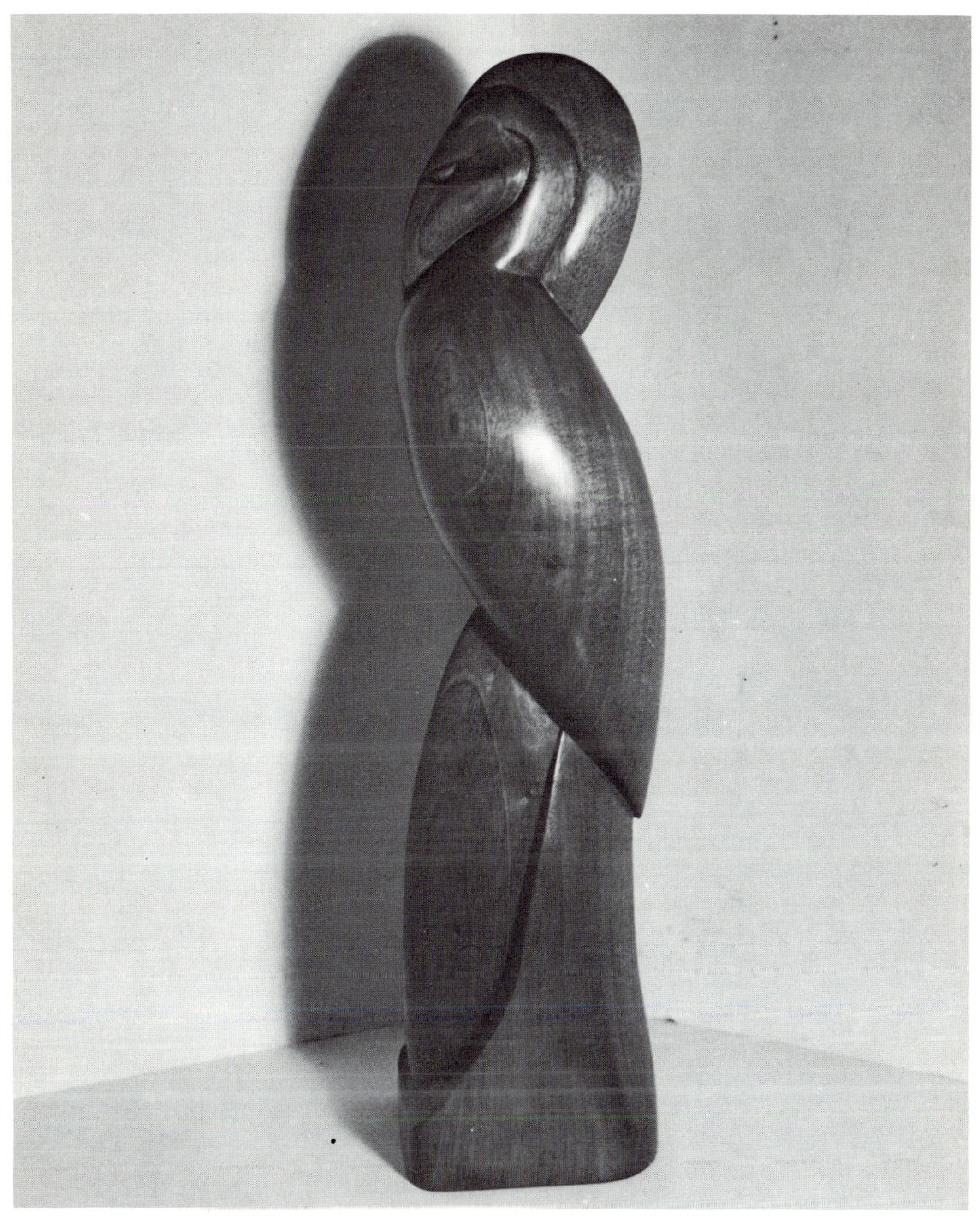

Figure 66. *Bird*—mahogany, by John Rood (1937).

Charles G. Chase

Mr. Chase could be considered one of the "egghead" members of the exclusive tribe of bird-carvers. He writes magazine articles; he is an explorer, economist, engineer and teacher. Two years ago, during one of his globe-hopping trips, he saw a Goliath Heron preening itself on the banks of the river Nile. He took motion pictures of the large bird and when he arrived home he used one of the film's frames to model the beautiful carving shown on the opposite page.

The Goliath Heron of East Africa is about 5′ tall, so the carving is about one-half size—actually 29″ high. It is carved in black walnut and given a clear natural finish.

The observer will note that this excellent example of sculpture is not pigmented in any way except where the sapwood shows. Also, the carving technique is smooth and free of feather and chip marks. Note, too, how the grain of the wood enhances the composition of the carving.

Mr. Chase is another "Down Easter," so the public may expect his "salty" nature to show through his formal polish. He certainly has savored his work to suit the discriminating taste of the connoisseur. It is truly a fine example of the wood-carver's art.

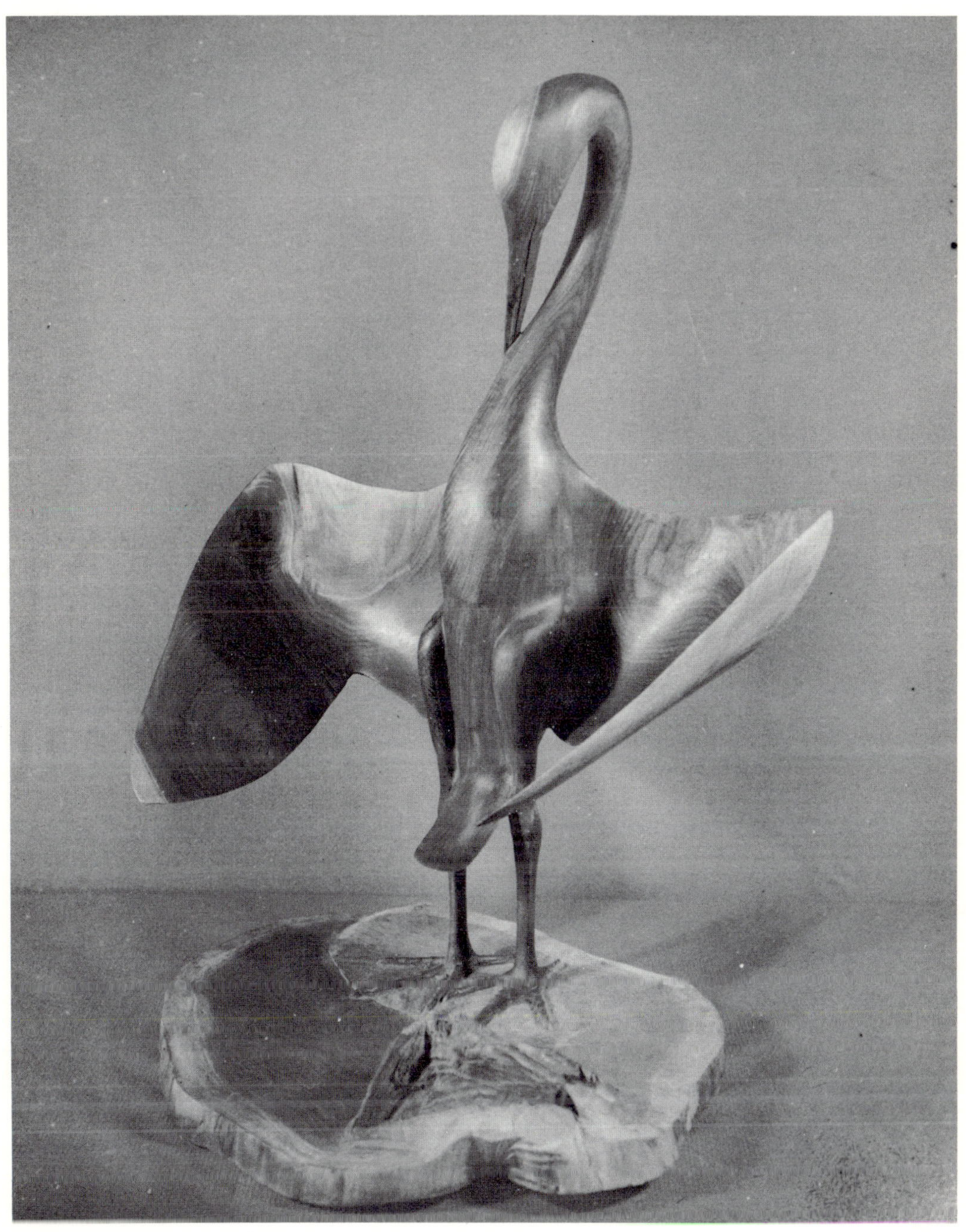

Figure 67. *Goliath Heron,* by Charles G. Chase.

The Ward Brothers: Stephen and Lemuel

There are few, if any, bird-carvers who have been in the business longer than Steve and Lem. They started more than fifty years ago and have been selling their work to discriminating collectors over the continent during those years.

The Ward Brothers have been featured in many national magazines, including the *National Geographic.* Thousands of individuals visit their modest shop annually. No fewer than six of the foremost carvers on the Eastern Shore have been influenced by their work—some of them actually have been taught their craft by these sensitive and masterful artists.

Lem does all of the painting. "Just don't have the patience for this kind of work," says Steve. But he compensates by keeping the saws and other tools razor-sharp. Both carve their birds and ducks from white pine or basswood.

The Ruffed Grouse is not native to the Creek community where the Wards live and create their superb models; so the photograph is of a bird carved to order for some admiring collector.

The Wards are two years behind in their orders, unable to keep abreast of the demands for their wildfowl carvings.

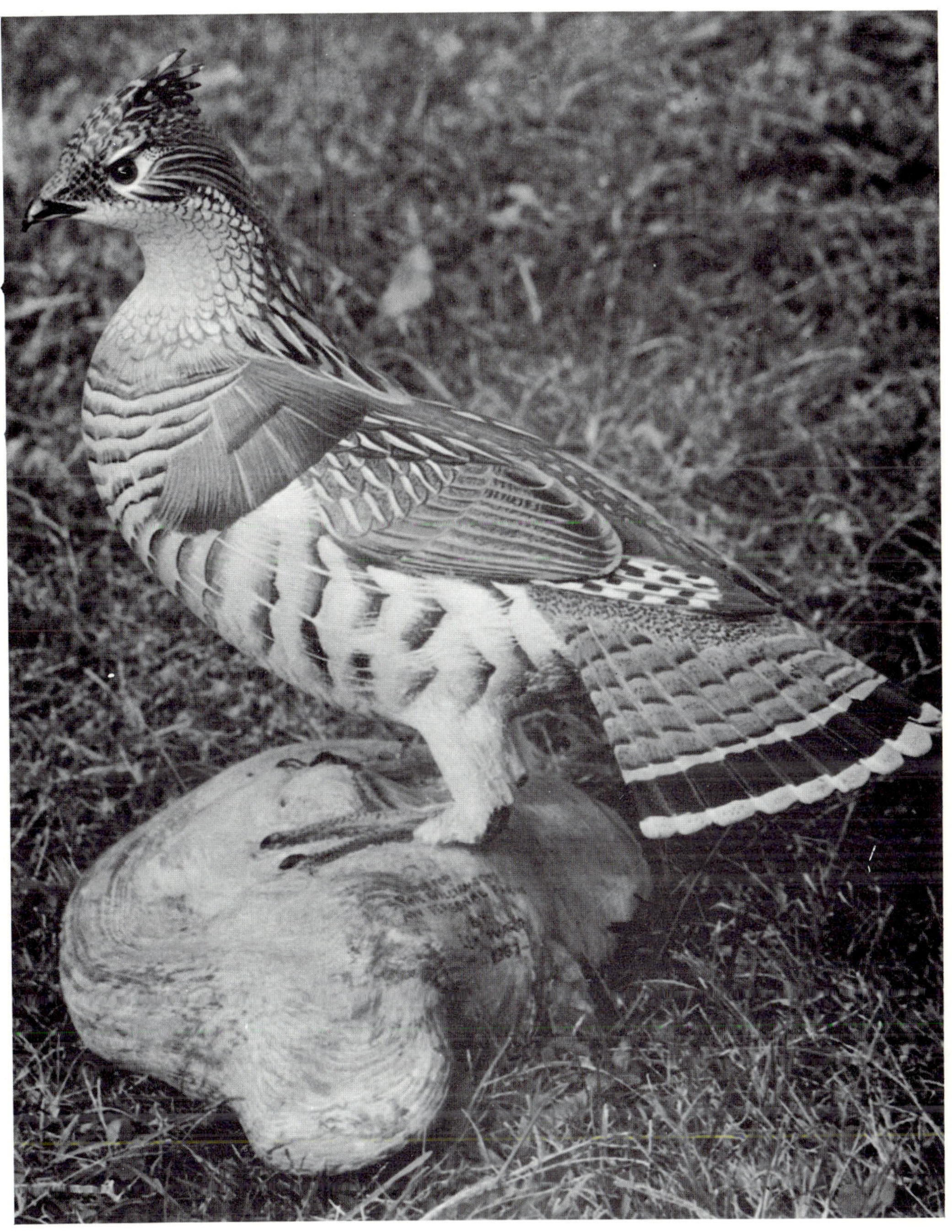

Figure 68. *Ruffed Grouse,* by Lemuel Ward.

Arnold T. Melbye

Mr. Melbye is one of the better known bird-carvers. His work is sought after by most connoisseurs of the art; his birds may be found in many private collections.

He is one of the few carvers to have the envious distinction of exhibiting in the Smithsonian Institute by invitation of its staff members. At this writing his birds, shown in the opposite photograph, repose in the diorama. The birds are all native to the fields and beaches of his community, South Yarmouth, Mass. The Evening Grosbeak is a subject seldom carved by wild-life carvers, but there he stands on a piece of driftwood in all of his yellow, white, and black splendor. Other birds in the photograph are: A pair of Pheasants (Quail), Ruffed Grouse, Chickadee, Blue Jay, Cardinal, Greater Yellowlegs, three Sandpipers, and what appears to be a Robin.

Mr. Melbye carves from natural models, usually birds he has shot and stuffed himself.

He has been called a "carver's carver," which is praise enough for any artist of the jackknife and chisel.

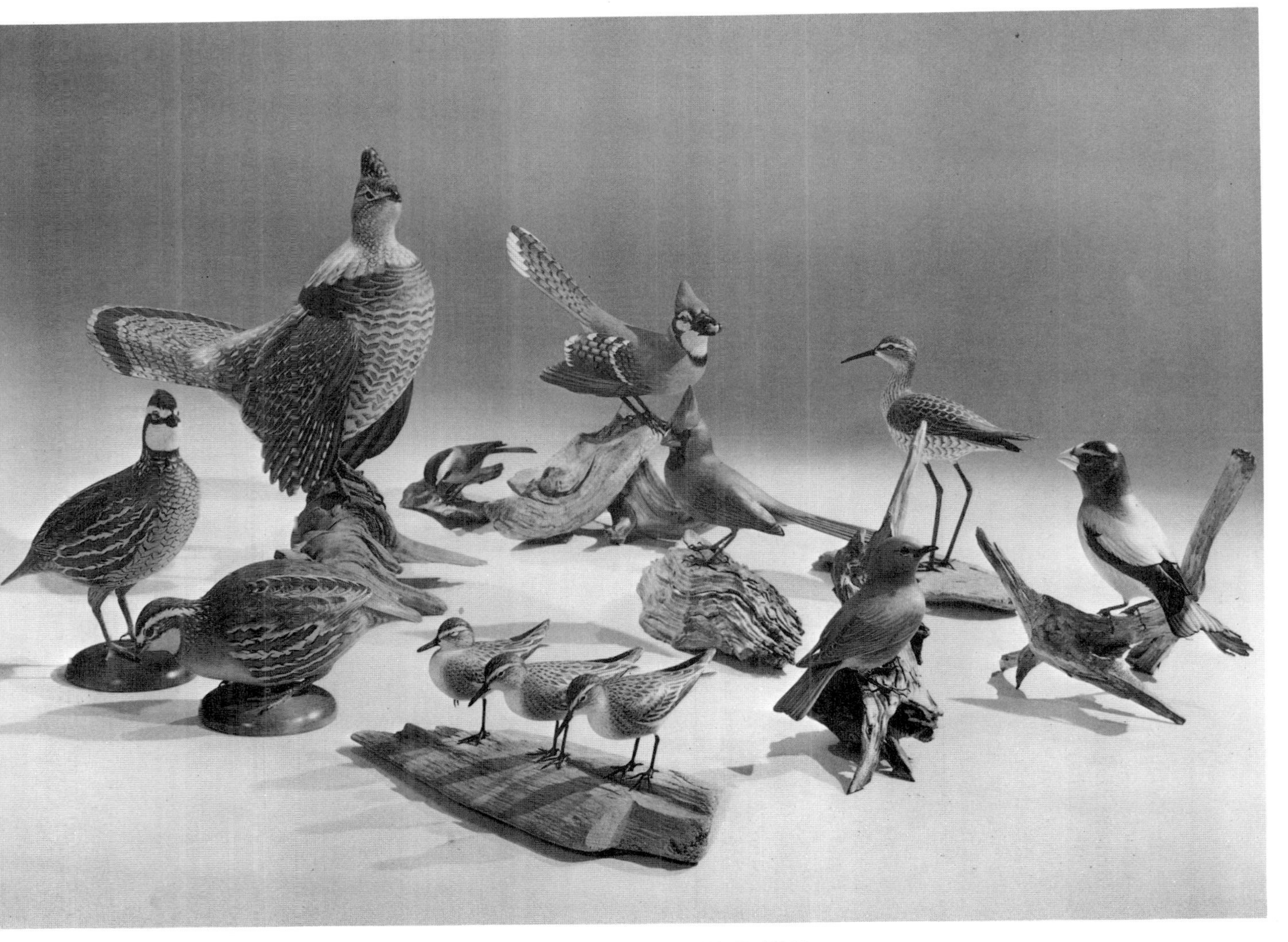

Figure 69. *Birds*, by Arnold T. Melbye.

Wendell Gilley

Mr. Gilley is the immediate past president of the National Wood-carver's Association. He is the author of *Bird Carving* and is an authority in the bird-carving art. I have quoted him on several occasions.

Mr. Gilley has carved over 5,000 birds and they are now scattered throughout the world. His latest commission was for an Eagle to be mounted on the bulkhead of the *Peloha,* a ketch being built in Holland. Presidents and governors own his birds. He carved his first one in 1930 and has been busy with his chisel and mallet ever since.

Mr. Gilley is a "Down Easter," too. His carvings and humor reflect his salty thinking.

The photograph is of a Bald Eagle carved life-size. All of the feathers are carved and each wing is made and carved separately, of wood 3″ thick. Head and tail are separate pieces of wood also. The bird measures almost 36″ from head to tail and the back wing measures nearly 48″ long. The Eagle is owned by Robert T. Thayer who lives near Mt. Vernon, on the Potomac.

Mr. Gilley sent his photograph reinforced with a piece of ½″ plywood and accompanied by this message: "I know how the Post Office Department bends up photographs. Let's see them bend this one!"

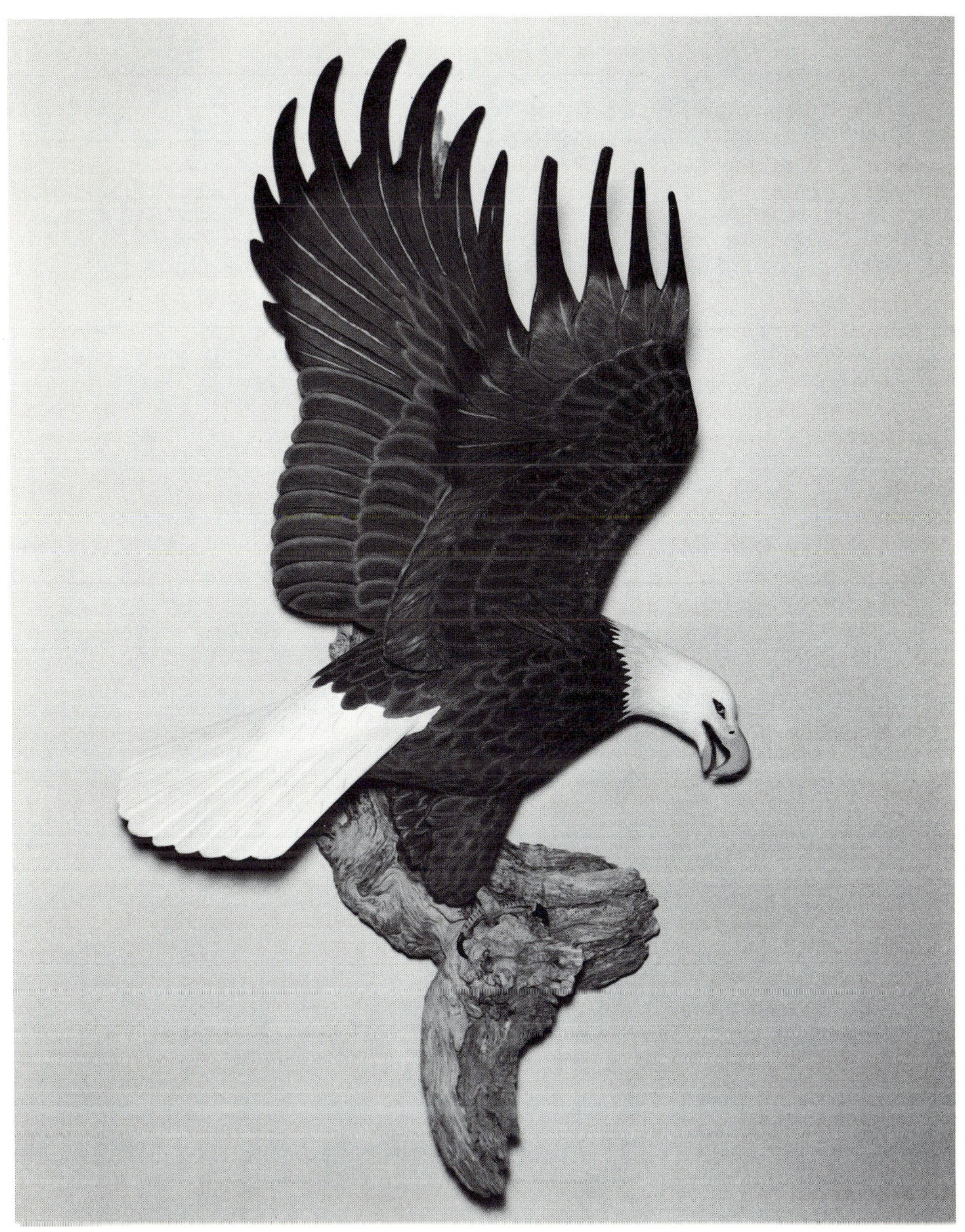

Figure 70. *Bald Eagle,* by Wendell Gilley.

Robert and Virginia Warfield

The Warfields have spent most of their lives in some form of art pursuit. For many years Bob made custom furniture and Virginia was an accomplished potter. After moving to New Hampshire they pooled their interests and began carving birds on a full-time basis. They work as a team, with Bob doing all of the carving and Virginia doing the more difficult part—painting the birds to look as realistic as possible.

Bob carves in basswood and Virginia paints with oils. The birds are usually carved in miniature, the smaller the bird the more likely it is to approach full-scale size. They have carved and painted the likenesses of many songbirds and waterfowl. The couple themselves probably do not know how many different kinds of birds they have created.

The output of the Warfields is prolific judging by the material sent to me. Bob says their most productive season is from early fall to late winter.

The Tern represented in the photograph measures 10″; the Pheasant, 19″.

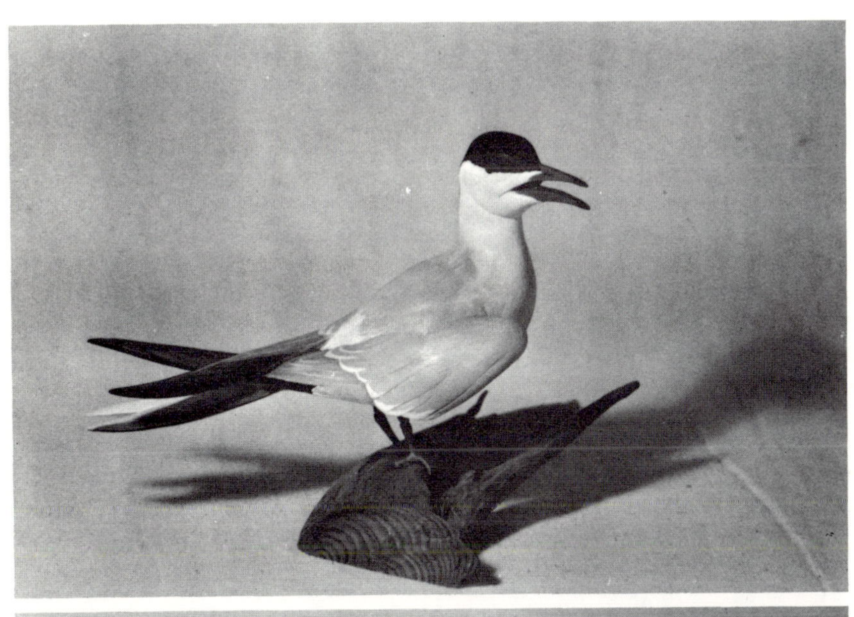

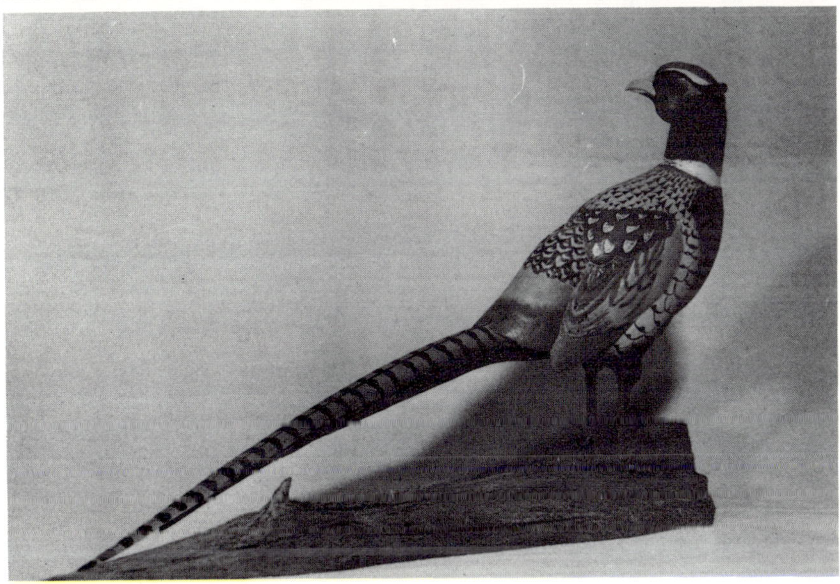

Figure 71. *Common Tern* (top), and *Pheasant* (bottom), by Robert and Virginia Warfield.

Gladys N. Black

Perhaps Rudyard Kipling was only expressing the findings of naturalists when he said: "The female of the species is more deadly than the male." This being so, why does the principle have a carry-over value in the manly art of bird carving? Imagine a woman carving birds of our fields, streams, and waterways and doing it as well—or better—than most men!

Mrs. Black seldom, if ever, takes a back seat among her carving peers. She is where the action is, performing her work on a high level with the best of them, irrespective of her sex. There are women painters, a whole raft full of them—but carvers—ah, here is the rub! At the moment only two other women wood-carvers come to mind: the exceptional Melvina Hoffman and Enid Bell. Both of these talented artists are sculptors, not bird-carvers. Mrs. Black has not had the mantle of a sculptor draped over her shoulders, but as a carver of wildlife she probably has no equal among her sex and few among the men carvers can do a better job.

An observer of Mrs. Black's work cannot fail to see the sympathetic understanding she has for her subjects, her delicacy of design, and the mastery she has over her carving tools. Her butterflies are the best evidence of her ingenuity and artistic ability. Her sensitivity to design is also reflected in the perches she selects for her birds. Could ever an old piece of "driftwood" be so ruggedly beautiful to offset the formal, cleverly carved and painted Hooded Mergansers! Experience spanning more than twenty-five years has coalesced into a sensitive artist who has climbed to the height of her profession.

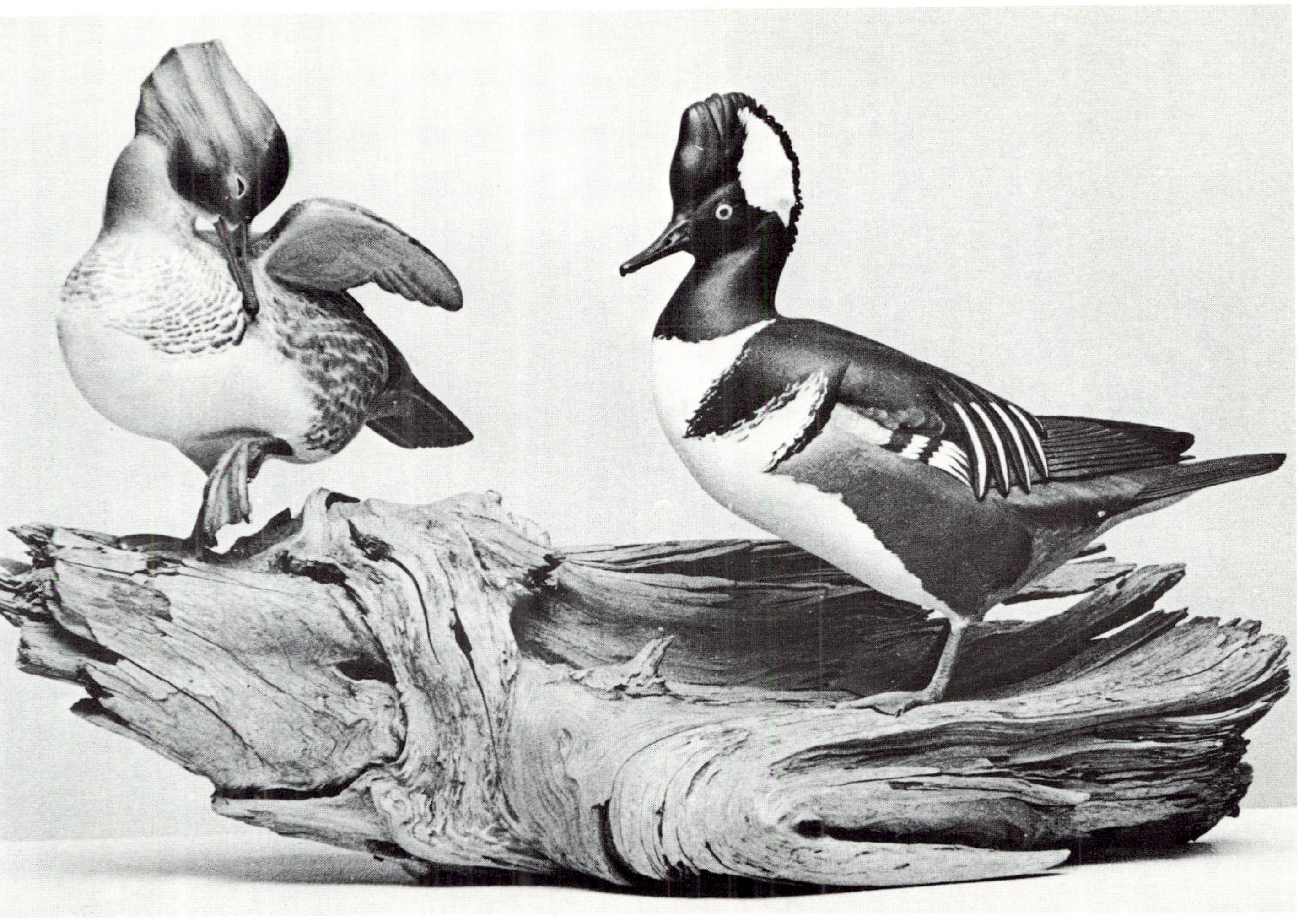

Figure 72. *Hooded Mergansers,* by Mrs. Gladys N. Black.

Davison B. Hawthorne

Davison Hawthorne is one of the best carvers on the Eastern Shore of Maryland. He calls his studio *Hawthorne House,* and no doubt collectors have beaten a path to his door. This year he has already won two "best in show" ribbons, one in the full-scale class with a hen Shoveller, and one in the miniature category with a half-size Yellowlegs. The occasion was the National Duck Carving Contest at Babylon, Long Island.

A mere glance at the Screech Owl shown in the photograph is convincing evidence of Mr. Hawthorne's knowledge of birds, and what is more, he knows how to use his chisel and mallet. Even without pigment the Owl would stand out as an example of expert carving precision. In fact, a sculptor would prefer the bird without finish. However, the judges in bird-carving exhibitions usually ignore a fine sculptural work in favor of a polychromed model. The collectors who have developed from decoy duck enthusiasts are chiefly responsible for this discrimination. If the bird appears ready to take off, they become interested. If it follows them around the room, they will purchase it.

Mr. Hawthorne's Owl has a quizzical expression. It appears to be sizing up the situation, trying to decide whether to fly away or just look wise.

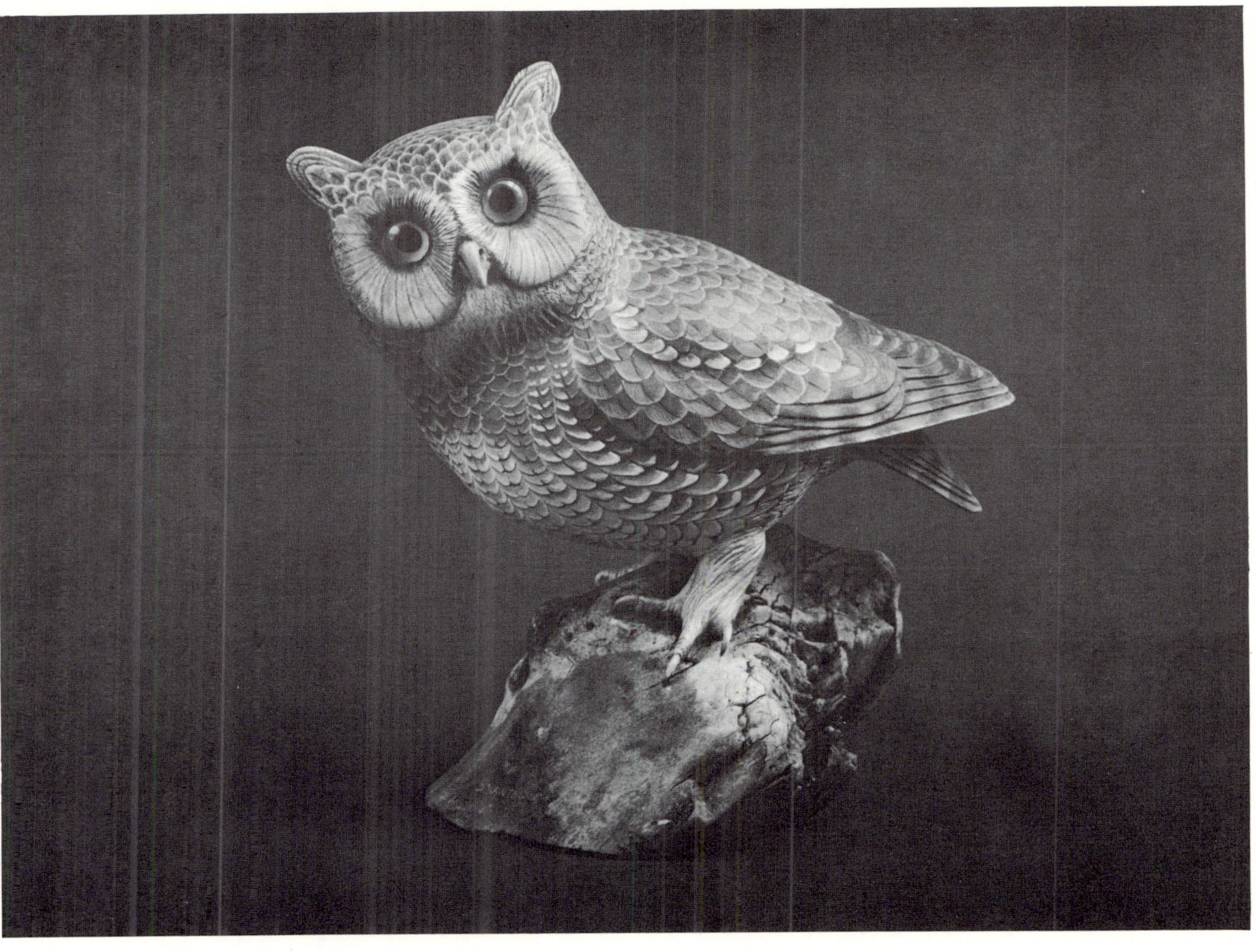

Figure 73. *Screech Owl,* by Davison B. Hawthorne (1968).

William L. Schultz

William Schultz has been associated with the Milwaukee Public Museum, Milwaukee, Wisconsin, for twenty years. What an ideal spot for a wildlife carver! He is versatile not only in forming his birds but in painting them. His skill with tools and paint probably accounts for his long tenure with the museum.

A study of the photograph will indicate his sensitive feelings for wildlife. Observe the poise of the uncommon Hudsonian Godwit preening its feathers. The more common Avocet stands proudly erect with slightly open bill. Both birds represent a happy combination of the painter's and the carver's art.

The perches seem to carry out the artistic scheme and lend a touch of the rustic to balance the otherwise formal carvings. The touch of the master carver has created two lovely birds, striking specimens of waterfowl.

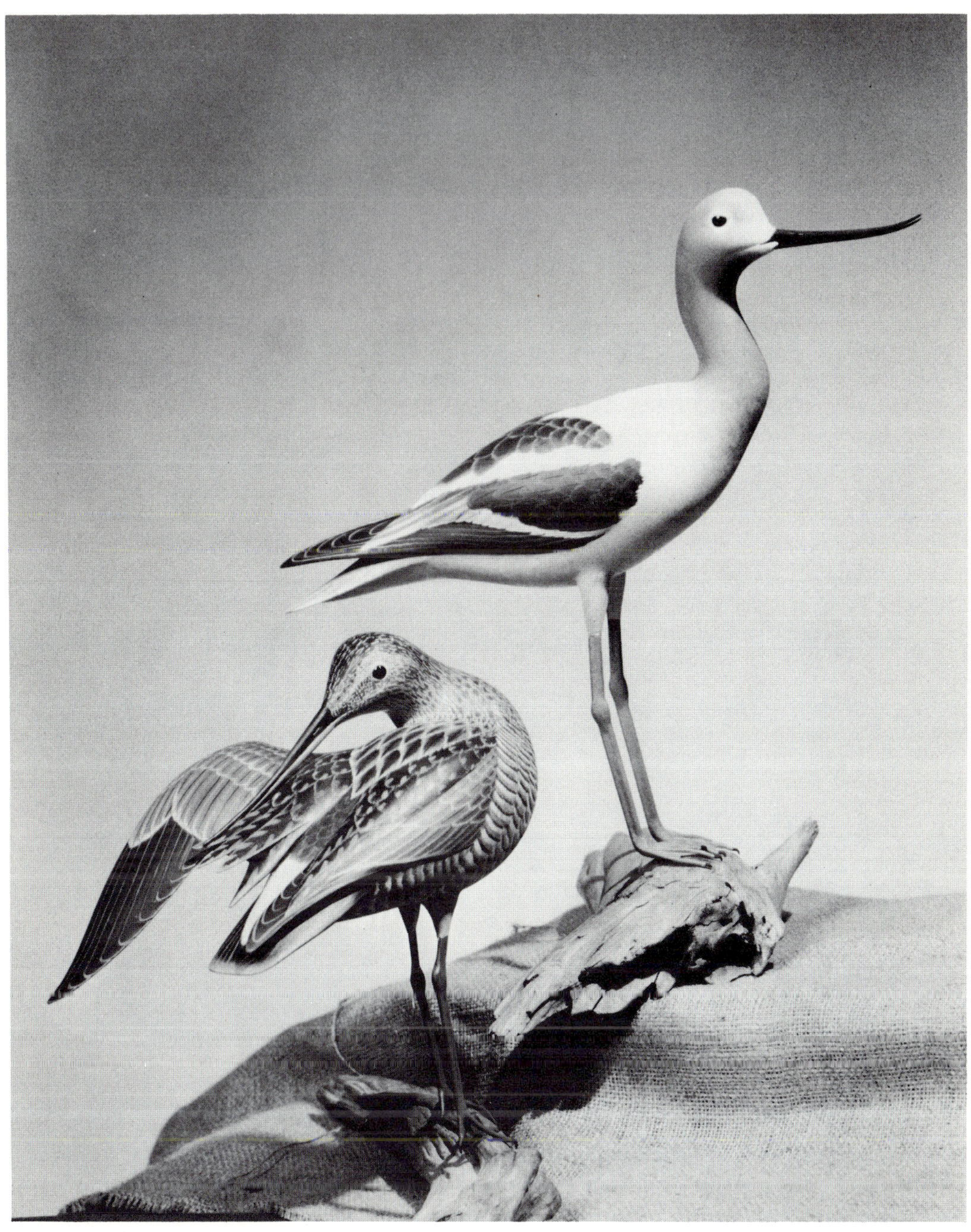

Figure 74. *American Avocet* (right), *Hudsonian Godwit* (breeding plumage) (left), by William L. Schultz.

Paul F. Nock

Paul Nock is another Eastern Shoreman, a versatile hobbyist and a wood-carver of the first rank.

When asked the trite question: "Where and how do you get your ideas?" he replied, "I don't believe there is any specific inspiration in my case. I love to carve; I'm fascinated by waterfowl, and I feel there is a real challenge to one's ability to carve and paint them in a realistic manner."

He also confesses, like all dedicated artists, that he is never entirely satisfied with his work. Nonetheless, his Drake Bufflehead won for him a first prize and best of the show at the National Carving Contest held at Babylon, Long Island, in June, 1967.

Mr. Nock uses white cedar and northern basswood for all of his carvings. They are all polychromed. His decorative birds are hollowed to within ½″ of their skin feathers to discourage checking (and, no doubt, with the flotation test in mind).

The drake Bufflehead measures 7½″ long; his drake Greenwing Teal measures 6″.

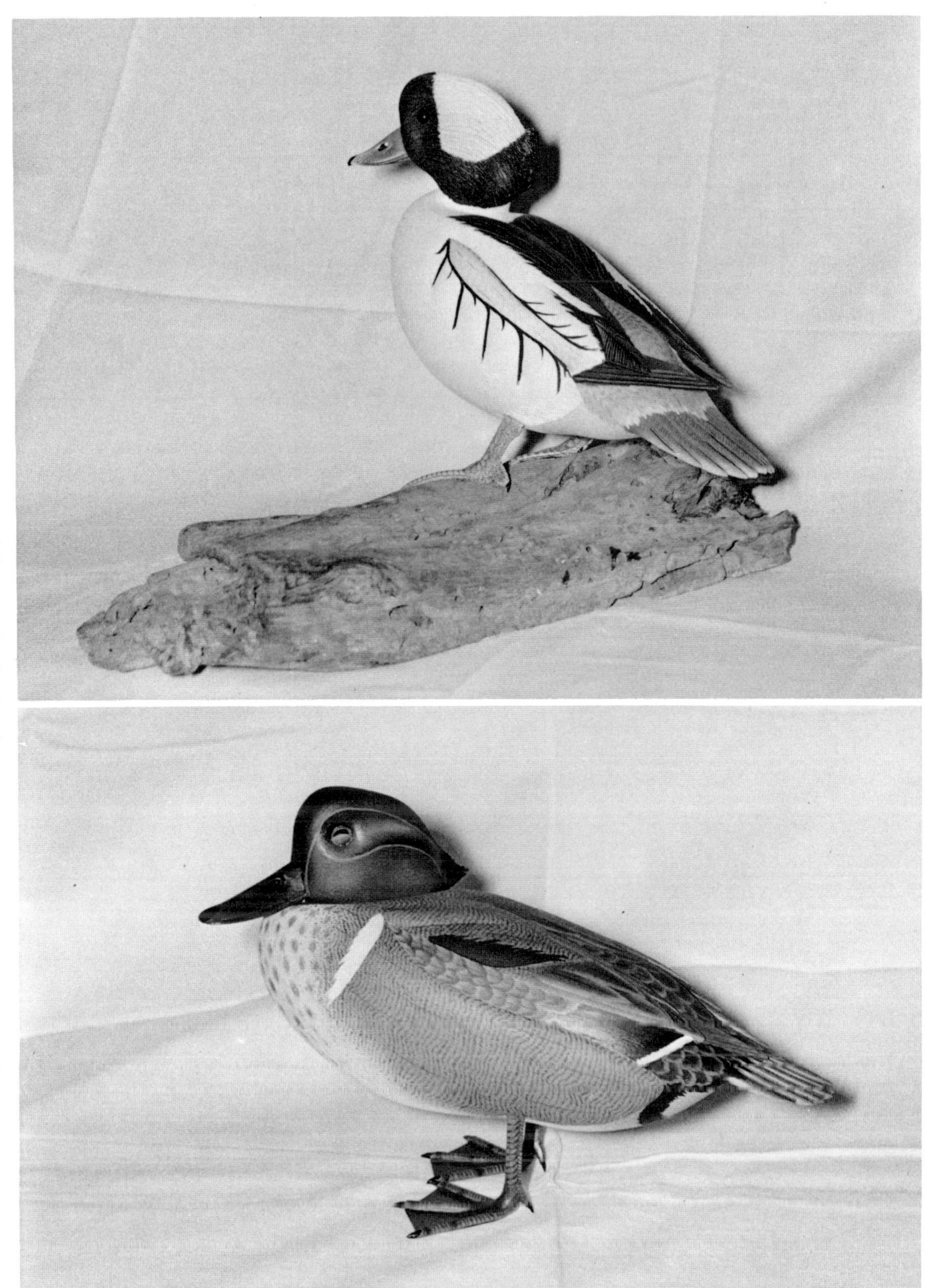

Figure 75. *Bufflehead Drake* (top), and *Greenwing Teal Drake* (bottom), by Paul F. Nock.

Harry V. Shourds

Harry Shourds represents the third generation of duck-carvers in his family. His grandfather was one of the first decoy-duck makers in southern New Jersey. His grandfather's and father's decoys are now collectors' items. With such an unusual background the fact that Mr. Shourds began carving at an early age is no accident. At the National Decoy Show, held in Babylon, Long Island, Mr. Shourds' carving of a Brant decoy won third place. "The thrill and excitement of this nearly bowled me over," he states.

Mr. and Mrs. Shourds operate a little shop which they call the "Duck's Nest." "I'm having trouble keeping up with the demands," he says—a problem not uncommon with popular bird-carvers.

As the photograph indicates, Mr. Shourds' decoys are painted in a stylized manner, a technique common among decoy-duck makers. The color markings are indicated but no attempt is made to paint in the feathers realistically. The head of the Mallard, however, is far from a stylized carving, indicating both skill and familiarity with his subject. He leaves the observer to guess how a wooden duck is able to "drop in" or take off without wires or some other hidden device in evidence.

The carving is full-size and is carved of soft wood.

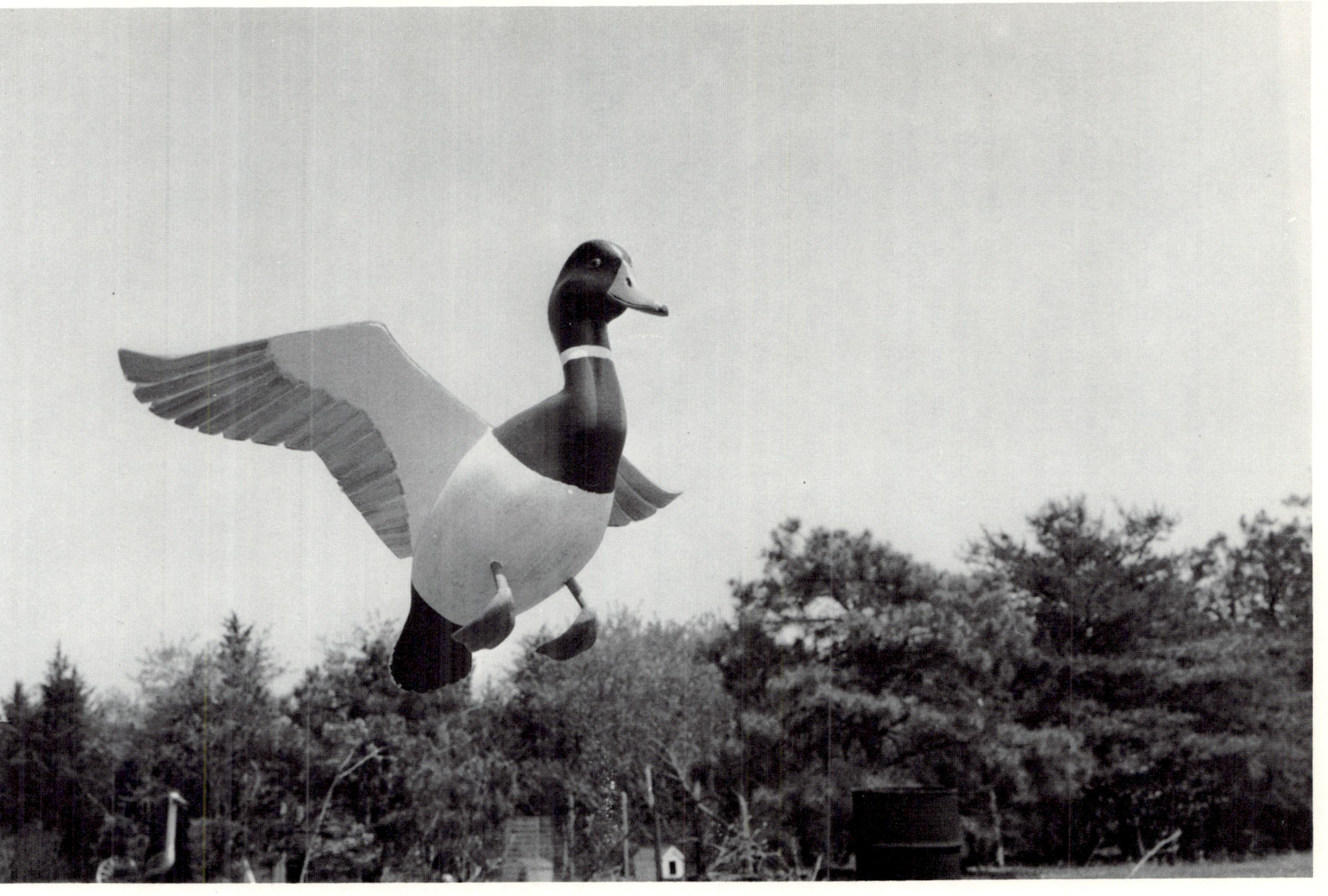

Figure 76. *Mallard Dropping In,* by Harry V. Shourds.

Homer D. Lawrence

Homer D. Lawrence is from Connecticut. He is one of today's foremost exponents of the fine art of bird carving, recognized as an expert in his own circles and by organizations interested in birds. He has been cited by the Audubon Society for his pair of Sicklebilled Curlews as representing the best examples of wood carving. His works are shown in all major exhibitions throughout the East.

Mr. Lawrence is one of the more formally trained bird-carvers. He studied at Silvermine College of Art. He was at one time a pupil of Karl Lang who, in turn, was a pupil of Gutzon Borglum, the man who chiseled from the native rock on Mount Rushmore the heads of four presidents—Washington, Jefferson, Lincoln, and Roosevelt—the largest modern sculpture in the world.

Mr. Lawrence carves chiefly from laminated basswood blocks. All of his work is polychromed, and to such realistic likeness that his birds appear ready to take off. No carver has painted wildfowl more expertly, but he modestly admits that this phase of his art work is done by a professional artist. Even so, Mr. Lawrence is one of the most sensitive individuals to the forms, characteristics, and color markings of the birds he carves.

The photograph shows a pair of Wood Ducks and a Ruffed Grouse. They are all full-size and made of basswood.

Note: Since this brief was written, Mr. Lawrence has passed on. He died suddenly while preparing for an exhibition of his work at the Wildlife Carving Show held in Salisbury, Md., in 1968.

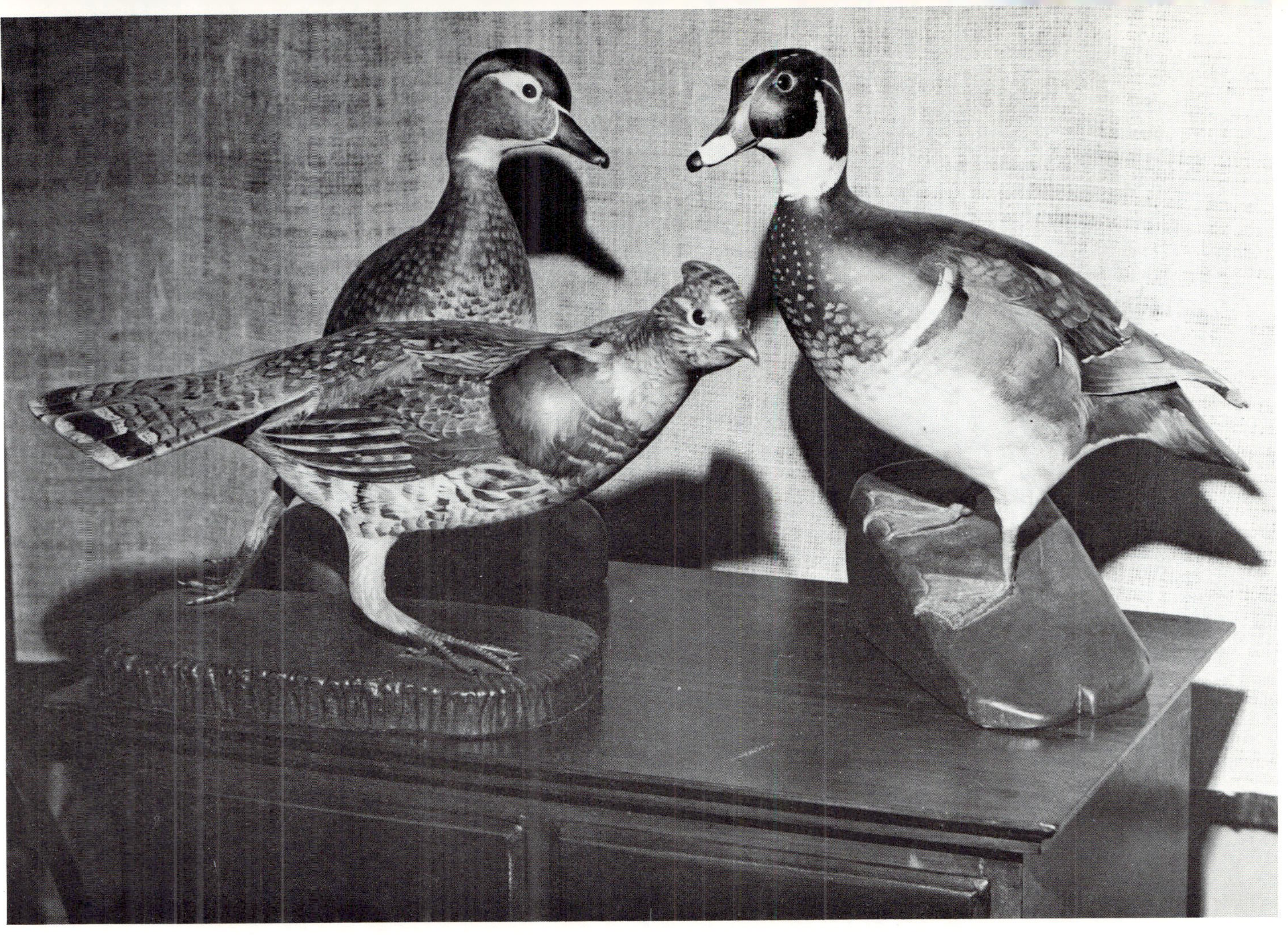

Figure 77. *Pair of Wood Ducks* and *Ruffed Grouse*, by Homer D. Lawrence.

William M. Birk

Working with wood seemed to be a natural characteristic of the Birk family. Mr. Birk's father was a lumberman and his grandfather was a cabinetmaker. Young Birk soon discovered that he was a "chip off the old block" and turned his talents to carving fiddles, or anything that appealed to him.

Without any formal training in the fine art of carving he taught himself to become a master decoy-duck maker. He carves working models, but his best work is represented by the decorative variety. The latter models are in such demand that Mr. Birk is already three years behind in his orders. One admiring collector has a standing order with him for at least one pair of his decorative ducks each year. Collectors are glad to pay $300.00 for a pair of his decorative decoys, but this price nets him less than the minumum Federal Government wage scale. It is the joy of carving, of creating a beautiful bird, that compensates.

Mr. Birk first came to the attention of collectors about eight years ago when his Canvasback duck entry won first place at the Syracuse Wildfowl Carving Exhibition. Since then he has won first-place ribbons all over the East Coast and as far west as Michigan.

Like most decoy-duck carvers, he hollows out his models for two specific reasons: (1) to discourage checking, and (2) to pass the flotation test, a criterion of the judging process. Models must float high out of the water like real birds or they are disqualified. Mr. Birk uses mainly white pine for his work, but unlike other carvers, he uses mahogany for the heads. He says that he can hold detail better with this wood.

In his younger days, Mr. Birk was an accomplished violinist. His bent for harmony and melody have now been sublimated in a visual channel to the enjoyment of his many friends and wildfowl lovers all over America.

The large duck in the photograph is a female Pintail. The miniatures are, left to right, a Canada Goose, of course, and what appear to be a Mallard, Black Duck, and Canvasback.

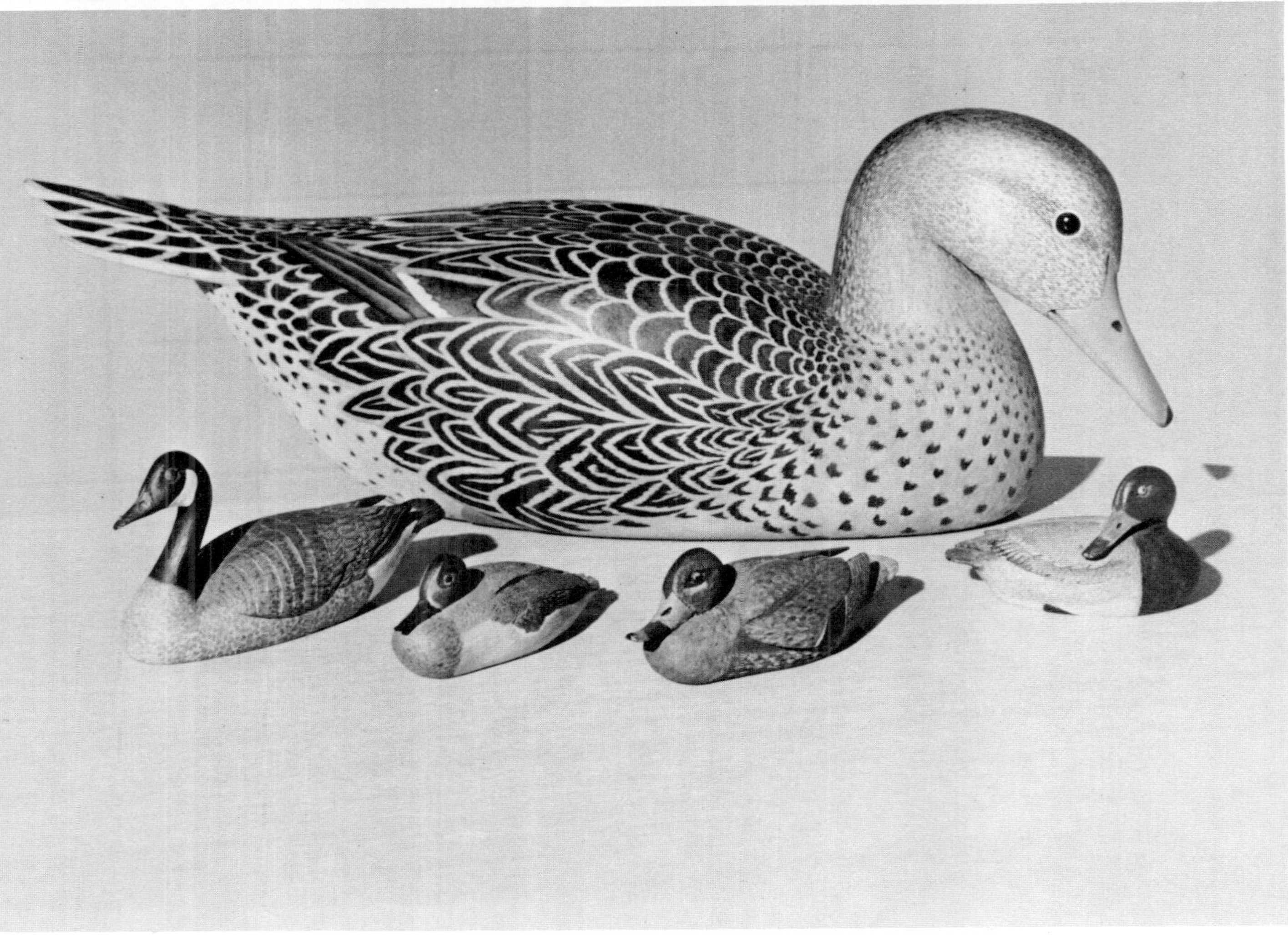

Figure 78. *Female Pintail,* by William M. Birk.

James N. Denny

Mr. Denny and I exhibited in the same show recently. He sold one of his ducks carved of redwood, and strangely enough it was finished naturally. I was impressed with his work and invited him to contribute to this chapter.

Mr. Denny's best work is in miniatures, small pins, similar to the birds used as a project in the first lesson of this book. They have considerably more detail and are carved more in the round.

Mr. Denny carves mainly in redwood and white pine. Since he has been carving for less than four years he does not consider himself as experienced as other Eastern Shore carvers represented in this chapter. But when I discovered his work I believed that his birds were of professional dimensions.

The reader can judge for himself the skill of this young carver by observing the Wood duck and Blackhead in the opposite photograph. Not only are they carved expertly but they are painted with a high degree of skill.

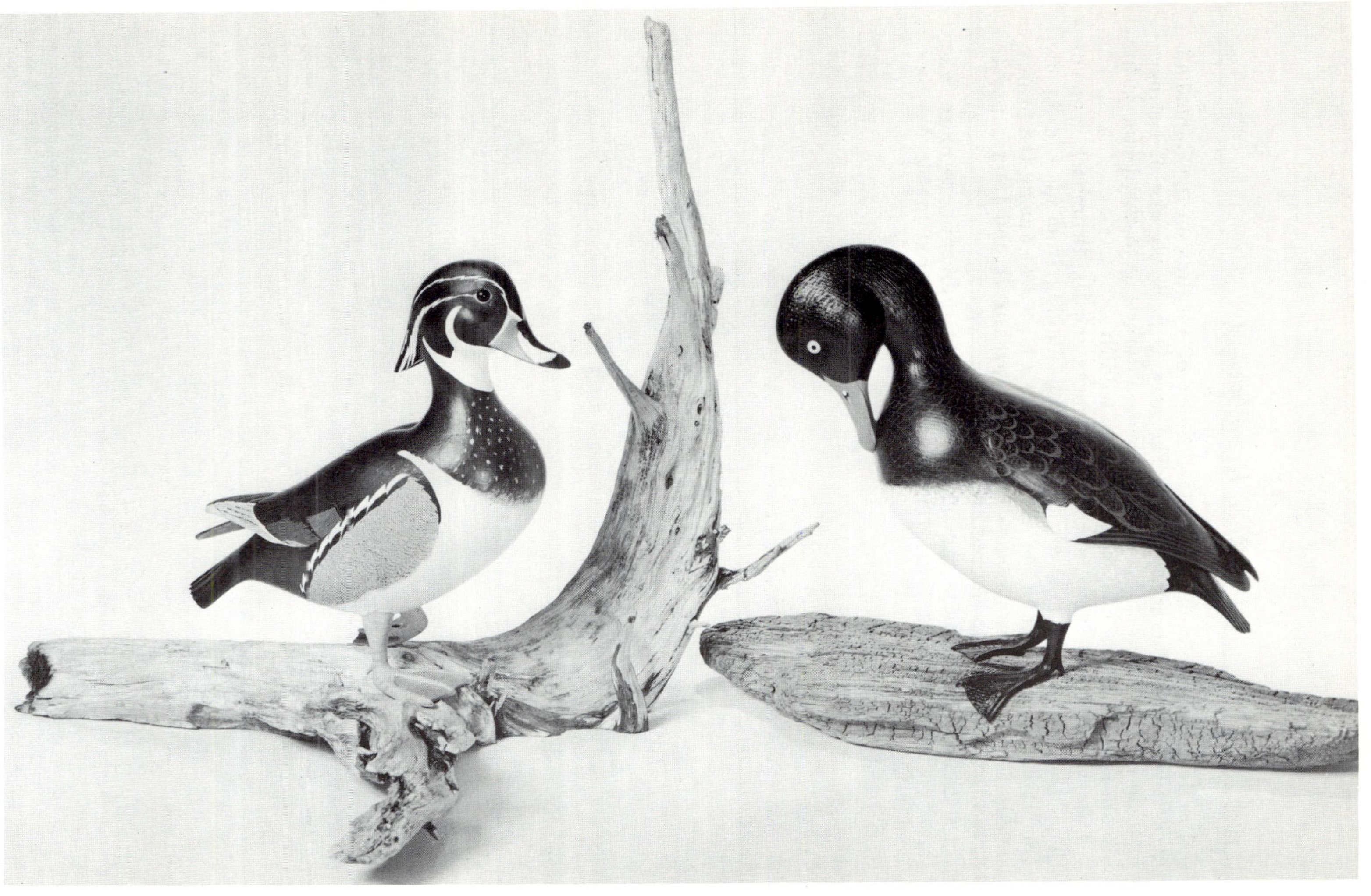

Figure 79. *Wood Duck* and *Blackhead,* by James Denny.

Dr. R. L. Brumback, Jr.

Dr. Brumback is from the Western Shore of Virginia on the Rappahannock River, near Chesapeake Bay. The area is probably one of the most historic in the entire state. What is more interesting to the doctor is his proximity to two popular waterways for wildlife.

I know of but two D.D.S.'s who carve ducks and Dr. Brumback is one of them. He claims to be only an amateur, but judging from his Old Squaw (male) in the photograph, he need not take a back seat among the professionals. His work shows evidence of a talented carver and I am happy to have his Old Squaw in my picture gallery.

Dr. Brumback has been carving for six years and carves no more than three or four pieces a year. He was recently featured in the *Virginia Wildlife Magazine.*

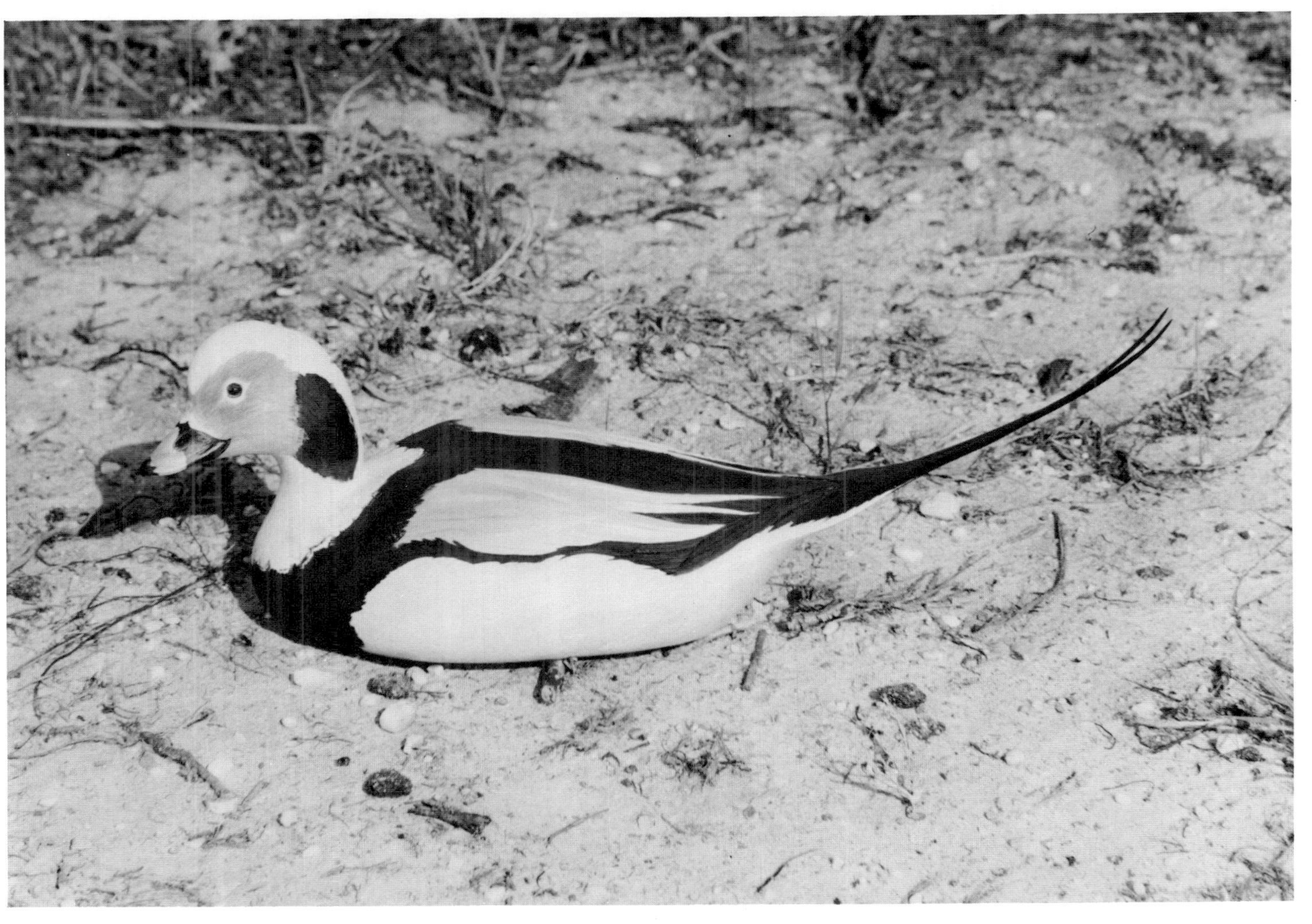

Figure 80. *Old Squaw* (male), by Dr. R. L. Brumback, Jr.

Horace L. Crandall

Mr. Crandall proudly heads his letters with a cut of a jackknife, the emblem of the National Wood-carvers Association. In offering his assistance, he remarked: "Us wood-carvers are a neighborly breed." He is just as enthusiastic about his carving efforts. He was born on Long Island, and fortunately for the City of the Angels, he took his talents with him to California.

Mr. Crandall exhibits all over the United States. Since the San Francisco World's Fair, 1940, he has exhibited in wildlife shows throughout the country. His work is frequently seen in hobby shows. Wherever bird carvings are exhibited, Mr. Crandall is likely to be represented.

He carves waterfowl life-size and upland game birds in miniature. He is an experienced carver who knows his work and is one of the few who gives his carvings a "pinch" of humor. The skunk will have little success in securing eggs for breakfast for mama goose is giving him fair warning. Papa gander is not standing idly by, either, and will surely get into the fray if the wood pussy bravely makes an assault. All in all, it could develop into a "smelly" situation.

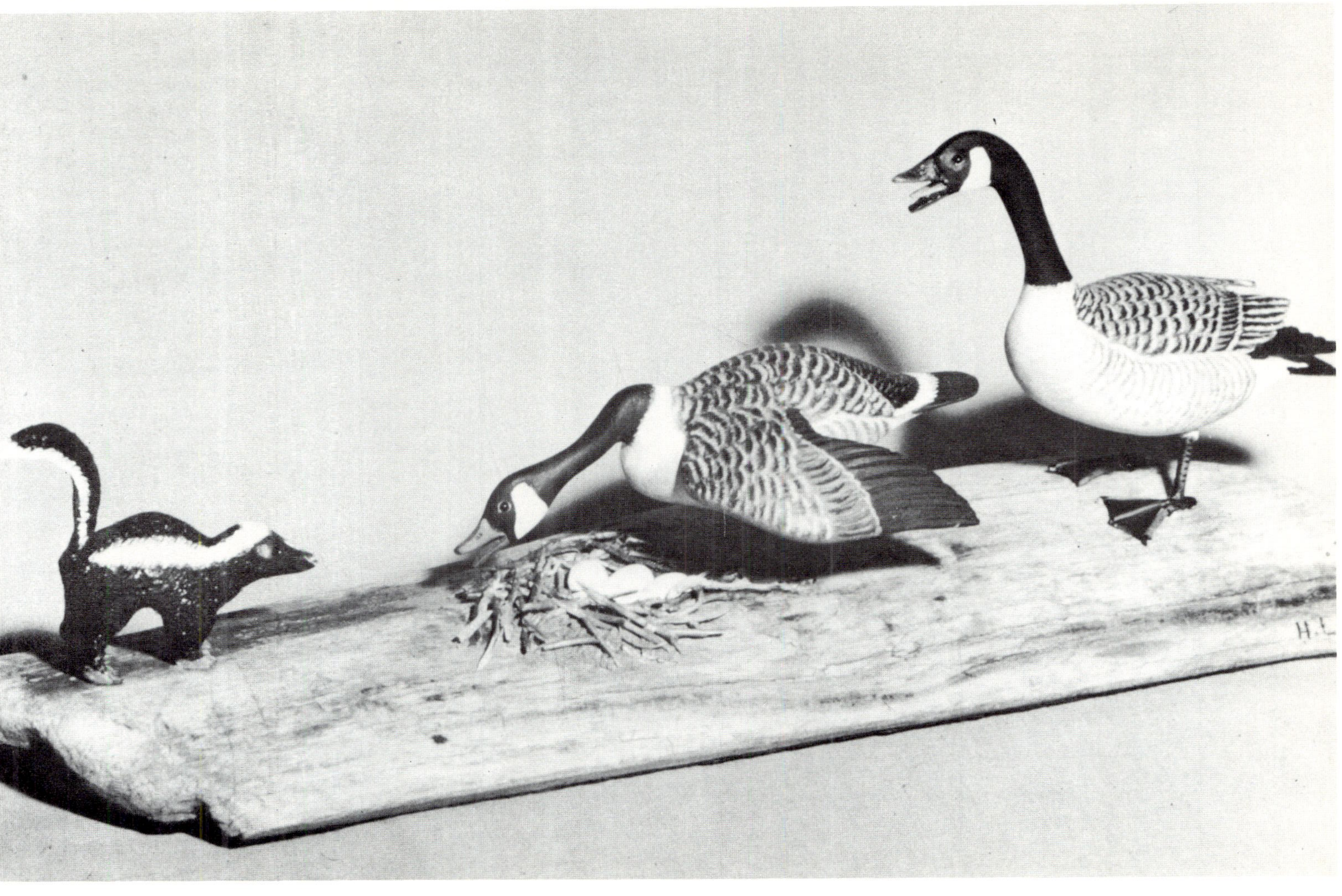

Figure 81. *Canada Geese,* by Horace L. Crandall.

Ted Hanks

Ted Hanks is fresh out of the Navy. He retired in May and, like so many seafaring men, has decided to become a "Down Easter." He says he will devote his full time to carving. "This I am looking forward to with great zeal and hopes."

Mr. Hanks' plaque adds variety to the picture gallery. It is three inches thick, 30″ wide, and 36″ high and an excellent example of high relief carving showing all of the finishing tool marks. Like a carpenter, a carver is known by his chips, so the work indicates the skill of this master carver. The work shown in the photograph is not the one requested by the author. "I have lost track of the person who purchased it," he said. Three plaques similar to the one illustrated here hang in the bar of the Robert Morris Inn in Oxford, Maryland. When touring this historic spot do not fail to visit the bar to observe Mr. Hanks' ducks—if for no other reason.

There are several special points of interest in *Ducks Dropping In.* The sweep of the right wing of the top bird is especially effective. The pure sine curve of the advancing edge is a beautiful line and located exactly right. The grain of the white pine showing through the clear finish is a fine example of the use of this natural feature of wood to enhance the carving.

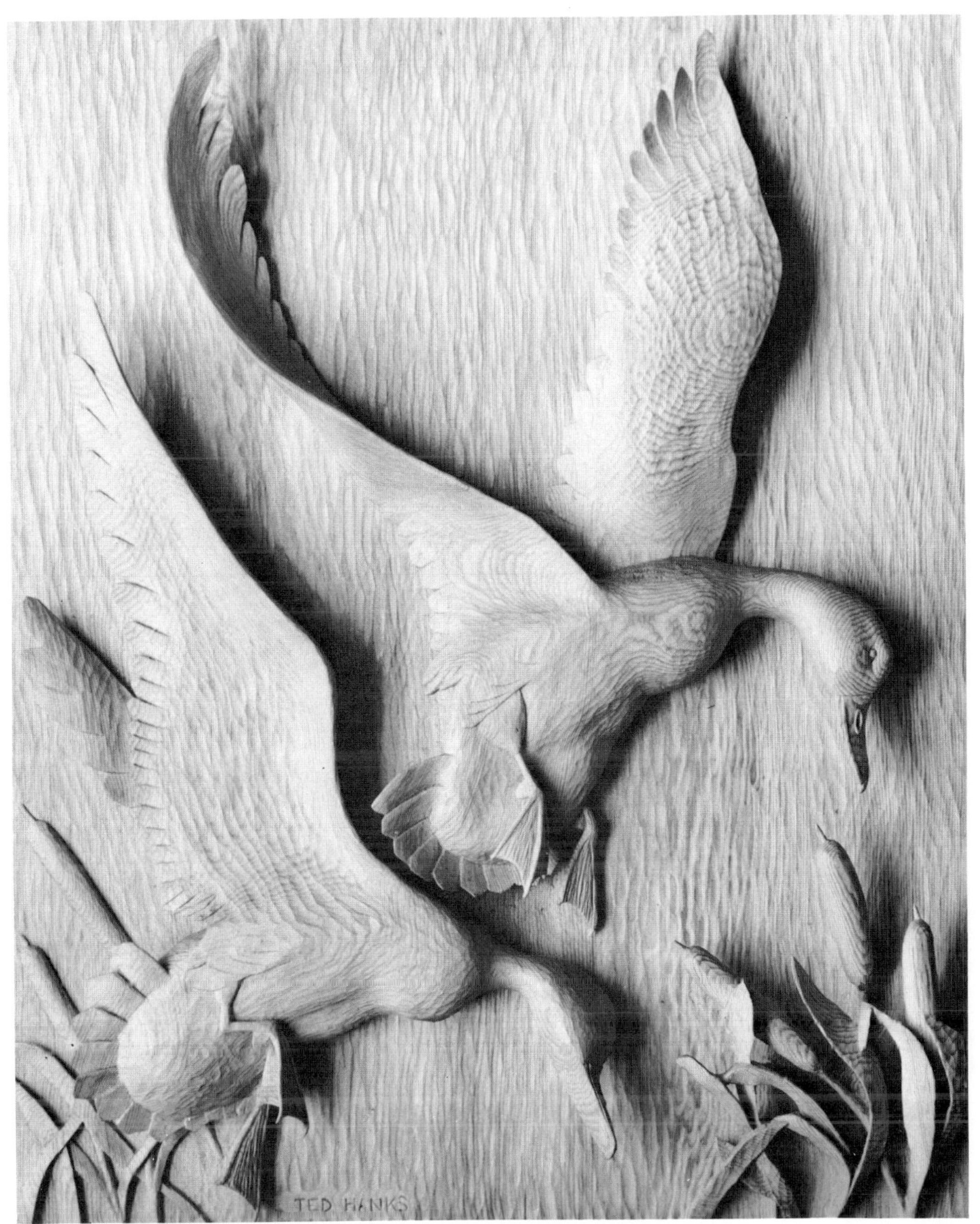

Figure 82. *Ducks Dropping In,* by Ted Hanks.

Captain Benjamin H. Riggs

Captain Benjamin Riggs retired from the Coast & Geodetic Survey (now ESSA) in 1952 after 32 years of service. He graduated from Lehigh University with a degree in Engineering. He started painting birds in Charleston, S.C., many years ago as a hobby; his carving began in Honolulu.

On retirement in Florida, Captain Riggs combined his painting and carving abilities originally for the easy identification of birds when he was president of the Audubon Society of the Everglades. The project has now become a business which has proved pleasant and profitable. "There are many gracious and delightful people in this field," he says.

Captain Riggs' photograph is of the Great Blue Heron, a favorite subject among wood-carvers. This interpretation shows the bird feeding, a pose not usually seen by observers as the Heron is an alert creature with head erect when it perceives a person in its field of vision.

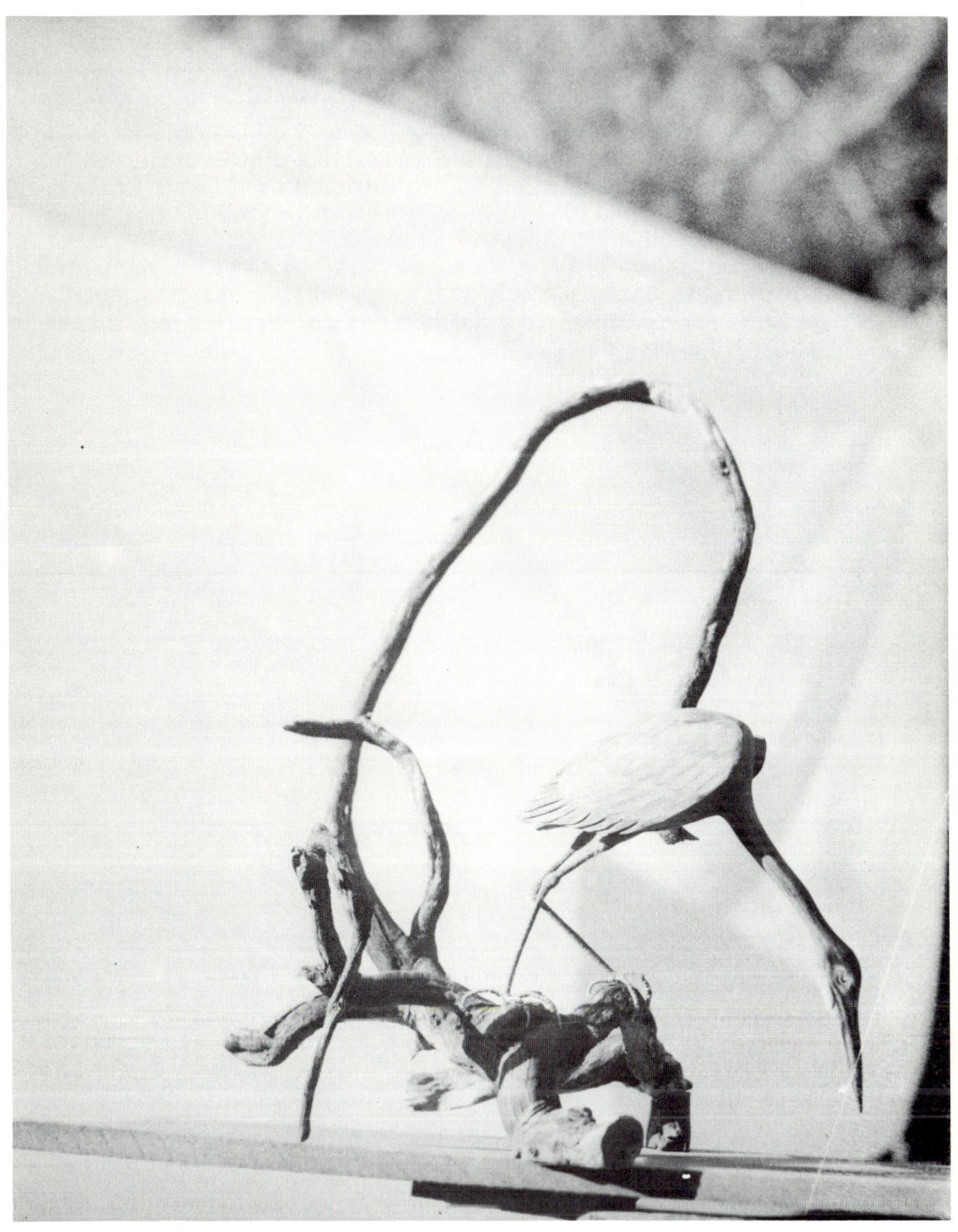

Figure 83. *Great Blue Heron,* by Captain Benjamin H. Riggs.

James T. Walker

Mr. Walker is a well-known carver of our great Midwest. Several years ago he began carving miniatures as a hobby. His carvings became so popular that he decided to specialize in full-scale models on a professional level.

Mr. Walker makes apologies for the wire holding the Canada Goose in place, but how else could a wooden goose be suspended in space? The Canada Goose is another popular carving model, although only two other of these birds are shown in the picture gallery. When carved in miniature they make a very decorative piece for that special niche or mantel space.

The perch is very effective; the bill is good; also the feet, held in the proper position for "taking off."

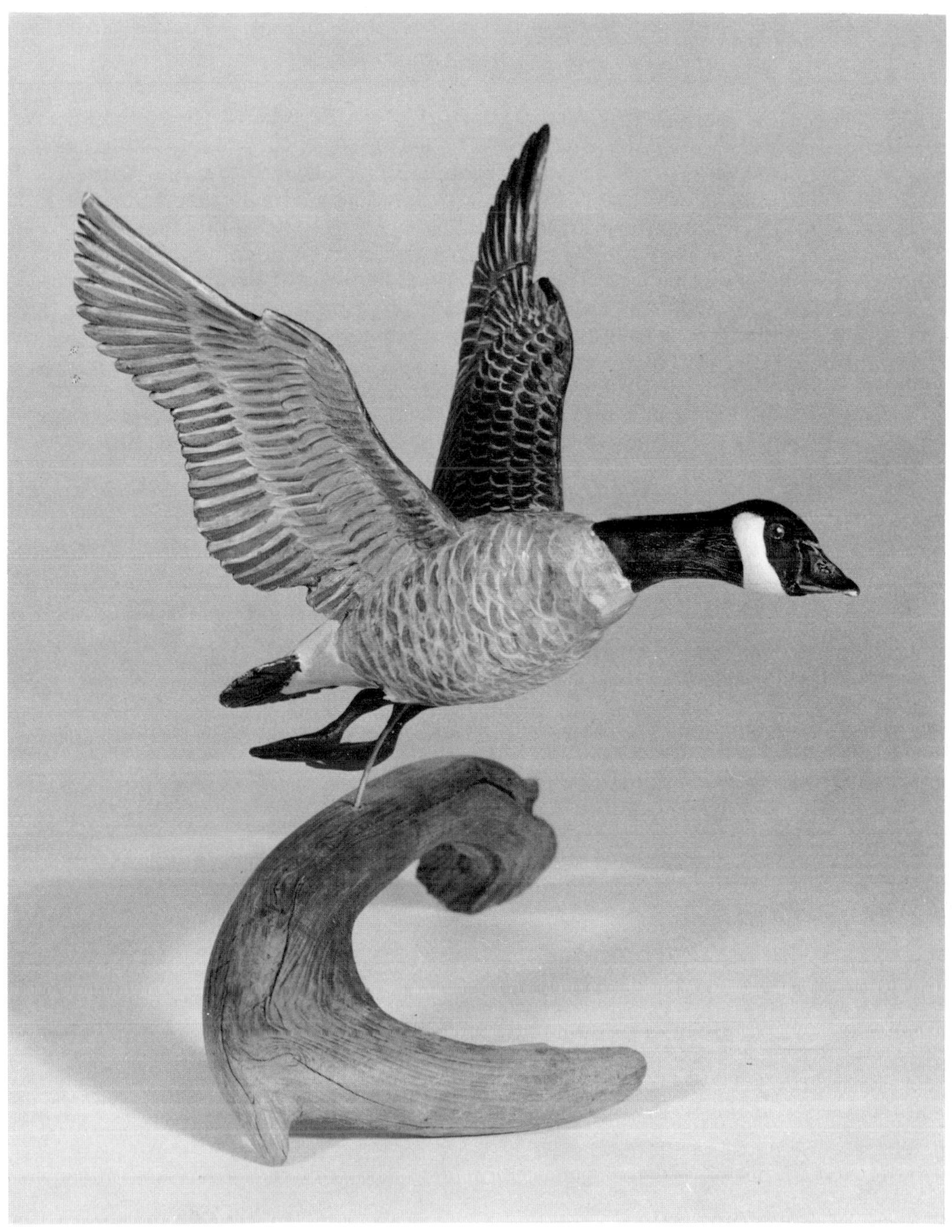

Figure 84. *Canada Goose*, by James T. Walker.

General C. Braddock deGavre

General deGavre is an Eastern Shoreman, too—from the Virginia end of the peninsula. He is situated so that he can observe waterfowl on both sides of his acres; Chesapeake Bay on his left (if he is facing north) is about five miles away, and about the same distance away on his right is the Atlantic Ocean with its inland waterways. The narrow peninsula is an ideal spot to observe wildlife. The General is a keen observer of birds and he likes to carve them as they appear in their natural habitat.

I remember the General saying that his Band-Aid kit was his most important tool; so he evidently does not always have his carving fingers in back of the cutting edge. He feels that the Great Blue Heron is not typical of his work. He specializes in ducks and geese, saying he is more familiar with them. We will settle for the Great Blue Heron. We are sorry that the colors do not show through the black and white photograph.

The attention of beginners is called to the perch which seems just right for the bird—a beautiful burl-like piece of "driftwood."

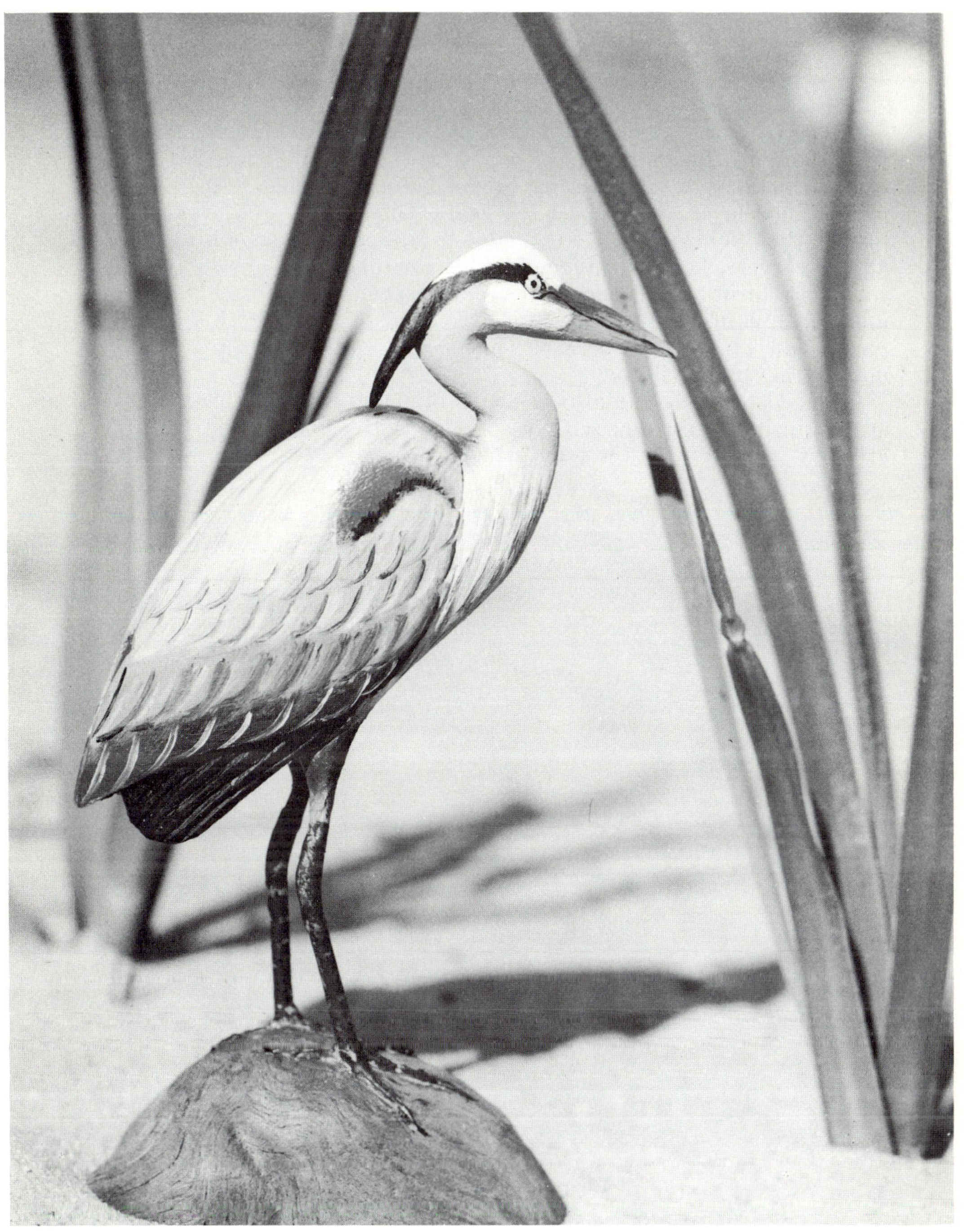

Figure 85. *Great Blue Heron,* by General C. Braddock deGavre.

Oliver J. Lawson

Oliver Lawson is another Eastern Shoreman. He resides a short distance from the Ward Brothers who have greatly influenced his work. He began to carve while only a small boy of thirteen years and has been carving on a professional level for the past ten years. Oliver is a prolific carver giving his full time to his work. He is unable to currently manage his orders. Like all top carvers, he is backlogged in his commissions.

Oliver's birds are authentic in every respect. He paints his models with uncommon skill. There is no effort required to recognize his birds on the part of an experienced person. The photographs mirror the skill of this master carver of wildfowl.

Oliver also carves miniatures—lapel pins and earbobs. These miniatures are exquisitely executed with respect to both carving and painting and are very popular with the ladies.

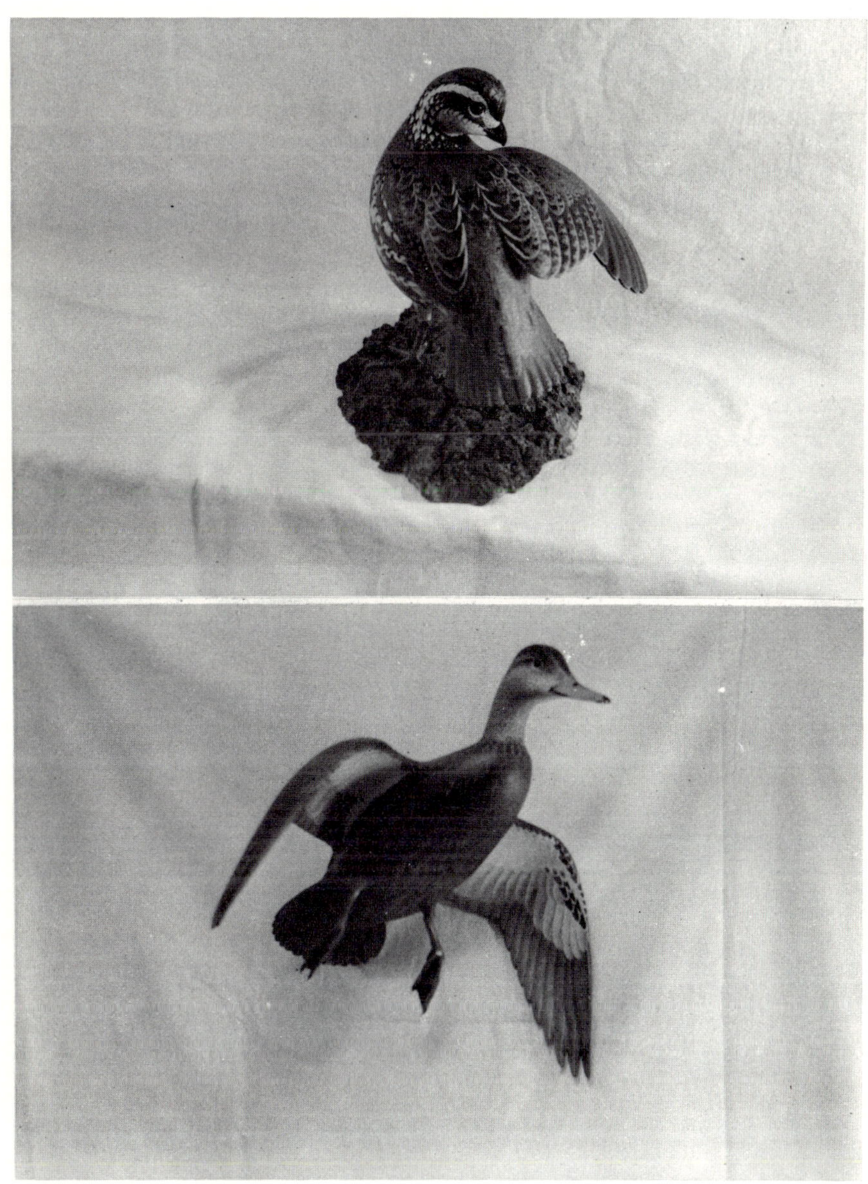

Figure 86. *Bobwhite* (top), and *Black Duck* (bottom), by Oliver J. Lawson.

Bruce Burk

"I know of no better person than Bruce to write the Foreword to your book. He is one grand person and a marvelous workman," says one of his Los Angeles admirers. Bruce is probably the best known bird-carver on the West Coast. His birds are sold by Kerr's of Beverly Hills and are sought after by collectors all over the world. There are few carvers who better depict in wood the wild birds of our streams and waterways. He is an expert in his field and has thorough knowledge of the birds he carves. He called attention to an erroneous detail of the Pintail in the manuscript: "You, like a number of illustrators have incorrectly located the neck stripes of the Pintail. They run up the neck and nearly meet in back of the eyes." Of course, he is right. He was also an able critic of my manuscript.

Birds carved by Bruce win prizes at exhibition contests. He won a first prize in the decorative class at the last National Open Decoy Contest at Iowa. His work created considerable interest at our show in Chestertown last year where many nationally known carvers were represented.

The birds in the opposite photograph are a pair of Canvasbacks. Note the high polish of the perch. Note, also, the legs, knee-joints, and the canvas-painted back of the bird in the foreground.

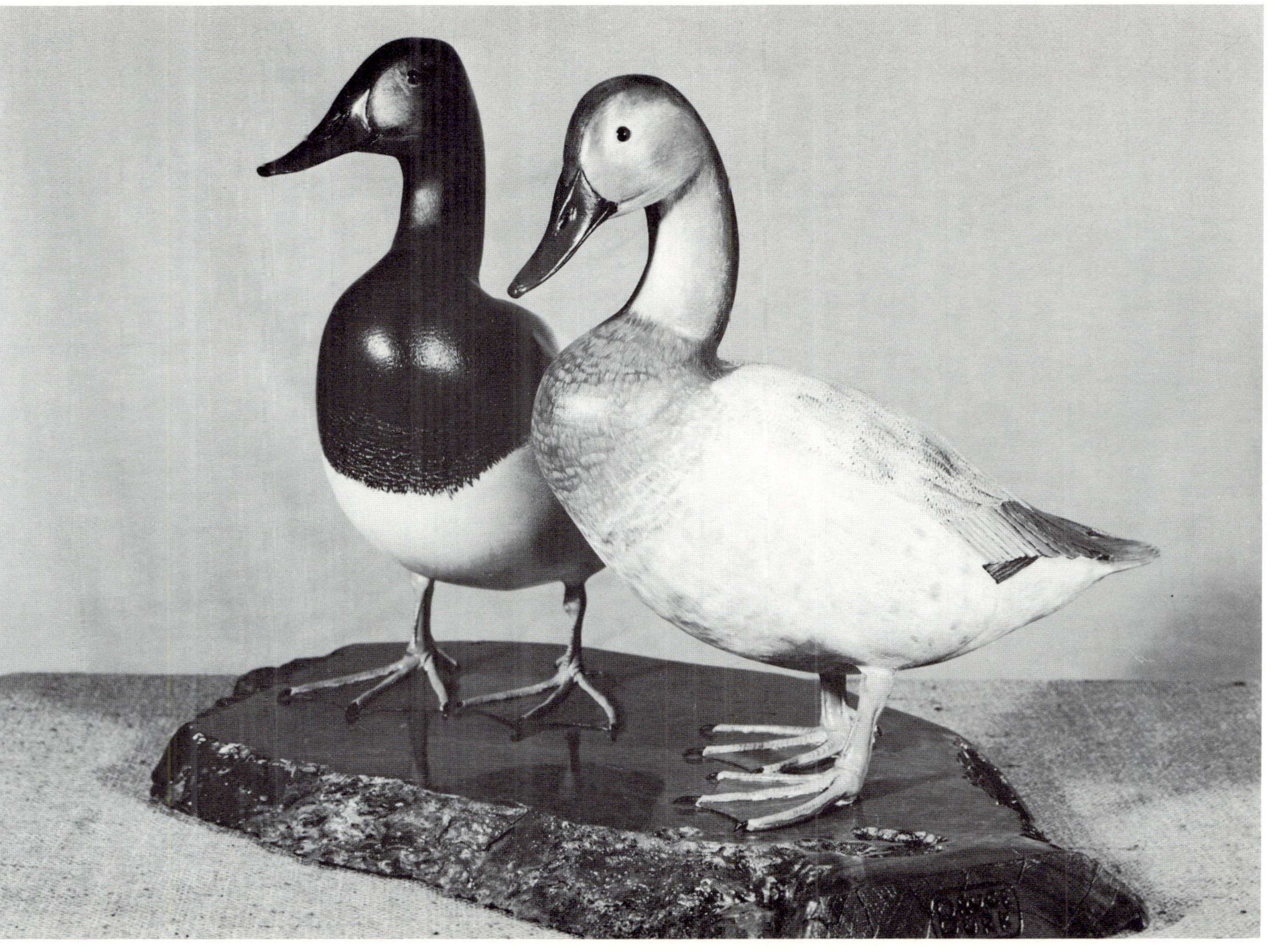

Figure 87. *Pair of Canvasbacks,* bv Bruce Burk.

Dan Brown

Dan seriously considered carving as a profitable career about five years ago. Before this time he had carved working decoys and repainted old models for his friends and others interested in collecting them. He learned that his hobby was rewarding in both pleasure and profit, so he began to carve more ornate models. His first blue ribbon, won at the International Decoy Contest, Davenport, Iowa, was sufficient incentive to spur him on in his carving efforts. Now, Dan is a full-fledged master bird-carver specializing in the birds and ducks that inhabit his native Eastern Shore of Maryland.

The duck shown in the photograph is a Pintail hen, a favorite model of most bird-carvers. I recently observed the carving at an art show and it is really more impressive than the photograph would indicate. The pose too is unusual—as if she were adjusting herself on her eggs. The perch for this position might be improved, however, but on the other hand she simply could be relieving a cramped wing.

The "Jacksnipe" is the Common Snipe. It gets its colloquial name from its twisting, skidding movements as it rockets itself into the air. Incidentally, the Pintail hen won second place at the National Decoy Show, Babylon, Long Island, this year.

In seven contests Dan has won 30 ribbons, including the best marsh duck and "Best in Show" in the Midwest Decoy Contest, at Detroit in 1967. Like all gifted artists, Dan is intrigued by the miracle of cutting away the waste wood from around his "brainchildren."

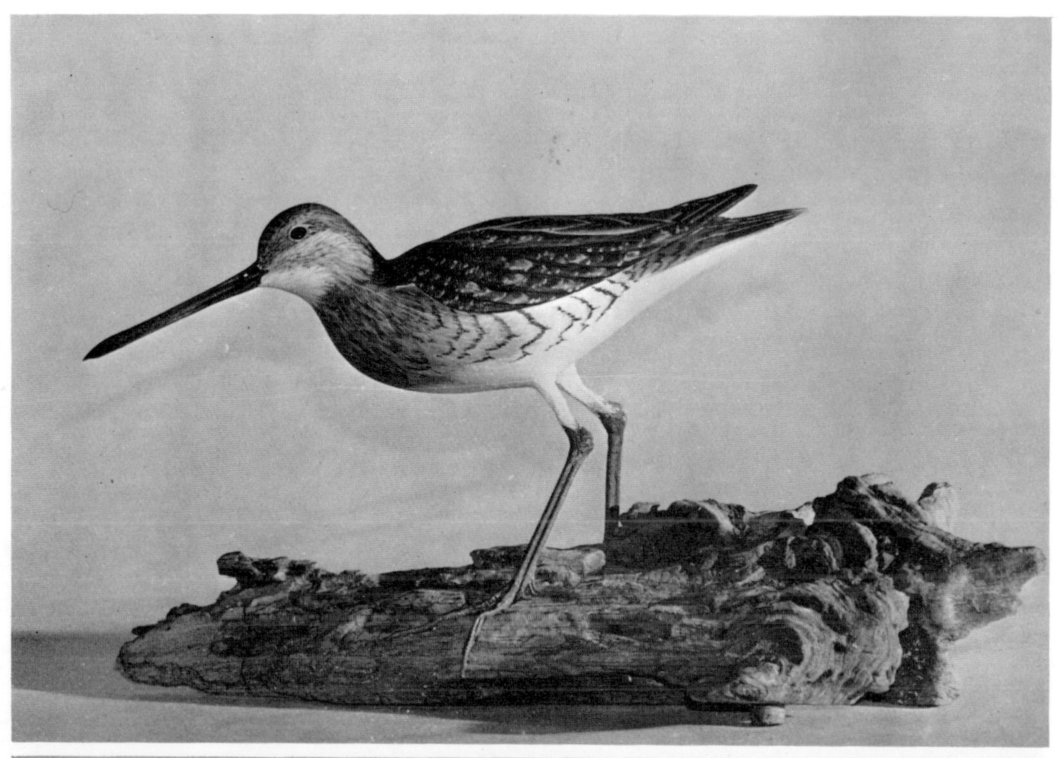

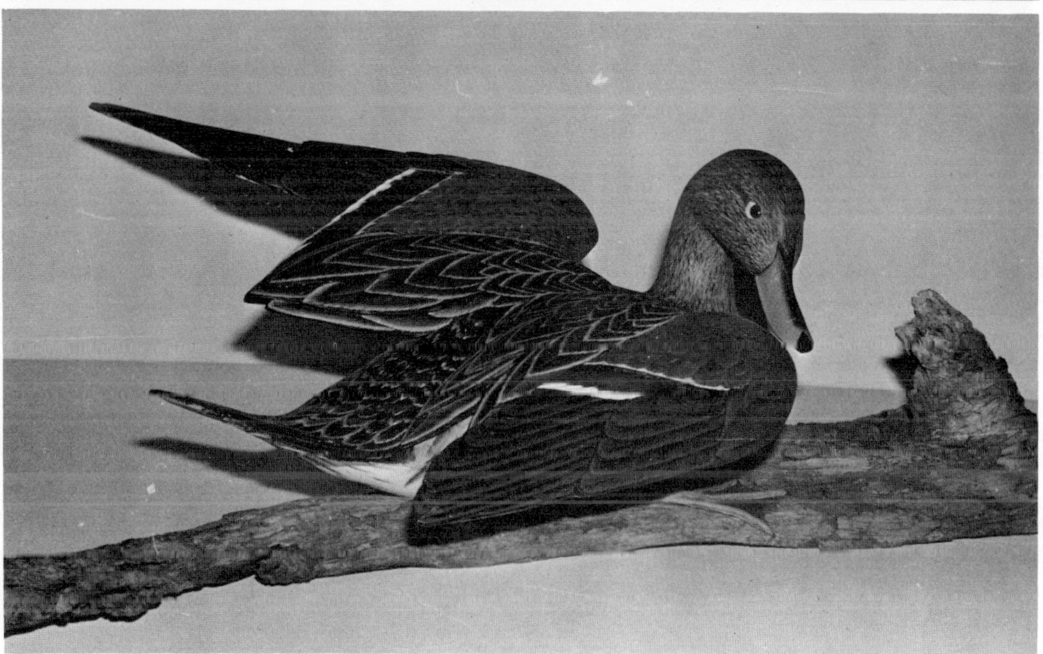

Figure 88. *Jacksnipe* (top), and *Pintail Hen* (bottom), by Dan Brown.

APPENDIX

Bibliography

Austin, Oliver L., *Birds of the World.* Golden Press, New York. (Illustrations by Arthur Singer)

Constantine, Albert, *Veneering Made Easy.* 2050 Eastchester Road, Bronx, New York, 10461.

Gilley, Wendell, *Bird Carving.* Bonanza Books, New York.

Graveney, Charles, *Wood Carving for Beginners.* Watson-Guptill, New York.

Kortright, F. H., *The Ducks, Geese and Swan of North America.* Wildlife Management Institute, Washington, D.C.

National Geographic Society, *Song and Garden Birds of North America.* Washington, D.C.

——— *Water, Prey and Game Birds of North America.* Washington, D.C.

Robbins, Chandler S.; Bertel Bruun; Herbert S. Zim, *Birds of North America.* Golden Press, New York. (Illustrations by Arthur Singer)

Rood, John, *Sculpture in Wood.* University of Minnesota Press, Minneapolis, Minnesota.

Slobodkin, Louis, *Sculpture, Principles and Practice.* World Publishing Co., Cleveland and New York.

Tangerman, E. J., *Whittling and Carving.* Whittlesley House, New York.

Catalogs

Woodcraft Supply Corp., 71 Canal Street, Boston, Mass. 02114 (Tools)

Craftsman Wood Service Co., 2727 S. Mary Street, Chicago, Ill. (Tools, Veneers and Wood)

Albert Constantine and Sons, 2050 Eastchester Road, Bronx, N.Y. 10461. (Excellent catalog)

Frank Mittermeier, Inc., 3577 E. Tremont Ave., P. O. Box 2, Bronx, N.Y. (Tools)

Buck Bros., Riverton Works, Millbury, Mass. (Tools)

Art Mart Inc., Clayton, Mo. (Large selection of supplies, including jewelry findings)

Crowe and Coulter, Cherokee, N.C. 28719 (Pre-cut Blanks and Wood)

Sculpture Supplies

Sculpture House, 38 East 30th Street, New York, N.Y. 10016

Sculpture Associates, 114 East 25th Street, New York, N.Y.

Ettl Studios, Inc., Ettl Art Center, Glenville, Conn. 06833

Birds' Eyes

J. W. Elwood Supply Co., 1202 Harney, Omaha, Nebr. 68102

Chauvin Taxidermy Studio, 4417 White Plains Road, Bronx, N.Y. 10470

Jewelry Findings

Rock Haven Art Metal Co., Box 8, Whitefield, N.H. 03598 (Local jeweler)

Miscellaneous

New York State Conservation Magazine. "Do a Decoy," Dec.-Jan., 1953-54.

Chip Chats. Magazine of the National Wood-Carver's Association.

Literature of "Ducks Unlimited, Inc.," P. O. Box 66300, Chicago, Ill.

INDEX